T0319924

Capitalism and Democracy

NEW HORIZONS IN INSTITUTIONAL AND EVOLUTIONARY ECONOMICS

Series Editor: Geoffrey M. Hodgson
Research Professor, University of Hertfordshire Business School, UK

Economics today is at a crossroads. New ideas and approaches are challenging the largely static and equilibrium-oriented models that used to dominate mainstream economics. The study of economic institutions – long neglected in the economics textbooks – has returned to the forefront of theoretical and empirical investigation.

This challenging and interdisciplinary series publishes leading works at the forefront of institutional and evolutionary theory and focuses on cutting-edge analyses of modern socio-economic systems. The aim is to understand both the institutional structures of modern economies and the processes of economic evolution and development. Contributions will be from all forms of evolutionary and institutional economics, as well as from Post-Keynesian, Austrian and other schools. The overriding aim is to understand the processes of institutional transformation and economic change.

Titles in the series include:

Evolutionary Economics and Environmental Policy
Survival of the Greenest
Jeroen C.J.M. van den Bergh, Albert Faber, Annemarth M. Idenburg and Frans H. Oosterhuis

Property Rights, Consumption and the Market Process
David Emanuel Andersson

The Evolution of Path Dependence
Edited by Lars Magnusson and Jan Ottosson

Economics, Culture and Social Theory
William A. Jackson

Deep Complexity and the Social Sciences
Experience, Modelling and Operationality
Robert Delorme

Creative Industries and Economic Evolution
Jason Potts

Institutional Variety in East Asia
Formal and Informal Patterns of Coordination
Edited by Werner Pascha, Cornelia Storz and Markus Taube

Capitalism and Democracy
A Fragile Alliance
Theo van de Klundert

Capitalism and Democracy

A Fragile Alliance

Theo van de Klundert

Tilburg University, the Netherlands

Edward Elgar

Cheltenham, UK • Northampton, MA, USA

Published by
Edward Elgar Publishing Limited
The Lypiatts
15 Lansdown Road
Cheltenham
Glos GL50 2JA
UK

Edward Elgar Publishing, Inc.
William Pratt House
9 Dewey Court
Northampton
Massachusetts 01060
USA

A catalogue record for this book
is available from the British Library

Library of Congress Control Number: 2012953538

This book is available electronically in the ElgarOnline.com
Economics Subject Collection, E-ISBN 978 1 78195 616 8

ISBN 978 1 78195 615 1

Typeset by Servis Filmsetting Ltd, Stockport, Cheshire
Printed by MPG PRINTGROUP, UK

For Michel, to remember   *somehow*

sometime

somewhere

Contents

PART II   HISTORICAL DEVELOPMENTS IN A
         THEORETICAL PERSPECTIVE

Map and figures

MAP

FIGURES

Tables

Preface

This book is the outcome of nearly lifelong learning. At the age of 17, I decided to study economics. Now, 60 years later, I am still fascinated by new developments taking place within the discipline. In the 1950s and 1960s neoclassical theory dominated the academic field. The theory of economic growth, which originated from this source, presented a rather optimistic picture of the real world. It appeared that sufficient welfare could be realized by an adequate amount of savings. Later on this picture had to be amended. On closer inspection technological development was not as self-evident as assumed in neoclassical growth theory. Starting from the alternative assumption that technological progress is endogenously determined by economic conditions, a whole new stream of publications could emerge.

From the beginning of my career the theory of economic growth has had my full interest, as appears from a number of publications, of which the most important ones are reprinted in Sjak Smulders (ed.), *Growth Theory in Historical Perspective. Selected Essays of Theo van de Klundert* (Edward Elgar Publishing, 2001). As an aside I would like to mention that – unlike most of my work – my first academic publication, written in 1961, focused on the analysis of a partial oligopoly. In Chapter 7 of the present book I refer to this article not as a kind of curiosum, but to illustrate the tenability of some of our insights.

Returning to the process of economic growth, I must conclude that the introduction of endogenous technological change in models of a neoclassical flavour is not the end of the story. Empirical research reveals that technological development exhibits strong irregularities. The introduction of complex systems in the form of general purpose technologies may induce long waves, which have large societal consequences. New wealth is created, but creative destruction may go along with poverty elsewhere.

This observation urges a closer inspection of capitalism. Karl Marx, and at a later stage Joseph Schumpeter, maintained that the accumulation of capital has radical consequences. These thoughts always triggered my interest, although I was well aware of the shortcomings in the analyses of both economists. Marx as well as Schumpeter predicted the collapse of the capitalist system, but reality is quite different. Capitalism is hit by many crises, but survives one way or the other by changing the rules of the game as the circumstances require. In his time Karl Polanyi (1944) understood better than anyone else the essence of capitalism. However, during the neoclassical era, which coincidences with an upswing in the terminology of the theory on long waves, there was no interest in analyzing the capitalist system. Even the term 'capitalism' was in decline as John Kenneth Galbraith (2004) observes in his last published book.

The 1990s witnessed a revival of institutional economics initiated by Nobel Prize laureate Douglass North (1990) and others. Institutional economics shows the shortcomings of neoclassical theory, thus setting the stage for a reappraisal of capitalism. In my book written in the Dutch language *Vormen van kapitalisme* (Uitgeverij Lemma, 2005) emphasis is put on the relevance of institutions under different historical circumstances. However, something is still lacking in this approach. Institutions are manmade and as such depend on the distribution of political power in society.

In this connection, thoughts may go again back to Marx, but the old ideas on the class struggle have to be replaced by a broader spectrum of opposing forces. In Western democracies citizens have equal rights, but this does not imply that everyone has the same influence in the political arena. Economic wealth and power can be used to acquire political power. As a consequence, in the course of history varying economic elites are confronted with citizens, who have to solve their problems of collective action. The resulting power balance strongly depends on the economic circumstances. In times of deep recession or even depression there may a majority opting for more regulation. In contrast, if extensive regulation stands in the way of innovation the call for more economic freedom may be loud and clear.

In modern Political Economy interesting mathematical models are constructed to illustrate the impact of economics on politics, but a canonical form is not yet developed. In this sense the theory falls short of neoclassical analysis, where many flowers breed on the same ground. Nevertheless, the basic notions of political economy as well as those of institutional economics have inspired me throughout the present book. I am also convinced that these notions may be useful in understanding the causes of the recent economic crisis.

In a comprehensive analysis of capitalism attention must be paid to different countries, giving rise to a number of questions. What are the causes of economic backwardness? Under which conditions are countries in a position to catch-up with or leap-frog the leading economies? To answer these questions again an appeal has to be made to institutional economics. Catching-up of developing countries in the course of time also has important consequences for the distribution of political power in the world as a whole. This could imply that the way the world deals with economic crises and the allocation of scarce resources (including climate change) will no longer bear a typical Western stamp. This makes it relevant to investigate whether different varieties of capitalism are viable. The question is not new as the discussion on the relative merits of the Anglo-Saxon model and the Rhineland model, to use the popular terminology of Michel Albert (1991), shows. In this respect our analysis builds upon the results discussed in *Vormen van kapitalisme*. A new aspect is the emergence of different varieties of state capitalism. Whether such varieties are viable in the long-run is a much debated, but still open question.

When writing the book I benefited from the critical and constructive comments of a number of colleagues with whom I worked together at Tilburg University. Henk van Gemert, Ad van de Gevel, Ton van Schaik, Sjak Smulders and Martin van Tuijl read all or most of the chapters in the course of time. I am extremely grateful for their penetrating questions and suggestions for improving the text. In the original set-up the book was written in Dutch, because this put me in a position to express my ideas making full use of what a language has to offer. As a first approach this is satisfactory, but after discussing matters it became clear that I had to change the language in order to reach a much larger audience. Very special thanks go to Martin van Tuijl and Sjak Smulders for their help with the translation into English while preserving the original intentions. In retrospect, the English version is better than the original, because the translation offered an opportunity to improve the exposition and to express my ideas in a more effective manner within the economic literature. Of course none of the colleagues mentioned above are at fault for any remaining errors and weaknesses.

The digital revolution came in a later phase of my life. Therefore, help with word processing and the construction of figures was more than welcome. Corina Maas, Ella Muñoz, Mirjam Schermij and Nicole van de Ven processed my text with dedication and professional competence. Without their unremitting efforts the book would never have been completed. I am also indebted to the Department of Economics of Tilburg University for providing me with the facilities necessary to do the required research.

In the final stage of the process things must run smoothly. Sjak Smulders of Tilburg University and Matthew Pitman and Elizabeth Clack, editors for Edward Elgar Publishing, helped me through this hectic period, for which I am very grateful.

Words can hardly express my gratitude to my wife Theresa, who supported me fully during the period in life that is supposed to be reserved mainly for leisure activities. I have dedicated this book to my eldest son Michel, who deserves nowadays more than anyone else a token of sincere sympathy.

Introduction

> *A question permeates much comparative political economy from the
> classics to contemporary scholarship: how is it possible to combine
> capitalism with democracy?*
> Torben Iversen (2006, p. 601)

MAIN ISSUES

Iversen's question takes a central place in our book. The friction between
capitalism and democracy can be explained as follows. Capitalism generates strong inequalities in the distribution of income and wealth, while
democracy divides political power in an egalitarian manner, under the
principle of one person, one vote. The majority may vote in favour of
redistributing income, and maybe wealth, from the rich to the poor. But
then the rich will resist by disputing the political power of the majority or
by curtailing their economic efforts. The consequences of such a struggle
are serious and may influence the viability of the capitalist system.

There is another aspect in the quotation above that needs attention.
Iversen refers to political economy but in economics, as the discipline
is usually called, there is no attention to the distribution of income and
wealth. In the dominant neoclassical theory emphasis is on the efficient
allocation of the production factors, taking account of the preferences
of economic subjects. Who owns these factors and receives the factor
incomes is irrelevant in this theory.

To understand why capitalism produces inequality a different approach
to studying the process of supplying goods and services is in order.
Capitalism implies that the owners of capital have the freedom to organize the production process to make as much profit as possible. Moreover,
competition forces capitalists to innovate new production methods or new
production processes which lead to temporary monopoly positions. This
process is reinforced by applying every opportunity to take advantage
of economies of scale with respect to the technological possibilities but
also with respect to the organization of enterprises. Not every attempt to
generate profits is successful. Moreover, existing economic activities may
be outcompeted by new developments. Such events are referred to as acts

of creative destruction. In the on-going process of capital accumulation there are always winners and losers. Losers may try to improve their fate. The question is then: what means do they have to change the course of development?

Redistribution of income through the political system is a possibility, as mentioned above. However, the problem should be placed in a much broader perspective. The relentless accumulation of capital is constrained by a set of rules. These rules of the game consist of laws, conventions and beliefs. It is customary to indicate these constraints on economic activities as economic institutions. Institutional economics analyzes the manner in which the rules of the game determine capital accumulation, economic growth and the distribution of income. After a long period of standing in the shadow institutional economics has regained the prominent place it had in the past. However, this approach is not sufficient. Institutions are man-made and how they come into existence must be analyzed. This task brings us back to the realm of political economy.

An important lesson of political economy is that there is a close connection between capitalism and democracy that goes both ways. Economic institutions and the redistribution of income are determined according to the distribution of political power. Political power depends on existing political institutions, such as the constitution and voting rules for parliament, and on the investments in political power by economic agents with sufficient wealth. Such investments may be profitable if the economic institutions can be changed in a way that is beneficial to the investors. Investments in political power can take very different forms. There are historical examples of landowners buying the votes of their labourers. In modern times capitalists may financially support political parties with programs that are attractive to them or spend funds for lobbying among politicians and civil servants. Moreover, capitalists may invest in public communication channels which may be profitable and at the same time instrumental in influencing the public opinion in a preferred manner. Moreover, it may be rewarding to join economic and political elites. The revolving door policy in the appointment of people in high places in business as well as in politics is a way of materializing such cooperation.

It should be noted that not all economic institutions can be adapted in the short-run. There is a certain degree of path-dependency, implying that institutional differences across countries are to some extent the result of decisions made in the past. Therefore, historical constraints have to be taken into account in political economy. In this connection it is important to observe that the capitalistic system is rather young. It emerged along with the Industrial Revolution in England after 1750. Before this event economic activities were embedded in social relations. The separation of society into an economic and political sphere is marked by Karl Polanyi (1944) as 'The Great Transformation', which paved the way for a self-regulating market system. Polanyi prefers the latter term to the now prevalent term capitalism.

The Industrial Revolution was made possible by ensuring property rights of merchants and entrepreneurs, without relying on a fully developed democracy. This is an important observation, because we will return to the question of whether capitalism and democracy have to go hand-in-hand in the course of our considerations. The coexistence of capitalism and democracy is not a matter of necessity as recent developments, for instance in China, make clear. The fast growth of the Chinese economy has been possible without the support of a democratic political regime. Nevertheless, secure property rights are a necessary condition for economic development in all circumstances.

Capitalist accumulation accompanied by Darwinian competition has brought a high level of welfare into the Western world. At the same time an uncontrolled form of capitalism is inherently unstable. This concerns not only financial instability but goes much deeper. The forces behind the relentless accumulation of capital are strong enough to erode the moral foundations of society. The process of creative destruction reaches further than the elimination of declining industries. The market system needs some form of regulation. This is part of what Polanyi (1944) calls the 'double movement'. On the one hand, for the market system to flourish capitalists and entrepreneurs need the freedom to experiment and to change things. On the other hand, society must protect itself for the pernicious effects of relentless accumulation. How this tension inherent in the capitalist system is solved must be revealed by studying economic history. However, at this point we encounter a methodological problem. As emphasized by Joseph Schumpeter (1942), a pure description of the facts without applying the results of rigorous economic theory is not sufficient. In the words of Schumpeter (1942, p. 44) one has to determine 'how economic theory may be turned into historical analysis and how the historical narrative may be turned into histoire raisonnée'. This is not an easy task as there are no rules to stick to.

According to Karl Gunnar Persson (2010) economic history traces the efficiency aspects of institutions by studying markets, property rights, and incentives of economic agents. Efficiency considerations are important without any doubt and many institutions make a significant contribution to the efficient allocation of the means of production. However, the concept of economic history as conceived by Persson is too narrow. Special interest groups with political power may extract rents from productive sectors in the economy for their own well-being. Moreover, social conflicts regarding the distribution of income are an important aspect of real life. More than that, the question of institutional origins needs to be considered, which often cannot be done without taking into account the historical conditions that give rise to them. To proceed in this direction Iversen (2006) stresses the idea of rooting actors in the structure of the capitalist economy. The project is referred to as 'new structuralism', whereby the success 'will depend on combining carefully identified historical constraints with rigorous theorizing' (Iversen, 2006, p.618).

With this statement in mind, we proceed by introducing a dialectic approach. In Part I of this book economic theory is discussed in a historical perspective. The theories selected for discussion are relevant for understanding historical developments. In Part II of our study emphasis lies on historical developments in a theoretical perspective. The theoretical results obtained in Part I are applied to interpret the observed historical facts. Each part contains four chapters. The main question of how capitalism and democracy are combined is worked out in two directions. First, we analyze the double movement, as identified in Polanyi (1944), in the context of the leading countries in the capitalist system. Here leadership is defined in technological terms. The leading country operates on the technological frontier. In this sense the leader stands for capitalism in its most advanced form. Second, we investigate the consequences of introducing capitalism in different parts of the world. The Industrial Revolution started in England, while other European countries followed in due time. Throughout the rest of the world the process of industrialization had to wait for a much longer time. Lagging behind implies that technology and institutions can be imitated from the leading country. Whether the catching-up process leads to a uniform global pattern or to varieties of capitalism in separate countries, with diverging economic and political institutions, is an important issue that deserves close scrutiny.

OUTLINE OF CHAPTERS

To explain the design of the book we present a short outline of the different chapters. Several economic theories are considered in Part I. In Chapter 1 the genesis of capitalism is discussed. The 'Great Transformation', in the terminology of Polanyi (1944), marks the beginning of the self-regulating market system by setting the political rulers at a distance. To eliminate the possibility of expropriation property coercion-constraining institutions have to be installed, as Avner Greif (2008) emphasizes. In addition, contract-enforcement institutions are needed to regulate production and trade. Contract-enforcing institutions can be installed by private parties or have a public character when regulation is enforced by the government. With the right mix of both types of institution the market system will flourish. However, this is not the end of the story. Since the Industrial Revolution in England capitalist development is based on technological change and creative destruction. As a result, things may run out of hand. Speculation, inequality and exclusion may undermine the stability of the system. Under these circumstances additional regulation is called for. This implies that a double movement exists in the words of Polanyi (1944), characterizing the design of the economy. Property rights and freedom of enterprise are necessary to foster innovation and economic growth. However, too much freedom can lead to aberrations, which need to be corrected by imposing appropriate rules.

The discussion in Chapter 1 makes clear that economic activities and political decision-making are interconnected. To analyze the implications of this symbiotic relationship we have to turn to the field of political economy. As Edward Glaeser (2005, p. 2) observes rightly: 'The insight that economics impacts politics as much as politics impacts economics lies at the heart of political economy'. Chapter 2 is devoted to an overview of the field. After positioning the process of allocation of the means of production in society at large, we turn to a discussion of formal models of political economy. As shown in Daron Acemoglu (2009) the allocation of production factors and the resulting distribution of incomes depend upon the political regime. Elites dominating the economy will extract rents by taxing productive activities. 'Business elites' will even impose higher taxes than pure political elites, as explained in François Bourguignon and Thierry Verdier (2010). Business elites also may invest in state capacity building to increase the revenues from rent extraction. In the case of a probability of losing power, elites will react by taking measures to prevent the shifting of power to the workers. The analysis becomes more complicated when political power between the elites and workers switches according to a stochastic pattern. In the model by Daron Acemoglu and James Robinson (2008) stochastic regimes switches occur between oligarchy with exploitation of workers and democracy with workers paid according to their marginal products. Such switches resemble, to a certain extent, the double movement as conceived by Polanyi. However, the dynamic forces of capitalism in the form of capital accumulation and technological change are not taken into account. To fill this gap we discuss the history of the US economy. The relevance of the double movement is illustrated by showing that plutocratic periods with unrestrained capital accumulation alternate with democratic periods exhibiting more regulation of markets. In sum, one could say that both methods, modelling and description, each in their own way elucidate what is at stake in political economy.

Technological change is the driving force of accumulation and growth in the capitalist system. In Chapter 3 we survey the different approaches dealing with this phenomenon. In the traditional neoclassical growth theory technological change is conceived as an exogenous factor. In the more recent literature technological change is explained by factors like learning-by-doing and investment in research and development. However, in most of the models technological change appears as a smooth process so that balanced growth paths with constant growth rates of the key variables can be obtained. Such a reassuring picture changes dramatically when the abrupt introduction of general purpose technologies (GPTs) is considered. A GPT is a technological innovation in the form of process innovation, product innovation or an organizational breakthrough with great potential of its own and numerous other applications and spillovers to other sectors. As shown in the model of Elhanan Helpman and Manuel Trajtenberg (1998) the introduction of a GPT may lead to a temporary growth slowdown, because a new constellation of productive activities has to be built. In the model the introduction of a new GPT requires the production of related input components, which takes time. However, the appearance of a new GPT induces changes in many aspects of daily life, like for instance capital accumulation, education, infrastructure, corporate governance and so on. Moreover, the introduction of GPTs follows a certain pattern over time, which can be illustrated with the logistic curve. GPTs may also overlap and reinforce one another. In short, to understand the full meaning of general purpose technologies a descriptive analysis, or appreciative theorizing in the terminology of Richard Lipsey, Kenneth Carlaw and Clifford Bekar (2005), is again of vital importance.

For backward economies technological change is, to a large extent, dominated by catching-up with the leader. As shown in Chapter 4, catching-up implies a growth rate of GDP per capita in excess of that of the technological leader. As the process evolves, the growth rate of the backward economy slows down to the level attained in the leading country. Nevertheless convergence may be incomplete in terms of the level of per capita GDP, if the initially backward country fails to make the required adaptions in due time. What this may mean, is illustrated in a sophisticated model constructed by Daron Acemoglu, Philippe Aghion and Fabrizio Zilibotti (2006). To realize complete convergence backward countries have to switch in time from an investment-based strategy towards an innovation-based strategy. The investment-based strategy is based on long-term relationships and large-scale investment projects. In the case of an innovation-based strategy the selection of managers with innovative capabilities is at the centre of economic activities. The decision to switch toward an innovation-based strategy is made by profit-maximizing capitalists, but institutions play a role in the background.

The government may make the investment-based strategy more attractive by subsidizing investment or by restricting competition. Less competition implies higher profits and therefore less reason to alter the strategy. The problems that backward economies have to cope with are more extensive than appears from a macroeconomic approach. Structural transformations with respect to the sector structure and the mobility of production factors that are rather drastic have to be made. Here again the government may play a vital role by stimulating the required changes. However, it should be stressed that institutions also have to be adapted when they are no longer efficient. Whether this will take place depends upon the political constellation and the political power of the groups concerned.

In Part II historical developments in a world characterized by capitalism are put in the forefront. The existence, meaning and impact of long waves of approximately 50 years are considered in Chapter 5. The existence of long waves is much disputed. There are two ways to proceed if one wants to show that long waves are an essential element of capitalist development. The direct method applies statistical techniques to time series of macroeconomic data to identify cyclical patterns. A recent example of the approach is a study by Andrey Korotayev and Sergey Tsirel (2010), using spectral analysis to decompose time series of the growth rate of world output into cycles of different amplitude and length. The authors show that for the period 1820–2007 five long waves, or Kondratieff-waves as they call them, can be discerned. However, the direct method offers no clues with respect to the factors causing the Kondratieff waves. Moreover, testing the hypothesis of the existence of long waves by applying the growth rate of world output seems rather farfetched. The indirect method of identifying long waves overcomes these drawbacks. The basic idea here is that long waves are caused by technological revolutions. This implies that to find evidence for long waves one has to look at developments in countries that are the technological leaders. Another implication is that one has to trace down the technological features which shape the history of frontier economies. Chris Freeman and Francisco Louçã (2001) identify long waves applying concepts like the constellation of technical innovations, carrier branches, core inputs, infrastructure and organizational changes. They also distinguish five Kondratieff-cycles. Carlota Perez (2002) finds similar results, but comes to a slightly different dating by emphasizing the idea that long waves are the result of the introduction of general purpose technologies with properties discussed in Chapter 3.

In another approach the existence of long waves is explained by the financial instability hypothesis of Hyman Minsky (1964). According to this view firms and banks take an overly optimistic view when the economy flourishes. Too much debt is incurred giving rise to asset bubbles, which burst as the real economy shows signs of stagnation. Ideally, the theories about technological revolutions and financial instability should be combined. However, until now no satisfactory attempts have been made, but Perez (2002) seeks to integrate financial developments into her theory, based on the appearance of GPTs. Although the existence of long waves as such remains under discussion the different theories and empirical observations reveal that the capitalist system is marked by forms of instability in the long run. This observation is corroborated by a periodization of capitalism, which builds upon the results presented in Chapter 2. The cyclical pattern in the real sphere of the economy is reflected in the political field, thus giving rise to a 'double movement' in the sense of Polanyi (1944).

In Chapter 6 capitalist developments in Europe and the US are compared. Somewhere around 1900 technological leadership shifted from England to the US. During the third great surge (1875–1928), in the terminology of Perez (2002), England failed to invest in new industrial sectors such as electricity, steel and chemistry. In the other European countries industrialization started later than in England. The Great Depression and the Second World War set the European countries at a great distance from the US in terms of productivity (production per hour). Catching-up with technological leader only occurred after 1950. Meanwhile the political power in Europe had shifted towards the left as labour unions and socialist parties gained political influence. According to Alberto Alesina and Edward Glaeser (2004) this was a result of the turmoil caused by the First World War. As a consequence, the welfare state was installed in Europe with a substantial redistribution from the rich to the poor in the form of transfers and social insurance. The differences with respect to redistribution show that capitalism can be designed in different ways. However, the discussion under the heading 'varieties of capitalism' mainly deals with differences with respect to the coordination of economic activities.

Peter Hall and David Soskice (2001) set the tone by distinguishing liberal market economies and coordinated market economies. In liberal market economies coordination in the sphere of corporate governance and labour relations is based on competitive market arrangements. In coordinated market economies coordination is to a large extent based on incomplete contracting, network monitoring and collaborative relationships. The group of liberal market economies consists of the Anglo-Saxon countries, whereas the group of coordinated market economies is composed of continental West-European countries supplemented by Japan. In the economic literature there is much discussion on the fundamental problem of whether the continental European model, also referred to as the Rhineland model, performs worse in macroeconomics terms than the Anglo-Saxon model with unconstrained markets. Empirical research does not lead to a definitive result. However, the discussion parallels the one in Chapter 4 with respect to the change from an investment-based strategy towards an innovation-based strategy in the case where convergence is under way. Therefore, the main issue is whether capitalist economies should be designed strictly as liberal market economies once innovation becomes the driving force of economic expansion.

Catching-up in the world at large is analyzed in Chapter 7. As unconditional convergence is not found on a macroeconomic level one could look for conditions that must be taken into account when studying the catching-up of a large sample of countries in the second half of the twentieth century. Barry Bosworth and Susan Collins (2003) present an update showing that convergence ultimately depends on where the individual countries stand initially. In contrast, Margaret McMillan and Dani Rodrik (2011) show that even unconditional convergence can be shown in manufacturing sectors. The authors restrict the analysis to the recent period of intensive globalization, 1990–2007, and apply a sample of only 38 countries. As manufacturing sectors exhibit relatively large productivity increases, economic development is stimulated by the expansion of these sectors. If labour is displaced from highly productive sectors towards activities with lower productivity the economy-wide growth suffers. McMillan and Rodrik show that this is the case in Latin America and Africa, while in Asia structural change increases the growth rate of the economy. The difference is explained by the policies followed in the countries concerned. For instance, the Chinese authorities want their dynamic sectors to be competitive in the world market, which can be accomplished by an undervaluation of the real exchange rate. In contrast, in Latin America and Africa overvaluation of the real exchange rate squeezes profits in traditional industries operating at tight profit margins in the world market.

Catching-up is self-limiting. Growth rates decline as progress is made. Barry Eichengreen, Donghyun Park and Kwanho Shin (2011) estimate the chance of a substantial growth slowdown applying a sample with a large number of countries. The chances of such a slowdown depend on per capita GDP and a number of other variables, such as openness to trade, the composition of spending and the pre-slowdown rate of growth. Applying the results to China, it is found that the chance that China will have to face a growth slowdown in the near future is 73 per cent. This result is not in accordance with other empirical studies, which project high growth rates for the Chinese economy in the foreseeable future. Whether developing economies will start or continue to catch up with the leading countries is of utmost importance, as it influences the balance of power and cooperation of countries at a global level.

Patterns of international cooperation and the implications for democracy are discussed in Chapter 8. According to Dani Rodrik (2011a) countries have to choose between three alternatives. Globalization in the sense of full-scale market liberalization can be realized in two ways. First, countries can give up a significant part of their national sovereignty. Second, globalization can be combined with the nation state if democracy is kept at bay. The third possibility is to reject, what Rodrik calls hyperglobalization in order to rescue democracy. In the latter case one settles for a 'thin' or 'sane' version of globalization, meaning that countries maintain the right to protect their own social arrangements, regulations and institutions. The purpose of international economic arrangements is then to determine the rules for managing the interface among national institutions. The big question is of course whether countries really have that choice or whether they have to accept hyperglobalization under the pressure of international competition. What is at stake is revealed on a smaller scale by the problems surrounding the economic integration of Europe. In this respect the viability of the European Monetary Union (EMU) is of special interest. A monetary union or currency area without political unification invites trouble. This is certainly true when core EMU-countries and periphery-countries face diverging price levels. As a consequence of too high price levels in the periphery the real problem is a lack of competitiveness of the latter group of countries. This implies that the debt crisis is in essence a balance-of-payments crisis in the GIIPS-countries (Greece, Italy, Ireland, Portugal and Spain). Hans-Werner Sinn (2011) proposes a number of measures to restore market discipline in these countries, and to provide temporary help. However, to really rescue the euro it may be necessary to give up a part of the sovereignty. To a certain extent this already applies in the context of the European Union (EU). In fact as Charles Sabel and Jonathan Zeitlin (2007) argue, the EU is already in a stage characterized by a 'new architecture of experimentalist governance'. In this respect Europe may be considered as a forerunner in the search for new forms of international cooperation.

It is also interesting to speculate what will happen in China. Will there be another variety of capitalism, not routed in democracy, but characterized by Confucian values? According to Christopher McNally (2011) *Guanxi* capitalism with a 'deliberate ambiguity' in human relations is a Chinese variety of state capitalism, which may survive in the future. That China will remain different for a long time to come is corroborated by Martin Jacques (2009) in his penetrating study of the Chinese culture.

The implications for international economic cooperation are difficult to guess but the role of China will be prominent as Jacques (2009, p. 431) emphasizes: 'A nation that comprises one-fifth of the world's population is already in the process of transforming the workings of the global economy and its structure of power'.

PART I

Economic theory in a historical perspective

1. Emerging markets

1.1. THE GREAT TRANSFORMATION

Markets have been ever-present. However, the dominant role of the market system in the process of production, allocation and distribution of goods started with the (first) Industrial Revolution in England. Karl Polanyi (1944) speaks of the 'Great Transformation'. Since then, markets have no longer been embedded in social relations. On the contrary, after this radical transformation the market system has determined social relations.

Polanyi's ideas are partly based on anthropological studies. He distinguishes between different forms of what he refers to as economic integration. The latter concerns the way the process of production, allocation and distribution of goods is organized and economic activities are coordinated. Before the (first) Industrial Revolution, economic systems were based on the fundamental principle of either reciprocity or redistribution, or on a combination of these two. Reciprocity or mutuality rests on the exchange of gifts in a symmetric situation. Redistribution presupposes a central authority that coordinates economic activity. Self-interest and status, resulting from the possession of goods, are of minor importance, as the following quotation makes clear:

> In this framework, the orderly production and distribution of goods was secured through a great variety of individual motives disciplined by general principles of behaviour. Among these motives gain was not prominent. Custom, law, magic, and religion co-operated in inducing the individual to comply with rules of behaviour which, eventually, ensured his functioning in the economic system (Polanyi, 1944, p. 57).

Critics claim that Polanyi attributes too high a significance to primitive economic systems, for example, the exchange of goods on the Trobriand Islands in Western Melanesia. These islands roughly form a circle, which determines the trade based on the principle of reciprocity. Another example of such a primitive economic system concerns the bureaucratic redistribution in the Ancient Kingdoms of Babylon and Egypt. The procedures in these economies diverged substantially from the state of affairs in the economy of England on the eve of the Industrial Revolution. In the English commercial system many were making a profit from trading goods. However, what matters for Polanyi is that markets were controlled by rulers or organizations, for example, the medieval guild system.

Another point of criticism concerns Polanyi's concept of man, which many commentators consider to be overly romantic. Reciprocity supposes kindness and generosity, whereas the market system emphasizes self-interest and rational calculation. According to Polanyi's critics, self-interest and pursuit of profit already played an important role in ancient times. However, in Polanyi's view, the market system or capitalism, to use that word, has not changed man fundamentally. For the motives that eventually determine the conduct of man depend on the system of economic integration that is in force. Such a system stimulates certain motives, while suppressing others.

Once put in motion, the market system generates its own dynamics. According to Daniel Friedman (2008) a dual 'positive feedback system' exists that consists of two parts. The first part of this dual system concerns the relation between markets and innovation. The application of recent inventions enables the functioning of markets. Conversely, markets stimulate innovative behaviour: 'Innovation is normally suppressed in traditional empires, but increasingly in Europe, it found wealthy supporters' (Friedman, 2008, p. 52). The second 'feedback' concerns the relation between market forces and moral behaviour. Moral behaviour is encouraged that enhances the well-functioning of markets, such as effort, punctuality, rationality and scepticism regarding authorities. Once present, this stimulates the functioning of markets: '. . . the new morals would spread, boosting and boosted by the new market system' (Friedman, 2008, p. 55). Remarkably, Friedman, following Max Weber, accentuates virtues, meanwhile ignoring the emphasis on self-interest at the expense of pro-social behaviour.

In Polanyi's (1944) vision, the 'self-regulating market' is comprehensive. This implies that land, labour and money are transformed into what the author refers to as 'fictitious commodities'. However, the consequences of this transformation cause tensions and resistance. Indeed, according to Polanyi, the market system is not able to preserve itself: 'Our thesis is that the idea of a self-adjusting market implied a stark utopia. Such an institution could not exist for any length of time without annihilating the human and national substances of society; it would have physically destroyed man and transformed his surroundings into a wilderness' (Polanyi, 1944, p. 3).

When discussing this issue, Polanyi does not confine himself to the inequality in the income distribution. He also analyzes various other kinds of disruptions. Unconstrained market forces result in a 'war of all against all', in the spirit of Thomas Hobbes (1651). Resistance does not only come from the workers, but it gets broader support. This implies that a 'double movement' is decisive for the functioning of the market system. On the one hand, efforts are made, aimed at stimulating the 'self-regulating market'. Polanyi considers the 'enclosure' of common agricultural property during the 1790s and the reform of the 'Poor Law' in the year 1834 in England as striking examples. On the other hand, regulating the market system proves to be necessary. Such regulation is inherent to the market system, as the 'self-protection of society' is also part of the 'double movement'. Examples include restrictions regarding the employment of women and children, the growing influence of the labour unions and the foundation of the Bank of England as the 'lender of last resort'.

Polanyi's work shows a close resemblance to the oeuvre of Marx. Indeed, as Fred Block (2003) puts forward, Polanyi initially belonged to the Marxian tradition. However, he gradually adjusted his vision while conceiving his book called 'The Great Transformation'. This even goes as far as adjusting the terminology used. He replaces the term 'capitalism' with the term 'market economy'. Furthermore, he makes no reference at all to concepts such as 'productive forces' and the 'ruling class'. When introducing the notion of 'fictitious commodities', Polanyi (1944) indicates that this has nothing whatsoever to do with the Marxian concept of 'commodity fetishism'. However, the answer to the question of whether 'The Great Transformation' fits in the Marxian tradition is not that relevant. For, in this book, Polanyi has recorded a number of fundamental characteristics of capitalism. This makes the book a work of lasting significance.

In more recent contributions, Douglass North, John Wallis and Barry Weingast (2006, 2009) reflect upon the Great Transformation from a somewhat different point of view, without even mentioning the work of Polanyi (1944). North et al. make a distinction between 'natural states' and 'open access societies'. A dominant coalition that relies on complementary elites holds power in 'natural states'. For, military, religious, political and economic elites form an alliance that maintains its power by means of the creation of rents and the distribution of these rents between them. Obviously, this is nothing else but the exploitation of the majority of the population by the minority. However, in the science of economics, the more neutral term 'rent-creation' is customary in this connection. A rent is defined as 'a return on an economic asset that exceeds the return the asset can receive in the best alternative use' (North et al., 2009, p. 19). An important aspect of 'limited access orders' is the creation and distribution of rents by limiting the ability to establish organizations. Organizations foster competition in the economic and political spheres. Natural states are characterized by market power, privileges and differences between elites and citizens.

The 'natural state' is stable, but not static. The stability is warranted by a 'double balance': a correspondence between the organization of the military and political power, on the one hand, and the organization of the economic system in relation to the political system, on the other hand. The dynamics of such a society is determined by unexpected exogenous shocks, which might undermine the balance of power.

The 'open access society' or 'open access order' is based on a different type of logic. In such a society, citizens are free to establish organizations in all possible areas. The state keeps the violent or military organizations under control. In turn, the state itself is controlled by political parties and other organizations. In the sphere of the economy, individuals and organizations strive for the creation of 'rents'. However, competition, in the economy as well as in politics, prevents individuals and organizations enjoying excessive revenues. The 'open access society' is featured by its own specific double balance: 'open access and entry to organizations in the economy support open access in politics, and open access and entry in politics support open access in the economy' (North et al., 2009, p. 19).

The transition from a 'natural state' to an 'open access society' is an important aspect of the analysis, or as North et al. (2006, p. 6) state: 'Understanding the transition is the Holy Grail, for it is the process of modern economic development'. This transition clearly resembles the 'Great Transformation' as described by Polanyi (1944). Nevertheless, the authors in this book do not relate this transformation directly to the Industrial Revolution. In their view, historical transitions occur, provided that certain 'doorstep conditions' are satisfied. These conditions imply that the dominant coalition has a clear interest in the expansion of the opportunities for 'impersonal exchange' in the direction of other elites as well. This requires an adjustment of the existing institutions. The 'door-step conditions' are a set of necessary conditions, but they are not sufficient for a 'Great Transformation'. Further developments must make it attractive for the elites to extend the impersonal exchange to other groups. The analysis is reminiscent of the theory of the 'punctuated equilibrium' in which one equilibrium is somewhat abruptly replaced by another equilibrium. Indeed, as the authors conclude: 'historical transitions occurred within relatively brief periods, typically about fifty years' (North et al., 2006, p. 27).

The difference with the analysis of Polanyi (1944) is crucial. Although Polanyi dismisses the ideas of Marx, he succeeds in exposing the essential characteristics of the capitalist system. North et al. (2009) do not even refer to Marx. In their interpretation of the social orders, the neo-liberal body of thought with respect to the functioning of markets forms a kind of background utopia. Moreover, Marx is criticized, because by postulating that material conditions determined political arrangements, he failed to see both sides of the 'double balance'. At some stages, their utopia comes to the fore, more explicitly when, for instance, the functioning of markets is idealized: 'The presence of competition within open access orders fosters impersonal exchange and enables the price mechanism to function ... Resources are, therefore, able to move to their highest-valued use and because prices reflect marginal costs and marginal benefits, resources can actually seek out and determine their highest-value use' (North et al., 2006, p. 45). In open access orders, there is competition between different kinds of economic organizations. But too much competition can destroy the whole system. The open access order can be associated with capitalism. However capitalism, as Polanyi reminds us, has the tendency to annihilate society. This essential property does not get proper attention from North, Wallis and Weingast. To conclude, we summarize the lessons to be learnt from 'The Great Transformation' in three points:

1) Polanyi calls attention to a fundamental change in the history of mankind. Before the Industrial Revolution the economy was always embedded in society. After the revolution the situation was turned around and society was subordinated to the logic of the market. Classical economists encouraged politicians to pursue a policy of fully disembedding the economy.

2) Polanyi argues that a fully self-regulating market economy requires human beings and the natural environment to be turned into commodities. This will induce resistance and the state must play an active role to reduce the risks of unemployment, poverty and financial instability. The capitalist system is characterized by a double movement. The movement toward a laissez-faire economy is opposed by a protective countermovement. It is interesting to note that Polanyi was aware that this could sometimes create a dangerous political-economic stalemate. 'His analysis of the rise of fascism in Europe', says Block (2001, p. XXVIII), 'acknowledges that when neither movement was able to impose its solution to the crisis, tensions increased until fascism gained the strength to seize power and break with both laissez faire and democracy'.

3) The anthropological studies of Polanyi illustrate that the system of economic integration that is in force determines ideas, beliefs and motives, to a large extent. Or as Block (2003, p. 300) argues: 'As Polanyi makes clear human beings are not born with Adam Smith's propensity to barter and trade. On the contrary, economic actors

have to be constructed; they have to learn how to behave in market situations'. Consequently, the ideas of market liberalism rooted into England, and by extension, the United States, could be adapted in the construction of market societies on the European continent and elsewhere.

Polanyi (1944) wrote a rich book in which he analyzed the essentials of a self-regulating market system. Writing in the US during the Second World War Polanyi was optimistic about the future. He saw Roosevelt's 'New Deal' as a model for a democratic system where regulation and control can achieve freedom for all. However, despite its merits Polanyi's analysis does not pay sufficient attention to technological progress, which is the main driving force behind the double movement, as we will argue throughout our book.

1.2. PROTECTION OF PROPERTY RIGHTS

A kind of 'double movement' also appears when analyzing the emergence of markets in the era preceding the Industrial Revolution. Traders need protection to be able to sell and buy commodities. At the same time, trade needs to be regulated to avoid abuse and conflict. The relation between trading partners is simple in the case of a single encounter between a buyer and a seller, and complete transparency with regard to the product that is traded. However, if such information is absent, the buyer runs the risk of purchasing something that does not meet his expectations. He may be cheated. Cheating may happen in different ways. First, the seller may deliver inferior products. Second, the buyer may disappear without paying. Third, the seller may not keep his promise to deliver goods in the future. These problems are less serious in the case of repeated transactions between a buyer and a seller. Then, both parties have a clear interest in establishing a solid reputation, as trade will cease if one of the parties cheats, putting an end to opportunities to make a profit. The reputation mechanism is important, certainly if one takes into account that reputation may be transferable. A trader who cheats falls into bad repute within the group of traders. As a consequence, no other trader wants to do business with him anymore. Obviously, the reputation mechanism will only work if the group of traders is fairly small. If the group becomes too large, an alternative has to be developed.

Institutions, aimed at the protection of property rights, originated in the beginning of the Middle Ages when trade started to prosper. The whole body of rules, codes and administration to stimulate commercial transactions in the Middle Ages is known as the *Lex Mercatoria*, or, in English, as the Law Merchant. The traders established this regulation all by themselves, as the central authority was either too weak or simply not capable of arranging this. These institutions were aimed at solving two problems. First, traders need to be adequately informed about the counterparty in a transaction, which enables them to punish in the case of fraud. Second, traders should be motivated to discipline the cheaters, even if this would come at a cost. Both conditions need to be fulfilled for the reputation mechanism to be effective.

Paul Milgrom, Douglass North and Barry Weingast (1990) develop a model that is inspired by the annual 'Champagne Fairs'. These fairs played an important role in the twelfth and thirteenth centuries as a *trait d'union* between economic activity in the North and in the South of Europe. As can be seen in Map 1.1, the county of Champagne is located between Paris and Dijon. Its attractiveness was determined by its location as well as by its liberal rulers. The fairs were held at the cities of Provins and Troyes. As Peter Spufford (2002, p. 144) notes: 'The geographical position of Champagne gave to its fairs, for a century-and-a-half, an important international position quite different from those of the vast number of other local and regional fairs that had been springing up all over Europe at the same time.' Specialized cloth-dealers from Flemish towns made week-long journeys to bring and sell their valuable merchandise. The Genoese and other Italian traders brought Italian goods and also products imported from the Levant to Champagne. Many of them spent a month in the region. The clientele of the Champagne fairs came from places in Germany, Italy, northern France and Flanders. The local currency with a mint established at Provins became of international importance. The same holds true for the 'troy weight' as a standard for weighing commodities, which was also applied in London as well as in Paris.

With so much economic activity, there was a need for institutions to settle disputes. This demand was easily met as Spufford (2002, p. 146) concludes: 'A whole organisation of overseers and courts for the fairs gradually evolved, so that cheap and rapid justice was available to settle commercial disputes, and enforced the payments of debt contracted at them.'

The analysis of Milgrom et al. (1990) builds on these empirical observations. The starting point is the notion that it is not necessary for every trader to know whether all other traders are honest. A system aimed at such comprehensive information would be far too expensive. It suffices for every trader to know whether his counterparty is trustworthy. To achieve this, the local ruler appointed an official with authority, who would collect information and intermediate in conflicts, the so-called 'Law Merchant'

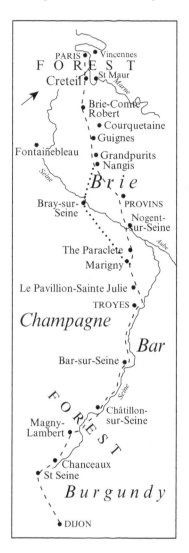

Source: Spufford (2002).

Map 1.1   *Routes from Paris to Dijon recommended by the Itenéraire de*
              Bruges, both going through Provins and, alternatively, avoiding
              it. Many goods were also carried down to Paris on the Seine.
              The map also indicates the various principalities, and the forest
              belts that the route passed through.

(LM) in the model by Milgrom et al. (1990). Traders could obtain information from the LM, for example, regarding whether their counterparty had outstanding debt. If this were the case, there would be no trading at all or additional security would be demanded. However, even if there were no unpaid bills, cheating remained possible. Traders could report fraud to the LM, provided that they had obtained information from this authority about the status of their counterparty prior to trade. Both obtaining information from the LM and filing a complaint with this authority were costly. If in a dispute between two parties the LM had reached the conclusion that one of the parties had cheated, damages were awarded to the injured party. The convicted party might pay this debt, or not. The LM did not possess any means of exercising power in order to enforce this payment. Execution of this arrangement was a matter of private initiative, because the government was mostly at too large a distance, in the literal and figurative sense. The LM did register unpaid bills, which provides an instrument to encourage honest trade.

It should be observed that the system described above only leads to honest and, therefore, efficient trade, if some plausible conditions are met. First, the amount of compensation ought to be sufficiently high to provide an incentive to file a complaint, since the latter action entails expenses. Second, the size of the compensation should be prohibitive for cheating. Third, the amount of compensation should not be too high, as this would probably rule out voluntary payment. Finally, it is important that the party who has to pay the compensation attaches importance to continuation of trade in the future. If this party does not intend to participate in future fairs, the damages will not be paid. Without the strong arm of the law, it is impossible to expel incidental cheating.

The theoretical model of Milgrom et al. (1990) meticulously shows how information can be collected, how this information can be dispersed and how this enables the reputation mechanism to perform its task. However, trust remains an important factor in economic activity. Milgrom et al. (1990, p. 19) are fully aware of this: 'Neither the reputation mechanism nor the institutions can be effective by themselves. They are complementary parts of a total system that works together to enforce honest behaviour.'

The game-theoretical exercise is not an exact account of the functioning of the 'Champagne Fairs'. Such an account would be neither possible nor necessary. The model makes clear that certain institutions are required to protect property rights, thus fostering the functioning of the economy. Such private institutions gained importance, as both the size and the intensity of trade increased, and cities claimed a more prominent role with respect to the regulation of markets in the late Middle Ages. At the end of this period in European history, the government got a stronger grip on the enforcement of socially desirable behaviour, owing to the formation of nation-states. The monopoly on violence retained by the state also leads to a decrease in the costs of the regulation of trade. For the sake of clarification, suppose that the government can settle conflicts at the same cost as the Law Merchant in the example above. Then, the additional costs attached to obtaining information from the LM about the behaviour of merchants in the past can be avoided. Therefore, intervention of the government in the economy has major consequences. As Milgrom et al. (1990, p.21) note: 'Thus our approach suggests that the importance of the role of the state enforcement of contracts was not that it provided a means of enforcing contracts where one previously did not exist. Rather, it was to reduce the transaction costs of policing exchange'.

Ownership and acquisition are not only important in trade relationships. The less protected the owners of goods are, the richer the loot that predators, if any, may extract. With no protection, anarchy prevails, characterized by Thomas Hobbes (1651) as the 'war of all against all'. Sellers of goods attempt to prevent looting by taking the necessary precautions. Such measures entail costs, so that a trade-off arises between protection and losses due to robbery. In an article titled 'Make Us a King', a title derived from the request of the people of Israel to the prophet Samuel, Herschel Grossman (2002) shows that the state is able to arrange this type of protection at lower costs than individual producers. Surprisingly, this does not stem from the cost-lowering effect of economies of scale. The latter may occur in reality, but, in that case, the argument is trivial. Grossman makes clear that the state is able to supply a public good, whereby the deterrent effects on potential predators are taken into account when establishing the level of protection. Individual producers do not take this externality into account in their decision on the level of protection. Therefore, if the government takes care of the protection of property rights, per capita income will be higher than under anarchy.

However, the state often serves the interests of the ruling elite. This does not necessarily mean that producers would be better off under anarchy. Grossman (2002) shows that per capita consumption may be higher in a 'proprietary state', in which the monarch (king) maximizes consumption of the ruling elite via the tax system. By monopolizing the protection of property rights, the state increases the tax base. As a result, government revenues rise. Of course, this cannot go on forever. As the government raises the tax burden or tax rate (τ) ever more, taking on the role of predator becomes attractive for more and more individuals. The government does not have a grip on these predators in the model and, thus, increasingly loses revenues. Thus, there is a limit to maximizing the consumption of the elite. This constraint can be illustrated by a 'Laffer curve', which

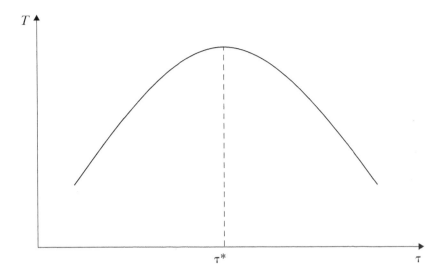

Figure 1.1　A Laffer curve

relates the tax rate (τ) imposed on economic activities to the tax proceeds (T) of the government. The curve usually takes the form of an inverted parabola as shown in Figure 1.1.[1] The optimal tax rate from the viewpoint of the government is τ^*. For tax rates $\tau > \tau^*$, tax revenue declines as more people curtail their legal economic activities.

The pursuit of power and wealth may seduce a 'rent-seeking' elite to raise government outlays above the level that is justified from the viewpoint of optimal taxation. This will lead to citizen resistance, which takes us back to the first aspect of the 'double movement' as described by Karl Polanyi (1944). In this context, it is of utmost importance that market participants may trust the government to respect property rights both in the present and in the future. Douglass North and Barry Weingast (1989, p. 803) concisely express what really matters: 'For economic growth to occur the sovereign or government must not merely establish the relevant set of rights, but must make a credible commitment to them'. If the sovereign might raise taxes arbitrarily in the future, then investing becomes less attractive. However, it remains an open question whether the government can commit itself in a credible way in order to provide the desired level of certainty.

North and Weingast (1989) describe how the 'Glorious Revolution' of 1688 seriously curtailed the power of the king in England. The king possessed virtually absolute power before this revolution unfolded. One should note that the parliament did not have any say at all with regard to government outlays. Its main influence concerned the approval of taxes raised for different purposes, for example, waging war against enemies. Besides, the king acquired revenues from different sources. Half of total revenues stemmed from large landownership. Sales of monopoly rights formed a special way to generate income. Patents were used 'to reduce settled industries to monopolies under cover of technical improvements' (North and Weingast, 1989, p. 820). The sales of rights to private individuals essentially came down to a high tax burden on current and future profits. Of course, this exerted a downward pressure on the return on investment, resulting in a lower level of entrepreneurial activity. Many other methods were available to the king to extract value. The ancient right of 'purveyance' offered the king the opportunity to purchase goods for 'public purposes', but at a price that was substantially lower than the market value. Furthermore, the king sold titles of nobility at high prices. Besides, the monarch frequently had to borrow money to cover his deficits. Regularly, he placed forced loans on his subjects. On top of that, the king often did not respect the agreement regarding the repayment of the principal. North and Weingast (1989, p. 810) note: 'The Crown's inability to honour its contractual agreements for borrowed funds is a visible indicator of its readiness to alter the rights of private parties in its own favour'.

The political institutions conferred great power upon the king. His royal prerogative enabled the sovereign to issue proclamations with respect to regulation without the (preceding) approval of Parliament. The Crown paid the judges and, thus, could appoint them at discretion. In the case of legal conflicts, the 'Star Chamber' had the final word, which enabled this institution to correct any verdict that was unfavourable for the Crown.

The arbitrary and avaricious behaviour of the king led to resistance and a Civil War, resulting in a temporary dismissal of the monarchy. After the restoration of the monarchy, King James II aimed at side-lining the opposition in the Parliament. In an attempt to draw all power to himself, however, the king turned on his own followers as well. This was the overture to the 'Glorious Revolution', which led to the removal of the king. James II was replaced by William and Mary. The Parliament conquered the power to reform the political institutions. Meanwhile, the power of the king was diminished. Henceforth, government expenditures had to be approved by the Parliament. Ruling by decree was no longer possible, while the independence of the judiciary was firmly rooted in the constitution. The new political institutions prevented the Crown from opportunistic behaviour. According to North and Weingast (1989, p. 816) the economy benefited: 'Political rights were seen as a key element of protection against arbitrary violations of economic rights'.

However, the majority group in the Parliament consisted of members of the rich elite, the owners of wealth in the pre-industrial era. The Whig Party ran the show and this party wanted to safeguard commercial interests by keeping government influence as small as possible. There was a balance of power, in which the Crown and Parliament were condemned to each other. Consequently, interest groups did not get the chance to push their goals through in the process of political decision-making: 'Any interest group seeking private gain had now to get approval from both the Crown and the Parliament' (North and Weingast, 1989, p. 819).

The 'Glorious Revolution' secured property rights in England. Yet, did it also lead to higher economic growth as compared to France, England's closest competitor of that era? Historical research makes clear that this was not the case prior to the (first) Industrial Revolution. However, the public finances of England were in a far better shape than those of France. This is one of the reasons why the French lost several wars against the English. The consequences were dramatic, as North and Weingast (1989, p. 831) put forward: 'The contrast between the two economies in mid-century is striking: in 1765 France was on the verge of bankruptcy while England was on the verge of the Industrial Revolution'. Nevertheless, it is not beyond doubt whether these considerations of North and Weingast really explain why the (first) Industrial Revolution took place in England. More than that, established property rights are a necessary condition, but probably not a sufficient condition for an industrial revolution. In Chapter 6, we will analyze more deeply the differences between England and the rest of Europe on the eve of the Industrial Revolution.

The institutions that we have discussed so far have to do with the protection of property rights. However, the studies discussed above depart from different assumptions. It is, therefore, useful to explore the taxonomy of institutions based on the work of Avner Greif (2005, 2008).

1.3. COMPATIBILITY OF INSTITUTIONS

Italian traders visiting a 'Champagne Fair' had two main worries. First, the assets they left behind in their home country had to be guarded against abuse by the local ruler. Second, on arriving at the fair with their commodities they expected to engage in a form of fair trade. As Greif (2008) observes, for markets to develop property rights must be secured and contracts must be enforceable. Moreover, as Greif emphasizes, the institutions regulating production and trade must be compatible.

In order to discuss these issues in more general terms Greif (2005, 2008) introduces the following concepts. Coercion-constraining institutions (CCIs) determine the costs and benefits for rulers of abusing property rights with the purpose of extracting wealth from economic agents. Property rights are protected, at least to a certain extent, if agents have the possibility to retaliate following an expropriation. This implies a cost for the ruler which may deter wealth extraction. Greif (2008, p. 3) provides the following examples: 'Merchants can flee with their assets once expropriation begins and craftsmen can respond by increasing the consumption of leisure or reducing the quality of their products'.

The exchange relations that people with secured property rights will go into are determined by the contract-enforcement institutions (CEIs). Contract enforceability is problematic as most economic transactions are inherently sequential. When time elapses between the *quid* and the *quo*, there must be some way of guaranteeing that contract obligations will be fulfilled *ex post*. Contract enforceability can be based on private regulations or institutions such as reputation, family loyalty or supernatural beliefs. Private CEIs are based on economic, social and coercive sanctions imposed by economic agents. The role of the 'Law Merchant' during the 'Champagne Fairs', discussed in section 1.2, provides an example of such a private arrangement. Contract enforcement in the public domain (public CEIs) may be based on legislation and administered by independent courts, as in modern constitutional states.

The analysis of Greif focuses on the interaction of institutions. More specifically, the following two questions need to be considered. To what extent are public contract-enforcing institutions compatible with different forms of coercion-constraining institutions? Can private contract-enforcing institutions stand in the way of public contract-enforcing institutions? Before turning to these questions it is appropriate to identify the factors that determine the effectiveness of coercion-constraining institutions. Throughout the discussion it should be kept in mind that the main issue is how institutions stimulate the emergence of markets in the course of time. According to Greif the analysis even generates testable predictions that are confirmed by developments in pre-modern England, Imperial China and Tokugawa Japan (1603–1868).

The effectiveness of CCIs depends upon three main characteristics of society:

1) Economic power (or 'mobility') can secure property rights, because mobility implies a cost to the rules. If these costs are sufficiently high, the ruler will be deterred from expropriation.
2) The distribution of coercive (or military) power determines whose rights are protected and to what extent. Coercive power is centralized when the military capacity of the ruler renders futile any response by economic agents (asset holders) following an abuse. When coercive

Table 1.1   Examples of coercive and administrative power distributions

Coercion	Administration		
	Minimal	Delegation	Autonomy
Centralized	China under the Qing	Bourbon France	Habsburg Spain
Dispersed	Armed caravans		
Coordinated	Tokugawa Japan	Early Ottoman	England
	European Feudalism		Early Modern

Source: Greif (2008).

power is dispersed, it matters whether there is coordination or not. In the uncoordinated case every group with military power has secured rights. In the coordinated case the ruler coordinates retaliation against any group that uses its military power against another group. The intention of the ruler is to maintain the balance of power. For this reason, a ruler might even find it attractive to protect the rights of agents without coercive power.

3) Administrative power is important as rulers have to implement policy choices, including abuses. The ruler needs 'administrators' for implementation in the form of armies, tax collectors, feudal lords, bureaucracies, self-governed provinces or cities, etc. The administrative structure determines the cost of abusing property rights. In the case of a minimal administration property rights are secured. Delegation of administrative services also influences the costs and benefits of abusing rights. When the ruler, for instance, depends on the services of financiers, who can credibly threaten to withdraw services, expropriation is not likely, as Greif (2008, p. 7) observes: 'Such threats seem to have secured the rights of the sixteenth century Genoese financiers of the mighty Habsburg kings. These financiers had a comparative advantage in the administration of paying the royal army in Flanders'. Historical examples of the distribution of coercive power in combination with administrative structures are presented in Table 1.1.

Coercion-constraining institutions are a necessary condition for markets to prevail. However, the extent of the market depends on contract-enforcement institutions. This brings us to the first question asked above: are coercion-constraining institutions always compatible with public order contract-enforcing institutions? It appears that not all combinations of both types of institution provide equilibrium solutions. The introduction

Table 1.2   CCIs' effectiveness to supply CEIs

Power	Deterrence		
	Low	Medium	High
Coercive	Centralized	Dispersed & uncoordinated	Dispersed & coordinated
Administrative	Minimal	Delegated	Autonomy
Economic	Immobile	Some mobility	Mobile

Source: Adapted from Greif (2008).

of a public-order CEI may undermine the property rights of economic agents if the administration of the government is weak. Establishing a CEI may require the building of an infrastructure, which afterwards makes it easier for the ruler to extract wealth from its economic subjects. The reason is that many CEIs reveal information about the wealth of agents to those with coercive power, thus endangering property rights. As a consequence, markets cannot expand by introducing public-order institutions when rights are secured only by a weak administration. In the same vein one can conclude that public-order CEIs are more likely to undermine the security of rights when coercive power is centralized and mobility is low. The argument is generalized by Greif (2008, p. 13) in the following statement: 'The more effective the CCIs are in securing the economic agents' rights, the more likely public-order CEIs are to expand markets'. The discussion is summarized in Table 1.2, presenting the determinants of the ability to effectively *supply* public-order CEIs. The higher the deterrence, the more effective CCIs are in supporting contract-enforcing institutions that are conducive to market expansion.

The second question asked above is: can private contract-enforcing institutions stand in the way of public-order contract-enforcing institutions? The introduction of public-order CEIs that do not undermine property rights nevertheless will not lead to market expansion when private-order CEIs are efficient. In the case of private contract enforcing, markets remain local and rather restrictive. The network externalities connected with large impersonal trade resulting from better information through price signals and lower search costs will not be effective if the number of market participants remains low. This leads to the possibility that economic agents opt for private order institutions which provide higher benefits. Rulers will then have no incentives to invest in public-order institutions: 'After all, creating public-order CEIs requires an upfront sunk investment in, for example, physical infrastructure and human capital, and requires inducing beliefs in the institution's effectiveness' (Greif, 2008, p. 16).

The efficiency of private-order CEIs depends on social and cultural factors. More specifically, it is relevant whether a society is more 'collectivist' or more 'individualistic'. In collectivist societies, social relations depend on characteristics such as kinship, tribe or religion. Moreover, these societies are usually 'segregated', in the sense that most of the time individuals interact with members of their own group. Private-order CEIs, therefore, take the form of intra-group regulations. This is different for individualistic societies which tend to be more 'integrated', implying that economic transactions will be mainly conducted among economic agents belonging to different groups. As a consequence, private-order institutions are then less effective in disciplining market participants in comparison with collectivist societies. Thus, the *demand* for public-order CEIs will be high in individualistic societies and low in collectivistic states.

Demand and supply determine the institutional design of society. Different equilibria may result with specific consequences for the expansion of the market system. This can be illustrated by exploring the developments in Imperial China and Pre-modern England applying the conceptual framework introduced by Greif (2005, 2008).

The explanation for the differences between the economic development of England and China in the pre-industrial era is well-documented. As shown in Table 1.1, the Chinese state was characterized by a centralized organization, but the rulers did not have an administrative apparatus at their disposal that could exploit the commercial sector. Land was taxed, but taxes on trade were low, as compared to Europe. Under such circumstances, it is not wise to make use of public CEIs. Indeed, in reality, this did not happen, since: 'the authorities invested little in commerce-related legal infra-structure and discouraged legal adjudication of commercial disputes' (Greif, 2008, p. 21). Moreover, the Confucian ideology implies that disputes should be resolved informally, without appealing to the law. Therefore, private CEIs did support trade. The collectivist structure of the Imperial Chinese society stimulated the efficiency of these institutions, resulting in the emergence of lively trade. Prior to the year 1500, per capita GDP in Imperial China was definitely not lower than European per capita GDP (see Angus Maddison, 1991, p. 10).

In England, CCIs were effective after the 'Glorious Revolution', as North and Weingast (1989) demonstrate. Therefore, public CEIs were able to play an important role in economic expansion. Greif (2008, p. 31) summarizes the development in England as follows: 'Given the prevailing individualism, relying on public-order institutions contributed to market expansion once the growing economy strained the capacity of its private-order institutions'. Whether China would possibly have followed the same path, remains an open question to Greif (2008). Military and economic conflicts with the Western hemisphere influenced the institutional development of China in the nineteenth century. The emperors raised the tax burden on economic activity, but corruption increased, while trade stagnated.

This might be true, but long before the conflicts with the Western hemisphere hampered the economic progress of China, the standard of living was higher and technology was more developed than in Europe. The question arises of why, unlike in England, no 'Industrial Revolution' occurred in Imperial China. Greif's explanation (2008) boils down to the claim that the protection of property rights in China was insufficient after all. For, the ruling class enjoyed absolute power, but they showed little or no interest in economic development. Admittedly, the Chinese economy grew, but solely owing to the private sector itself taking care of adequate institutions. However, this type of institution impeded a large-scale development. Greif (2005, p.767) summarizes this issue as follows: 'It was the relative absence of the state from the commercial sphere that hindered further development and led to an institutional evolution that was different from Europe's.'

Following Richard Lipsey, Kenneth Carlaw and Clifford Bekar (2005), we cite the renowned China-expert Wen-Yuan Qian (1985, pp.103–4), in order to clarify the functioning of the Imperial Chinese society:

> In traditional China, a territorially unified autocratic rule was effectively aided by and symbiotically combined with an equally unified system of ideological control. Its philosophical spirit was introspective, its academic scope was officially limited and exclusively politics-ethical, and its basic attitude discouraged innovative practices and rationalistic inquiries. This politico-ideological situation contrasted sharply with European pluralism, which was fully embodied in its feudal separatism, national rivalries and religious disputes.

The Chinese ideology prevented the large-scale application of new technologies from taking off. The following example may serve as an illustration (Lipsey et al., 2005, pp.285–6). In the beginning of the fifteenth century, more than 2100 seaworthy ships were built on government-owned shipbuilding yards, exceeding the production possibilities of this sector in Europe by far. Large fleets were sent to several destinations in Asia. The purpose of these tours was to make the Chinese culture generally known and to spread the glory of the emperor among the 'barbarians'. Admittedly, these expeditions took goods with them, but these goods had to serve as gifts rather than to be exchanged. Later on, trade missions were sent, but a new emperor soon finished these endeavours. The elite around him despised trade and wanted to avoid contact with the 'barbarians' as much as possible. From 1500 onwards, the building of ships with more than two masts was strictly forbidden. A quarter of a century later, the authorities even ordered the demolition of all seaworthy ships. This example demonstrates both the success and the failure of Imperial China. A great technological performance did not cause a cumulative development of the economy. By the way, the same holds true for the development of knowledge. In the absence of universities and libraries, there was 'nothing to provide a collective memory for scientific discoveries that would preserve them and allow them to be built on cumulatively' (Lipsey et al., 2005, p. 282). This also meant that scholars had no shelter from the caprices of the imperial court. The totalitarian Chinese state, controlling all ideology, did not even allow the commencement of modern science. As a consequence, the intellectual foundation for an industrial revolution, as it took place in England, was absent.

Returning to the analyses of Greif (2005, 2008), one additional conjecture deserves attention. The author states that CCIs which are conducive to public-order CEIs motivate rulers to establish political assemblies through which parties constraining the power of the ruler have a political voice. Such a democratic institution is in the interest of the ruler, because communication and negotiations with commercial parties may be less costly than solving conflicts. Such a conjecture has interesting implications as observed in Greif (2005, p. 729): 'The views that market development requires appropriate political institutions and that political developments follow the expansion of markets are too simplistic. Markets and political institutions co-evolve, reflecting the dynamic interplay between coercion-constraining and contract-enforcing institutions'. In Chapter 8, we will return to this topic.

1.4.   EVALUATION

Traditionally, trade has always been a very important economic activity. Many things may go wrong in exchange transactions. Frequently, delivery and payment of the goods are not made simultaneously. The quality of the goods cannot always be determined sufficiently at the marketplace. Sometimes, goods only reveal their true value when put to use. The granting of credit creates future obligations. In short, substantial regulation is necessary, certainly if the physical distance between the buyer and the seller is large, while they do not know each other. Sometimes, the involvement of intermediaries (agents) is necessary to make trade possible. However, the relation between the principal and the agent raises its own issues.

In many cases, trade has a repetitive character. The same economic agents meet to conclude a transaction in the present and in the future. Of course, then the reputation mechanism may provide fair trade. One may propose a penalty on the failure to honour one's obligations. Furthermore, one does not want to proceed with any person who cheats. However, the reputation equilibrium is not unique. How many 'mistakes' is an agent allowed to make before he gets punished? Is exclusion maintained if trade is highly profitable? The problems become even bigger if trade takes place with different people at different times. Then, for the reputation mechanism to function adequately reputation should be transferable. However, is everybody willing to carry out a punishment, even if someone else is the party who has been harmed? Thereby, the temptation to repudiate is large if profitability is high.

In the past, parties have made arrangements (institutions) to deal with the problems mentioned above. We have discussed one example in section 1.2, regarding the role of the 'Law Merchant' during the annual 'Champagne Fairs'. In the terminology of Greif (2005, 2008), which we presented in section 1.3, these provisions are indicated as private-order contract-enforcement institutions (CEIs). Such institutions may also be helpful in the case of 'principal-agent' problems. In the eleventh century, the Maghribi tribe appointed agents from their own circle for their seaborne trade, as pointed out by Greif (1989, 1993). In the case of fraud, everybody was aware of this. This system functioned well, even if the recruitment costs of agents were higher as compared to market-based recruitment. The disadvantage of private CEIs follows from the fact that punishment cannot be imposed with legal force. In contrast a government, in whatever way it is organized, has a monopoly on violence. Therefore, solving problems and disputes connected with large-scale trade requires 'public-order contract enforcement institutions'. Legislation, justice and the implementation of sanctions, all in hands of the government apparatus, are the main elements of these 'public-order' CEIs.

If one invokes the assistance of the government to manage trade, one runs the risk of moving the proverbial Trojan horse inside. For, who will check the government? (*Quis custodiet ipsos custodes?*) Suppose that a political elite exists, which aims at capturing a maximum amount of wealth from the traders. In that case, involvement of the government is less attractive. However, the protection of property rights and maximization of the consumption of the ruling elite may be compatible. In the model of Grossman (2002), which we discussed in section 1.2, the protection of property aims at countering predation. In the model, the government is able to execute this in a more efficient way than producers separately (anarchy). Even if the level of consumption of the elite is maximized, everyone is still better off, as compared to anarchy. In addition, generally the premise holds true that the introduction of public CEIs is based on the idea that the government is able to protect property rights in a more efficient way than the private sector. However, this does not mean that the government is able, under all circumstances, to resist the temptation to capture an excessive amount of wealth. In that case, the private sector is exploited and economic growth is hampered, as investment becomes less profitable.

Using the terminology of Greif (2005, 2008), 'coercion-constraining institutions' (CCIs) are then required, to keep this exploitation within limits. In a modern democracy, one is entitled to assume that such institutions are present. In a feudal society, the power of the sovereign and his proximity is large. Under such circumstances, property rights are not secured. In section 1.2 we have explained, based on North and Weingast (1989), how king and parliament kept each other in balance in England after the 'Glorious Revolution' of 1688. It is impossible to determine with any degree of certainty whether this provided a solid foundation for the Industrial Revolution, six decades later. However, it is crystal-clear that the institutional design of England contrasted favourably with the institutional design of Imperial China.

An impressive expansion of the market system accompanied the Industrial Revolution. The economy dissociated itself from society. A 'self-regulating market' emerged, with a different type of society than before. Polanyi (1944) refers to this development as 'The Great Transformation', as we have indicated in section 1.1. However, according to Polanyi, unbounded market forces may cause chaos. It is not possible to transform everything into tradable goods. Labour, land and money are so-called 'fictitious commodities'. These commodities require appropriate institutions in a market economy. It may be expected that such institutions will be enforced in a democratic society, if market forces cause deprivation of people and degeneration of society. 'Self-protection of society' is a part of the unavoidable double movement in the theory of Polanyi.

The characterization of society by Polanyi shows close resemblance to the tension between freedom of individuals and potential repression by rulers that Greif (2005, 2008) identifies. This being said, important differences between the ideas of Polanyi and those of Greif are also noteworthy, as can be deduced from Table 1.3. Greif discusses the problems in the pre-capitalist, autocratic era. The main issue is then to safeguard the property rights of the traders. Expropriation by the government ought to be prevented. At the same time, the necessary conditions for fair trade should be created. An adequate mix of institutions (CCI/CEI) ought to deliver the desired effect. In England a combination of institutions that

Table 1.3   A comparison of concepts

	Greif	Polanyi
Political system	Autocracy	Democracy
Contraposition	Market versus ruler	Market versus community
Institutions	CCI/CEI	SRM/SPS

stimulated a large-scale expansion of markets was operative on the eve of the (first) Industrial Revolution. However, the capitalist system which arose subsequently, raised new issues, as Polanyi (1944) emphasizes. In essence, the 'self-regulating market' (SRM) is a utopia. The market is not able to take care of everything. Society has to protect itself (SPS) to avoid deprivation and degeneration. Democracy, in a broad sense, creates the conditions for correction by citizens, as well as for protection of the latter. Apart from political institutions, private law arrangements are important, too. For example, employers and labour unions can negotiate on regulation within the legal system in force. However, a high degree of regulation (protection) might slow down economic expansion. This will provoke protests, possibly inducing deregulation. Thus, the tension between capitalism and democracy is featured by its own specific dynamics. This leads to a sequential repetition of moves, as far as the institutional design of the economy is concerned. In the following chapters, we will deal with these movements in more detail.

NOTE

1.   The curve was named after Arthur Laffer. However, as Laffer (2004) makes clear, he was not the first inventor of the relation between the tax rate and total tax proceeds.

2. Political economy revisited

2.1. THE BROAD PICTURE

Modern economics emphasizes the concept of scarcity. The object of the science of economics is the way in which society deals with scarce resources. In this view, economics is an aspect science. However, as we have seen in Chapter 1, the functioning of an economy requires regulation. If the scope of economics is on the allocation of resources only, it is often implicitly assumed that the prevailing institutions are adequate. After the Great Transformation, the economy is out there on its own. In this context, North, Wallis and Weingast (2009, p. 112) argue: 'An important property of open access orders is the seeming independence of economic and political systems'. Economic organizations need not participate in the political process to secure their rights. Contracts can be entered freely. If necessary, execution can be enforced. The *raison d'être* of organizations is not based on privileges, while the probability of expropriation is equal to zero.

With established institutions, economics can focus on the functioning of markets. It can be shown that a perfect functioning of all markets leads to an efficient allocation of resources. In that case, no economic agent can directly exert influence on prices, while no externalities occur. Such externalities are present if economic activities influence the position of others, outside of the market. An appealing example is the environmental pollution resulting from the production or consumption of certain goods.

In the case of an efficient allocation of scarce resources a Pareto-optimal situation results. Deviations from the Pareto-optimum will not improve the position of any economic agent, without harming at least one other economic agent. From a moral point of view, this situation is usually characterized as the 'principle of minimal benevolence'. This qualification suggests a high degree of consensus with regard to the desirability of such an efficient allocation of resources. However, something more important is going on during the transition from a non-efficient solution to an efficient situation. Most of the time, the income distribution changes as well. This immediately becomes clear if the government, in the presence of environmental pollution opts for regulation. For example, if a producer is confronted with rising costs to satisfy the legal requirements, profits will fall. Consumers are better off, owing to a cleaner environment. Yet, the producer is worse off, even if he passes on the higher costs to the consumer. This result illustrates that measures aimed at improving economic efficiency have distributional consequences most of the time. Cases in which there are no losers are rare. In the case where the measures taken lead to a potential Pareto improvement, winners can compensate losers. Whether this will happen is a matter of political choice, but the distributional consequences of changing the rules are not always made sufficiently clear.

In contrast, if the emphasis is put on the issue of the distribution of income and/or wealth, then one may expect economic agents to exert pressure, either to maintain regulation to their own advantage or to change it into that direction. In this context, a distinction can be made between the redistribution of already generated income, on the one hand, and rent-seeking in the sphere of income formation, on the other hand. The majority of the citizens may choose for the redistribution of income in a democratic system. According to the 'median voter theorem', this will happen if the income of the median voter is lower than the average income. This theory rests on a number of simplifying assumptions. The problem of redistribution seems to be more complicated, as one has to take political systems and diverging opinions with respect to the organization of society into account. We will deal with this issue at length in Chapter 6.

Rent-seeking or rent-creation occurs in every society, also in the open access society in the sense of North et al. (2009). However, in the theory of the open access society, rent-seeking does not get out of control, as both the market system and the political system are featured by a sufficient degree of competition. Moreover, the economy is dynamic. Vested interests are overthrown by a Schumpeterian competition of new firms, new products and new consumption patterns. According to the authors, a similar competition mechanism is operative in politics. If the power of the existing parties becomes too big, citizens will organize themselves in alternative ways, so that the power is curtailed. Free access to the political arena warrants the dispersion of power. In this way, the economy and politics keep each other in balance: 'seeming independence reflects equilibrium independence' (North et al., 2009, p. 146). However, this equilibrium is not a static one. Society is subject to all kinds of shocks, but competition between organizations in the distinguished domains induces adjustments. Thus, the open access society is featured by adaptive efficiency.

The analysis of North et al. (2009) is a step forward in comparison with the usual analysis of the allocation of scarce resources, which seems to ignore institutions completely. The authors take us back to the political economy, as the branch of science has been referred to traditionally. Politics and the economy are intertwined, as classical authors, with Adam Smith as a forerunner, were already aware of. Mark Blaug (1962, p. 58) makes this unmistakably clear, while characterizing the author of the *Wealth of Nations*:

> In his refreshingly cynical manner, he returned again and again to the theme of class conflict and to the weapons of 'ideology' – false consciousness – which the classes wielded in the struggle for political supremacy. It is in this quality, combined with his understanding of the 'rule of law' provided by the price system, that makes the *Wealth of Nations* a masterpiece of political economy.

The term political economy might evoke the mistake that the discipline is capable of making normative statements. Alfred Marshall (1890) is aware of this. Therefore, he advocates a positivist conception of the discipline. His main concerns are the exploration of goals people want and the ways to realize these goals. Political preferences need to be kept out. That is the way science ought to be. 'And it is better described by the broad term "Economics" than by the narrower term "Political Economy"' (Marshall, 1890, p. 36).

Indeed, the current name is economics, but the statement that this term covers a broader terrain than the notion of political economy is not beyond any doubt. Evidently, a scientific approach requires a positivist approach. The mutual relationships between economics and politics can be exactly analyzed in such a way. The term political economy emphasizes that the allocation of resources takes place in a societal context. The object of economics is broader than the one based on the traditional viewpoint. The domain of the political economy is depicted in Figure 2.1, using a scheme of causalities (arrows). Exogenous influences are ignored for convenience. The focus is on the design of the economy: in particular, the way in which economic activities in society are organized and coordinated. The organization is determined by the state of the technology, the institutions in force and the preferences of consumers. Preferences are usually assumed to be exogenous, so the latter factor has not been included in the scheme above. This assumption does not seem to be realistic, but we will follow it, at least for the time being. Technological progress is, as we shall see in Chapter 3, partly endogenous and partly exogenous. Therefore, in Figure 2.1, the state of technology has been taken into account.

The organization of the economy determines the allocation of the factors of production. Thus, it is also the ultimate determinant of the primary distribution of income between categories (viz. capital and labour), as well as between persons. Obviously, the way in which this primary distribution comes about depends on the formal and informal institutions in society

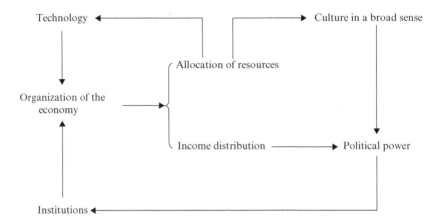

Figure 2.1   Scheme of causalities

as well. In the above scheme, it is assumed that formal regulation is an endogenous variable. In this context, the regulation primarily concerns economic activity. The political power that is necessary to make economic institutions get off the ground is determined by political institutions (such as the voting system), the culture in a broad sense, and the economic power of organizations and persons. In the scheme, the relationship between economic power and political power is linked to the income distribution, which follows from the organization of the economy. A wealthy elite in society may use its means to exert influence on decision-making via several channels. Moreover, it may be in the interest of the elite that the institutions keep the existing distribution intact. Low-income groups may change the income distribution to their advantage provided they can solve the problem of collective action. As Mancur Olson (1982) observes there is a paradox involved in the case of large groups. Because the revenue from contributing to the common goal for each individual is small, rational behaviour induces members of the group to free-ride on the efforts of others.

Culture in a broad sense refers to the body of opinions and beliefs that play a role in society. Such beliefs influence the political decision-making. In turn, opinions and beliefs are partly determined by economic factors. Dominant economic positions may be used to influence the public opinion through investment in education, research institutes and media. Culture in a broad sense may also include informal institutions that exert influence on the economic process. Research demonstrates that such institutions are historically determined (see Guido Tabellini, 2010). A lucid example concerns the degree of trust in society. In this respect, South-European countries diverge structurally from countries in the northern part of Europe.

Path dependency is a reason to categorize such informal institutions as exogenous. Anyway, a clear link to other variables in Figure 2.1 is absent. Rent-seeking is not aimed at the adjustment of informal rules, but it flourishes owing to the opportunity to influence both the introduction and the application of formal regulation. The large number of paid lobbyists in Washington DC and in Brussels forms the living proof of this.

As stated in Chapter 1, North, Wallis and Weingast (2009) make a distinction between the natural state, in which certain elites, sometimes in varying compositions, run the show, and the open access order, in which free entry to the economic and political system determines the state of affairs. As noted in Chapter 1, open access systems are Western democracies with a mature economy. Much can be said against the implicit assumption made by the authors that there is no specific room for elites in these societies. We will return to this issue in section 2.3, when we will describe the economic history of the US. Prior to that, we will discuss the state-of-the-art concerning the theory of political economy.

2.2. MODELS OF RENT EXTRACTION

Elites that dominate the economy will extract rents by imposing a tax on the productive activities of other agents. This gives rise to a number of interesting issues. First, as discussed in section 1.2, taxation may lead to a reduction of economic activities. However, an increase in the tax rate may at a certain point lead to a lower tax revenue. Elites have to take account of the well-known Laffer curve. In the case of a purely political elite the optimal tax rate will be found by maximization of the tax revenue. Things are more complicated in the case of a 'business elite', in the terminology of François Bourguignon and Thierry Verdier (2010).

In the model of Bourguignon and Verdier the economy consists of two groups. In each group, members own assets that contribute to the production of goods. Members of the elite own a fixed amount of capital. Members of the working class dispose over one unit of labour. There is one final product (output) that can be produced in two ways. In the formal sector, which is subject to taxation, output is produced by employing labour and capital according to a standard neoclassical production function. The formal sector is assumed to be competitive. In the informal sector output is produced by workers who escape taxation. The lower the after tax wage rate in the formal sector the higher will be the amount of labour allocated to the informal sector. This assumption clearly limits the possibility of the elite to extract a rent income.

Taxation by the elites differs according to their 'business interest'. The decisive factor is whether these 'business interests' are complementary to labour. This distinction is important for understanding why elites may behave in different ways as Bourguignon and Verdier (2010, p. 3) argue: 'elite-dominated economies relying primarily on mineral natural resources are likely to behave differently than elite-dominated economies relying on manufacturing exports'. If rent extraction is based on the exports of a natural resource labour input may be negligible and the optimal tax rate is found by maximization of rent income. In this case the familiar Laffer curve again determines the outcome. According to Bourguignon and Verdier, such situations can be observed in some autocratic African countries and in several elite-dominated oil exporting countries.

If the elite has to rely on manufacturing, labour will be a complementary factor with important consequences for rent extraction. The reason is that total income of the elite then depends on a market income as well as on a rent income. The market income depends on the marginal product of capital, which will be lower if less labour can be employed. Therefore, taxation has a positive impact on rent income, but a negative impact on market income. The optimal tax rate will then be lower than the rent maximizing level of the tax rate. The situation is illustrated in Figure 2.2 adapted from Bourguignon and Verdier (2010). The specific Laffer curve of rent extraction in Figure 2.2 (above) shows rent income as a function of labour employed in the formal sector (L). There is a one-to-one correspondence between the tax rate (τ) on labour income and the volume of labour employed in the formal sector that is under control of the business elite. The equilibrium allocation of labour when there is no taxation ($\tau = 0$) is indicated by L_0. At $L = 0$ there is no tax base. The market income (marginal productivity of capital) of the elite is shown in Figure 2.2 (below). The marginal product will be higher the more labour is employed. The optimum rate of taxation corresponds with L^*, which is the volume of labour for which the sum of both sources of income is at a maximum. For business elites there is a trade-off between the rent extraction motive and the market income motive.

The model of Bourguignon and Verdier (2010) is extended in the following directions:

1) Elites with limited state capacity can invest in building additional state capacity to facilitate rent extraction. Limited state capacity implies that the group in political control has an administrative problem in extracting rents by taxing other groups. Historical examples of states with weak administrative power are presented in Table 1.1.
2) In the analysis above it is assumed that the elite cannot lose political control. However, as Bourguignon and Verdier (2010, p. 9) observe:

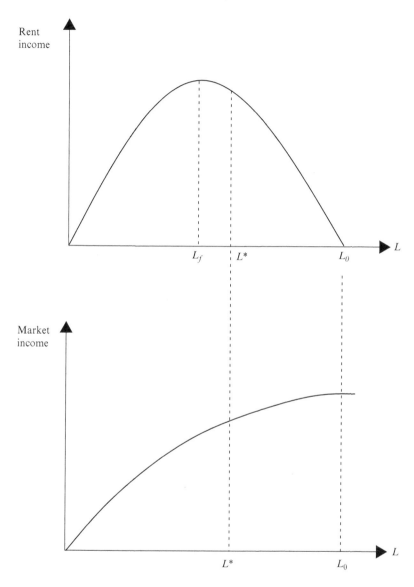

Source: Bourguignon and Verdier (2010). Reproduced by permission of UNU-WIDER.

Figure 2.2 Rent income (above) and market income (below)

'In reality losing political power is often one of the major concerns of elite groups'. The important point here is that such possibilities may not be independent from the redistribution operated by the elite while in power.

3) The structure of the economy becomes more sophisticated if instead of two classes a distinction is made between the political elite owning capital, a group of skilled workers and a class of unskilled workers. A neoclassical production function with three factors gives rise to a taxonomy with respect to factor complementarity or factor substitutability.

These extensions complicate the model from a technical perspective. To avoid the technicalities we limit ourselves to a discussion of some conclusions that are intuitively plausible:

● Assuming constant marginal cost of investment in state building the elite intends either to maintain this capacity at a minimum or raise it to a maximum. The threshold level is found by equating marginal benefit and marginal cost of the investment in state building.

● In the case of a significant probability of losing power, the elite will not invest in state capacity because it might be used against it, if the working class seizes power. It should be noted that the working class when in power will choose a redistributive policy that also trade-offs the 'market income' motive against the 'rent income' motive by the same logic as in the case of elite power.

● It may be assumed that the probability of the elite staying in power depends on the loss for the working class if they are under the rule of the elite compared to being in command of the economy themselves. The optimal tax will then be less biased against the workers than in the case with an exogenous thread of power shifting. By taxing less there is less 'incentive' for the workers to start a revolution.

● In the three factor model the elite can tax skilled and unskilled labour at different rates. As a full characterization of the elite problem is difficult. Bourguignon and Verdier focus on the role of substitutability and complementarity between the assets of the different classes. To simplify, the discussion is in first instance restricted to economies with weak state capacity levels. Then the elite has no motive for rent extraction, but in the case of a 'strong substitutability' of capital and skilled labour, the substitute factor (skilled labour) may be taxed to increase the return on the own factor (capital). This policy is known as 'factor price manipulation'. Unskilled labour is not taxed because in the so-called 'substitution

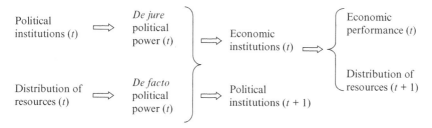

Figure 2.3   Acemoglu's dynamic framework

business elite' economy capital and skilled labour are substitutes, but capital and unskilled labour are complements. The analysis gives rise to some comment. First, effective taxation in an economy with weak state capacity may be dubious. A weak state is characterized by 'the inefficiency of bureaucrats in charge of levying taxes and channelling its proceeds' (Bourguignon and Verdier, 2010, p. 5). As taxing labour income is assumed to be effective in the analysis, the assumption of a weak state requires a different interpretation. Second, the discussion on the complementarity/substitutability issue in the context of a three factor neoclassical production function is rather technical. The factor price manipulation mechanism can be explained in a more direct manner as shown in Acemoglu (2009, Chapter 22). In the model, members of the elite as well as of the middle class can become entrepreneur and produce the final good in their own way. The elite can impose a tax on the output of the middle class. The revenue extraction motive is put aside as in the analysis by Bourguignon and Verdier. The idea is now to hurt the middle class as much as possible so that they reduce their demand for labour. As a consequence, equilibrium wages decline and the elite benefits. Acemoglu (2009, p. 795) summarizes the result in the following manner: 'It is also worth noting that, unlike the pure revenue extraction case, the tax policy of the elite is indirectly extracting resources from the workers, whose wages are being reduced'.

Thus far the analysis is static, but political and economic institutions change over time. Moreover, they are endogenous as emphasized by Acemoglu (2009). To see what this means the author develops a conceptual model in the form of a dynamic framework as shown in Figure 2.3. There are two state variables, political institutions and the distribution of resources, which change relatively slowly. To analyze the changes in institutions, Acemoglu (2009) introduces the distinction between *de jure* political power and *de facto* political power. On the one hand, *de jure* political power concerns existing legislation and the opportunities to enforce this legislation. On the other hand, *de facto* political power is obtained by gaining influence, one way or the other, within the existing political framework. Elites who possess abundant funds are capable of either bribing opponents or side-lining them. In contrast, the masses may exert influence because they are numerous if they are capable of organizing mass protests, which the rulers have to take into account. If obtaining *de facto* political power is at stake, the crowds always face a larger problem than the elite, in getting all noses pointing in the same direction. This is the problem of collective action that we have discussed in section 2.1. If the group is large, many people will simply wait for others to do the unpleasant work. Indeed, 'free-rider' behaviour is a well-known phenomenon.

The arguments presented imply that the distribution of resources has a huge impact on generating *de facto* political power. Ultimately, political power is the sum of *de facto* and *de jure* power. This power factor determines economic institutions and, thus, the distribution of wealth and income in the course of time. The dynamics of the model can be summarized as follows. At time t, the political institutions are given, while the distribution of resources is also known. The prevailing balance of power determines the economic institutions at that point in time as well as the political institutions at time $t + 1$. Establishing or adapting institutions such as parliamentary surveillance, constitutional rights, voting systems, or non-democratic rules is more time-consuming than changing economic institutions. The economic institutions determine the allocation of resources in period t and the resulting distribution at $t + 1$. The latter assumption implicitly refers to the fact that physical and human capital accumulation takes time.

The conceptual framework can be used to structure the description of historical events or applied to construct formal models of political regime switches. In Daron Acemoglu, Simon Johnson and James Robinson (2005) historical examples are given to illustrate the theoretical notions. A prominent case is the development of property rights in England after the Glorious Revolution of 1688. During the Middle Ages political power was in the hands of kings and various types of hereditary monarchs. The rulers had every incentive to protect their own property rights, but they did not generally enforce the property rights of others. The result was that 'economic institutions during the Middle Ages provided little incentives to invest in land, physical or human capital, or technology and failed to foster economic growth' (Acemoglu et al., 2005, p. 393).

Under these circumstances it would be beneficial for the parties involved to strike a deal. However, credible commitments by the ruler are not possible. No one can be sure that an absolute monarch will not renege on his words. However, history took its own course. Major changes in economic and political institutions in the seventeenth century paved the way for the development of property rights in England. The increased fortunes of the gentry and merchants increased their *de facto* political power. This induced a change in political institutions that stripped the king of much of his political power. These political changes led to major changes in economic institutions that spurred financial and commercial expansion, culminating in the Industrial Revolution.

As observed above, the conceptual framework also can be used to construct formal models of institutional change. In Daron Acemoglu and James Robinson (2008) a model of regime switches between oligarchy and democracy is presented. There are two groups of people. Workers produce goods without applying capital. So there are no hold-up problems. The marginal product of labour is constant. The political elite when in power represses labour and captures a share of aggregate income. This share is fixed and is therefore not optimally chosen by the elite. Such a simplification is made in this model, because emphasis is put on the analysis of regime switches. A distinction is made between two political regimes. In a democracy, the citizens (workers), forming a majority in comparison with the elite, ensure that workers will be paid according to their marginal product. In contrast, if the elite are in power, the workers are exploited and the wage is lower. In the terminology of Acemoglu and Robinson, in this case a non-democracy prevails, but, such a situation might also be typified as an oligarchy.

The purpose of the model is to analyze political regime switches along the lines set out in Figure 2.3. Both groups invest in *de facto* political power, but the elite always invest more than the citizens, since the stakes are higher for the former. Citizens could obtain more power, if they would succeed in solving their collective action problem. In the model, it is assumed that this source of *de facto* political power is stochastic and fluctuates in the course of time. Consequently, these fluctuations will cause equilibrium change in political institutions. Society is characterized by a Markov regime-switching structure, in which democracy and oligarchy and the accompanying economic institutions succeed each other, based on endogenous, state dependent, switching probabilities.

The probabilities that the elite holds power under respectively democracy and oligarchy are indicated by $P(D)$ and $P(O)$. Now suppose that democracy prevails, then there is still a chance $P(D)$ that the elite can repress labour and install political institutions in the next period. In the case of an oligarchy the chance that the elite determine the economic and political institutions is $P(O)$. In the baseline model we have $P(D) < P(O)$. As a result of this there is some persistence with respect to political systems. The chance that democracy follows democracy $(1 - P(D))$ is higher than the chance that democracy follows oligarchy $(1 - P(O))$. In the special case that investment in power by elites is as effective under democracy as under oligarchy the model generates the outcome $P(D) = P(O)$. Acemoglu and Robinson (2008, p. 287) characterize this situation using the term 'invariance': 'A special case of our model leads to an extreme form of effect, which we referred to as invariance; even though political institutions change along the equilibrium path, the stochastic distribution of economic outcome remains invariant'. The authors note that these results may explain historical cases, as the enfranchisement of former slaves in the south of the US or the end of colonization in Latin America. In both cases the change in political institutions was neutralized by different forms of *de facto* political power of the ruling elites.

In extending the model it is assumed that it is far more difficult for the elite to change political institutions than it is to change economic institutions. This may give rise to what is called a 'captured democracy'. If a democracy prevails the investment in *de facto* power by the elite may be such that the chance that they can determine the economic institutions is far greater than the chance that they can switch the political regime. A change of the political regime by the elite in the case of democracy is costly, but the elite may invest enough to determine with a high probability how the economic institutions will be designed in a democracy. In this case there is a more or less persistent democracy with a large probability that labour is repressed. This possible pattern is, according to the authors, illustrative for historical situations such as the persistence of economic institutions after the decolonization in Latin America.

This may be true, but the question arises, whether the explanation for such cases requires such rather complex models. This does not mean that these exercises are without merit. The contribution in Acemoglu and Robinson (2008) makes clear that the political conflict between citizens and elites may lead to diverging outcomes with respect to the allocation of resources and the distribution of income. Formal models along the lines set out in the paper may contribute to the acceptance of conflict theory in economics. This being said, we note that the dynamic content of the model is somewhat meagre. There is no place for economic development based on the accumulation of capital and wealth. This is not satisfactory, as a description of the economic history of the US in the next section will highlight.

2.3. HISTORY OF THE US ECONOMY

Many historians point at the alternation of democratic and plutocratic periods in US history. The term 'plutocracy' refers to the true power being in hands of the money magnates. Obviously, the concept of oligarchy is a broader one; it indicates that the political power rests with the elite, who may or may not have economic interests of their own.

In a plutocratic period, trade and industry dominate and entrepreneurs are not thwarted in any way. Income inequality is large. The idea that capitalism is capable of putting its stamp upon democracy has dawned upon many commentators after the recent economic crisis of 2008. Bill Emmott (2003) ventilates in *The Economist* what may go wrong in this respect as the following quotation makes clear:

> Close ties between business and government are detrimental to democracy, and to public trust in democratic government. Companies pose a problem for democracy by their very existence, for through their command over resources, persuasive power and many legal privileges they unavoidably carry much more political weight than do individual citizens. Similarly, political equality is challenged by extremes of wealth, for with more money may come more political power.

However, it should be emphasized that the power of the rich is subject to major changes in the course of time.

Kevin Phillips (2002) describes how large private wealth positions are accumulated in the American economy and which responses this wealth accumulation triggers from the majority of the population. Following Joseph Schumpeter (1939), the important role of the financial sector in the whole is highlighted. Steve Fraser and Gary Gerstle (2005) complete the analysis of Phillips by pointing at the fact that elites succeed each other in capitalism: 'The challenges to the rule of particular elites have come from other elites as well as from democratic pressure' (p. 19). At such a reversal of power, ideas often change as well, particularly if self-satisfied and egocentric elites give way to groups of leaders who have an eye for justice and for the public cause. However, elites remain in power and the class struggle has never really got a foothold in the US. From the democratic perspective, there is an important difference between Europe and the US: 'Genuine class warfare is almost impossible in the heterogeneous United States, but stalwart popular opposition to self-serving economic elites is as American as apple pie' (Phillips, 2002, p. XX). In Chapter 6, we will deal with the difference in the functioning of democracy between Europe and the US.

To avoid not seeing the wood for the trees, Table 2.1 depicts the history

Table 2.1 Historical survey US

Shock	Effect	Period
Civil War (1861–1865)	Gilded Age (p)	1875–1890
Populist resistance (1890–1900)	Progressive Era (d)	1890–1917
First World War (1914–1918)	Roaring Twenties (p)	1920–1930
Great Depression (1929–1930)	New Deal (d)	1930–1947
Second World War (1940–1945)	Golden Age (d)	1950–1970
Vietnam War (1965–1970)	Neo Liberalism (p)	1975–2007

of American capitalism from 1861 to 2007 in a schematic form. The classification in periods is based on Phillips (2002). A certain historical shock, often in the form of a war, induced a change in capitalist dynamics. In the column 'Effect', the periods following every shock are denominated, while the distinction between plutocratic periods (p) and democratic periods (d) is indicated between brackets. Wars play an important role in this scheme. Mostly, they heralded periods of unrestrained capitalism, in which the political system exhibits all the features of a plutocracy. The Second World War forms the proverbial exception to this rule. This war caused a strengthening of regulated capitalism, which set in with President Franklin D. Roosevelt's 'New Deal' in the 1930s.

The Civil War (1861–65) led to a realignment of American wealth, which set the stage for the rise of even greater fortunes during the Gilded Age. Railroads and steel laid the preconditions for scale and scope as documented in Chandler (1990). Capitalism showed its full dynamic force and no one seemed able to steer things in a different direction as Phillips (2002, p. 42) observes: 'Whether presidents were Democrats or Republicans mattered little in philosophy or management of the economy between the mid-1870s and 1896, because the nation's political culture was in the grip of laissez-fair and social Darwinism – the mock-scientific notion that millionaire capitalists represented a "survival of the fittest" selection process'. No wonder inequality increased substantially as is confirmed by a set of data (Phillips, p. 43). According to a certain calculation, one per cent of US families held more than 50 per cent of the total wealth in 1890, compared to about 29 per cent in 1860. Compilation of data at the state level provides a similar message.

In terms of income distribution, the entire nineteenth century shows a uniform pattern. The accumulation of wealth coincided with rising inequality. In the early days, a democratic period, there was still resistance, but 'industrialism was too powerful a feature to be stymied' (Phillips, 2002, p. 31). From the perspective of institutional design and its consequences the whole nineteenth century can be considered as one long period of free enterprise and accumulation of capital and wealth. As Phillips (2002, p. 31) observes: 'It did take half a century for the national reaction to industrialism – and with it, to "predatory wealth" – to crystallize'.

Public concern and indignation grew to critical mass during the Gilded Age. No wonder the turnaround came just over the new century's horizon with a number of remarkable institutional changes. In 1903, the US Department of Commerce and Labor was established with the possibility to investigate corporate behaviour. Railroad legislation was extended in 1906, in the form of the Hepburn Act, giving more power to the Interstate Commerce Commission. In the same year President Theodore Roosevelt offered a substantial reform plan with income and inheritance taxes and prohibition of corporation political funds. These were years of high growth and gains for farmers and workers. Income statistics are still in short supply, but as observed by Phillips (2002, p. 54): 'they do support a significant probability: that the Progressive Era brought modestly significant changes in wealth and income to match its political rhetoric'.

The Progressive Era did not last very long and the old economic elites recaptured political power under the impact of the First World War. Nevertheless, research has attached a special importance to this period. The Gilded Age was a period of totally unrestrained capitalism, in which large firms and their owners (the 'robber barons') enjoyed nearly unlimited power. The significance of the latter is expressed by Djankov et al. (2003, p. 606) as follows: 'The rise of railroads and large firms increased disorder; these firms maimed passengers and workers, destroyed their competitors through aggressive and possibly wasteful tactics, and occasionally poisoned and deceived customers'. Disputes could be fought out in court, but the 'robber barons' influenced the appointment of judges or simply bribed them. The resistance among many layers of the population led to regulation of the economy in the form of antitrust legislation, the promotion of food security and responsible medicine use, as well as improvement of labour conditions. This implied a fundamental change in capitalism: 'the regulatory state was born in the US' (Djankov et al., 2003, p. 606).

As observed above, the First World War (1914–18) put an end to the Progressive Era. The interaction of antitrust suspension with federal subsidies for wartime research stimulated big business. After the war, tax cuts were welcomed and the dynamics of the 'Roaring Twenties' were determined by the interaction of consumer demand and commercial momentum. More than any other innovation, automobiles dominated the 1920s, causing substantial relocations of almost everything, from plants to residential patterns. The speculative nature of the boom ended with the unexpected stock market crash in 1929 followed by a severe depression.

This induced subsequent reforms known as Franklin Roosevelt's New Deal in the 1930s. As Phillips (2002, p. 68) puts it: 'The 1920s' admiration for wealth would become 1930s' distrust'.

Restrictions in the capital market and tax measures contributed to a climate of egalitarianism, whereby unionization and blue-collar prosperity rose together. The effects of the New Deal lingered through the late sixties and into the early seventies, 'years that remain the zenith of twentieth-century American egalitarianism' (Phillips, 2002, p. 69). However, the 1966–1982 period was one of uncertainty and malaise. Productivity growth was slow or absent and corporate executives were pessimistic about the future of the American free enterprise system. Inflation soared and interest rates were high, thus contributing to the 'hidden depression'.

Things changed with President Reagan coming into office. Tax cuts and permissive regulation heralded a new era of liberalism. Supply side economists wiped out Keynesian ideas, and new initiatives were taken in finance and construction. At the same time, in Silicon Valley and elsewhere, the foundations were laid for a technological revolution. The great technology mania of the 1990s induced the Internet bubble in the stock market and the subsequent crash in 2000. But this time economic recovery lay around the corner. The elimination of moral hazard through bailouts and rescues by the Federal Reserve and US Treasury made a fundamental difference in comparison with financial problems experienced in the past. But the balance of power in politics did not shift in favour of reformists.

The classification as shown in Table 2.1 is corroborated by Fraser and Gerstle (2005). The authors discuss American history in terms of changing ruling elites. Centres of power are challenged from below by workers and farmers but also by upcoming elites and new oligopolistic power groups. Historical development is characterized by several moments of crisis of the ruling class and succession by other elites, often with a different view on public responsibility and the need to regulate capitalist expansion.

The first moment of crisis and succession occurred in the decade following the ratification of the Constitution (in 1789). The Federalists wanted to establish a British-style aristocratic republic in the US. They imposed repressive measures that caused the democratic opposition to coalesce. The Federalists were beaten by the democrats and: 'subsequent elites had to accommodate themselves to a democratic politics that had become a defining feature of the American republic' (Fraser and Gerstle, 2005, p. 20). However, buccaneers, industrialists and financiers, who emerged during and after the Civil War caused a second moment of elite crisis and succession. These men did not think of themselves as public men. On the contrary, the new elite of the Gilded Age was both ignorant and contemptuous of the public realm.

The populist reaction to crony capitalism of the Gilded Age triggered a third moment of elite crisis and succession. The new leaders showed an interest in the commonweal that the robber barons had never possessed. The Progressive Era promised: 'a capitalism supervised by the state that would ensure profitability for the owners of capital but also impose democratic checks on the ability of the wealthy to influence politics and dominate the economy' (Fraser and Gerstle, 2005, p. 18). However, after the First World War things changed dramatically as elites chose to roll back democratic achievements. As Dawley (2005) points out, two features mark the change of climate. First, 'by turning plutocrats into patriots, the war temporarily furthered the upper-class quest for legitimacy' (p. 171). Second, reforms in the labour market were looked upon with suspicion against the background of a communist revolution in Russia and disorder in Europe. As a result, 'the distribution of wealth reached something of a Mount Everest of inequality in 1929, when the gap between rich and poor was wider than at any other time in the twentieth century' (Dawley, 2005, p. 174).

The Great Depression put an end to unrestrained accumulation and speculation, and laid the foundation for the New Deal order 'in which the state managed to ensure corporate profitability, high wages, and social welfare for those unable to live off their own labor' (Fraser and Gerstle, 2005, p. 23). A more recent moment of elite crisis and succession occurred somewhere between the 1960s and 2000, when the New Deal coalition was overthrown by the conservative movement. What made this crisis particular was the emergence of the South as the centre of economic and political power. As Lind (2005, p. 253) observes: 'The southernization of American society was visible in many realms, from civil rights, where political polarization along racial lines came to define national politics, to economics, where the age-old southern formula of tax cuts, deregulation, free trade, and commodity exports came to define the national mainstream'.

Arthur Schlesinger Junior (1986) analyzes the patterns of alternation in American history from a political perspective. In his view there exists an endogenous cycle of about 30 years, exhibiting alternations between the attention paid by people to the public cause and the predominance of private interest. Periods in which the public purpose has a large impact on politics are characterized as democratic, whereas periods in which private interest stands central are marked as capitalist. The classification of history in Schlesinger corresponds roughly with that in Table 2.1, with the exception of the 1950–70 period. As the author notes: 'in the 1950s, as in the 1920s, public purpose receded, private motives predominated' (Schlesinger, 1986, p. 32). However, as the Eisenhower years were over a rush to public commitment in the 1960s led to a new era. As a consequence, the cycle in this case is of a rather short duration, because Schlesinger has to admit that a more conservative climate emerged somewhere around 1975. Wars do not play a decisive role in the description by Schlesinger. Political cycles are considered to be endogenous, because they are deeply rooted in human psychology. In the case of acceleration in the rate of social change people get tired of it after some time. The changes are more than they can bear, so that passion, idealism and reform recede. Periods of private interest domination also led to contradictions in the course of time. Then these periods are characterized by dissatisfaction and resistance, culminating in a breakthrough into a new political era with people again seeking meaning in life beyond themselves.

Such a psychological explanation of cycles in American politics completely ignores the relationship between economic and political power that occupies a central place in the studies of Phillips (2002) and Fraser and Gerstle (2005). However, also in the latter mentioned publications emphasis lies on description rather than on the development of a theory explaining cyclical economic growth. Indeed, much attention is paid by the authors to the changes in the capitalist regime, but few causal relationships at all are presented. Maybe it is not the task of historians to explore causal relations, but to gain further insight into the motion of capitalism theoretical elaborations are indispensable. Therefore, in Chapter 3 technological progress, as the main engine of accumulation and growth, will be put under close scrutiny.

2.4. EVALUATION

In North et al. (2009), a distinction is made between natural states, on the one hand, and open access societies, on the other hand. This distinction broadly corresponds with the contrast between an oligarchy and a democracy in the theory of political economy. This theory investigates, among other things, the effects on the economy of the political power of the elite. In this respect, one may think either in terms of a purely political elite, or in terms of an elite with their own economic interests. In the latter case, the elite has an alternative option, next to capturing income via taxation (rent extraction). Heavily taxing competitors forces the latter to reduce the level of output, which decreases labour demand and, therefore, wages. Such factor price manipulation enlarges the income of the elite, since the average production cost falls.

As observed by Greif (2008) states may lack the administrative power to tax their citizens effectively. Consequently, elites have an incentive to invest in building state capacity, so that levying taxes and channelling its proceeds work out more efficiently. Bourguignon and Verdier (2010) show that the elite will raise state capacity to a maximum beyond a certain threshold. However the elite will not invest in state power at all, if there is a significant probability that it will lose political power to the working class. In such a case the chance is great that the strong administrative power may be used against the elite in a later stage. The probability of the elite losing power may depend on the difference in welfare of workers under elite rule compared to their being in command of the economy. The optimal tax imposed by the elite will then be less biased against the workers than in the case of an exogenous probability of power shifting.

Institutions change in the course of time, which calls for a dynamic approach. According to North et al. (2009), the transition from a natural state to an open access order involves a more or less gradual increase of impersonal exchange, which provides new elites with the opportunity to employ economic activities. Once certain doorstep conditions are satisfied, the transition from a natural state to an open access order can be settled fairly quickly. Acemoglu and Robinson (2008) analyze the transition of political systems based on a social conflict between the elite and the citizens. Both groups invest in *de facto* political power. As a consequence, the actual balance of power is not exclusively determined by the existing legislation. The introduction of a Markov process, which simulates the solution of the problem of collective action by citizens, contributes to changes in political power. As a consequence, oligarchy and democracy succeed each other stochastically in the course of time. Moreover, if it is assumed that the transformation of political institutions is relatively difficult, the elite can determine the economic institutions in a democracy during a long period. Following the adopted terminology, this is a case of a captured democracy.

In the model of Acemoglu and Robinson (2008), there is no attention paid to capital accumulation and technological progress. In reality, these phenomena may induce fluctuations in political power and therefore in the accompanying institutions. Historians like Phillips (2002), as well as Fraser and Gerstle (2005), describe the alternation of democratic and plutocratic periods in the US ever since the republic has come into being. Such a description sheds light on the actual development, but it also suggests that the dynamics are determined by a scheme of action and response that can be described as follows. If capitalism is not regulated, then capital accumulation involves various negative effects. The income distribution becomes less equal and external effects gain importance, while moral values erode. After a while, this triggers a broadly supported response, which may induce an adjustment of the institutions. However, a large degree of regulation may then hamper innovative behaviour, which slows down economic growth. This leads to resistance against a surplus of regulation and to liberalization of markets. The unrestrained capitalist expansion can start all over again. The cyclical motion is then completed.[1] The descriptions of Phillips (2002) and Fraser and Gerstle (2005) correspond with the notion of a double movement in Polanyi (1944), referred to in Chapter 1.

Attention for the specific characteristics of the technological development is absent in the historical reflections discussed above. In the traditional literature, the significant impact of the technological development on the degree of regulation in the economy is only recognized sporadically. For example, Djankov et al. (2003) point at the connection between the transition from the Gilded Age to the Progressive Era in the US, on the one hand, and the emergence of large enterprises that undermined the constitutional state, on the other hand. In the view of the authors, this led to inefficiency, which made state intervention imperative. However, it seems unlikely that institutions come into existence merely because of efficiency considerations. As Acemoglu (2009) correctly observes, social conflicts often underlie changes in the area of regulation. Technological change is an important element in capitalist development as stressed in Polanyi (1944). It is therefore desirable to reflect on the characteristics of technological progress to understand what is happening under capitalism. In the next chapter different theories on technological progress will be discussed. In the theory of the long wave, which we will discuss in Chapter 5, the different lines of thought are brought together.

NOTE

1. In Van de Klundert (2010), the concept of recurrent cycles is modelled by applying the Lotka-Volterra model of predator and prey.

3. Engines of growth

3.1. FROM EXOGENOUS TO ENDOGENOUS TECHNOLOGICAL CHANGE

Growth theory has assumed large proportions since the 1950s. Amongst others, Acemoglu (2009) provides a detailed survey of the state-of-the-art. Evidently, technological progress takes a dominant position in growth theory. Remarkably, the position of technological progress has changed substantially in this body of thought. First, it was taken as given, as something that simply had to be taken into account. In a later stage, technological progress itself is completely explained from economic factors. From *exogenous* to *endogenous*, as the title of this section indicates.

In the standard neoclassical theory, economic growth follows from three explanatory factors, viz. capital accumulation, population growth and technological progress. The latter two factors are assumed to be exogenous. It is assumed that population and employment expand at the same rate. Therefore, the growth of output is explained by the growth of employment (number of workers), the growth rate of the capital stock and the rate of technological change. The relation is obtained by differentiation of a standard neoclassical production function with respect to time. Capital accumulation depends on the saving ratio.

Without exogenous growth factors in the form of either population growth, or technological progress, or both, the accumulation of capital causes the marginal product of physical capital and, hence, the rate of return on capital, to decline. However, population growth offers a way-out, as it makes physical capital relatively scarce, so that its rate of return does not need to fall. It can be shown that a long-run equilibrium exists, in which labour and physical capital exhibit exactly the same rate of growth. As a consequence, this growth rate also applies to production, implying that per capita output remains constant. A long-lasting increase in living standards, in the form of a higher per capita output, would require technological progress. In neoclassical growth theory it is often assumed that technological progress is Harrod-neutral, which means that it can be conceived as labour-augmenting. In this set-up, capital accumulation neatly adjusts and per capita output and, hence, welfare increase exactly

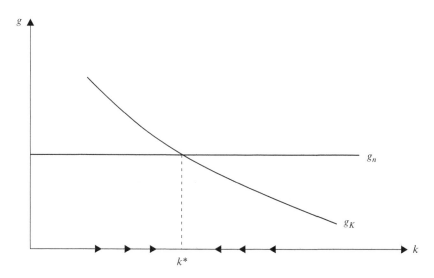

Figure 3.1   Transition towards the long-run neoclassical equilibrium

in line with the exponential rise in (labour-augmenting) technological knowledge. This result is known as the balanced growth path.

The transition process towards this long-run equilibrium path is illustrated in Figure 3.1. Along the horizontal axis the ratio of capital (K) to labour potential (AL) is measured. The ratio is usually referred to as the *effective* capital-labour ratio ($k \equiv K/AL$). Labour potential is the product of the volume of labour (L) and the effectiveness of this factor in the production function (A). Therefore, the factor A augments the labour potential. Both L and A grow at a fixed rate. The sum of these growth rates is called the natural rate of growth (g_n). It is indicated by a horizontal line in Figure 3.1. The growth rate of capital (g_K) depends on the exogenous savings rate and the endogenous productivity of capital. When the effective capital-labour ratio is low, relative capital scarcity results in a high return on investment. Consequently, the growth rate of capital is high and exceeds the natural rate of growth ($g_K > g_n$). In this situation, the effective capital-labour ratio increases as indicated by the arrows along the horizontal axis. The opposite happens if capital is abundant. Then we have $g_K < g_n$ and the effective capital-labour ratio declines. At $k = k^*$, the ratio is constant. Capital, labour potential and output (Y) then grow at the same rate (g_n). As a result, output per capita ($y \equiv Y/L$) grows at the rate of labour-augmenting technological progress. It should be noted that the assumption of strictly labour-augmenting technological change is specific. Empirical research reveals different results with respect to the character

Table 3.1   Models of endogenous growth

Characteristics	Type		
	A K-model	Product variation	Schumpeterian
Engine of growth	Learning process	R&D	R&D
Competition	Perfect	Monopolistic	Direct
Equilibrium growth	Too low	Too low	Too low or too high

of technological change at different times in economic history (see for instance Paul David and Theo van de Klundert, 1965).

The neoclassical theory of economic growth was developed in the mid-1950s. It is usually ascribed to the American Nobel-prize-winning economist Robert Solow (1956). However, others have contributed to the development of this body of thought. The work of the Australian economist Trevor Swan (1956), who launched the neoclassical framework simultaneously with Solow, deserves attention as well. The neoclassical growth theory is not satisfactory, since it does not provide an explanation for the rise in living standards. Technological development is autonomous. This has triggered some characteristic statements in the economic literature. For example, technological development would be provided by 'God and the engineers' or it ought to be considered as 'manna from heaven'.

Despite earlier attempts, it took economists until the 1980s to endogenize technological development in a satisfactory way. In the meantime, neoclassical growth theory has been extended in various ways, without altering the conclusions fundamentally. Different specifications of the production function, the distinction between sectors for the production of consumption goods and for capital goods (investment goods) and decision-making of economic agents under 'perfect foresight' enriched the structure of the theory. Although these extensions increased our understanding of economic growth, they did not throw a new light on the process of technological change.

If technological development is explained from other economic variables, while population growth is ignored, everything becomes endogenous in the theory of economic growth. Meanwhile, there is a large literature on models of endogenous growth. Here, again, we refer to the standard work of Acemoglu (2009) for a compact survey of models of endogenous growth. In Table 3.1 we classify these models by their main type and indicate the distinct characteristics. The table can be used to keep track in the discussion below.

The first and simplest version of endogenous growth theory is based on a microeconomic structure that does not diverge essentially from the traditional neoclassical model of economic growth. In a pioneering contribution, Paul Romer (1986) introduces knowledge spill-over effects between firms that neutralize the diminishing returns resulting from capital accumulation. As in the standard neoclassical model, competition is perfect. Technological knowledge is supposed to be linearly dependent upon the stock of physical capital. The line of reasoning behind this is clear. For, the level of knowledge is determined by a learning process in which all firms are involved. Firms are assumed to learn from past experiences. In this context, the aggregate stock of physical capital functions as a measure. Thus, technological knowledge is related to this variable. Knowledge is supposed to determine the productive potential of labour. Under the usual specification of the neoclassical production function, a linear relation between output and the capital stock results, known as the AK-model. Here, K refers to the aggregate stock of physical capital and A is a constant.[1] Growth is fully endogenous, it depends on the accumulation of capital. Firms take technological knowledge as given and act correspondingly, but the rate of return on capital does not decline under the impact of capital accumulation, owing to positive external effects. With positive externalities, the resulting equilibrium growth rate of output is too low compared to the social solution based on maximizing the welfare of economic agents. In this sense, the equilibrium is sub-optimal.

In the AK-model, technological knowledge is formally endogenous, but firms are not required to make specific efforts to develop knowledge. In reality, entrepreneurs spend much time and effort on 'research and development' (R&D), either to lower production costs (process innovation), or to introduce new products (product innovation). This phenomenon is at the heart of the extension of the endogenous growth theory. Thereby, one should be aware that entrepreneurs have to earn back the costs of R&D. For example, if an entrepreneur has developed either a new product or a new product variant, then some form of imperfect competition will be required. The entrepreneur will then charge a price for the new product or the new product variant that exceeds production costs. The resulting surplus or profit is the compensation for the expenditure on R&D. Moreover, the entrepreneur must obtain a patent on the new product or the new product variant, in order to safeguard these profits by preventing imitation. Models of expanding varieties come in two forms. First, a final good may be produced by many inputs, each with its own variety. Second, different qualities of the final good are sold to consumers, who have a taste for variety. Both constructions generate comparable results.

Endogenous growth models based on R&D and monopolistic competition can be solved analytically, provided that the relationships are well specified. In this context, the efficacy of expenditure on R&D is of vital importance. The effectiveness of spending on R&D should be sufficiently large, both at present and in the future. In other words, the 'engine of growth' ought to be strong enough to warrant uninterrupted growth. If scarce factors are used in the process of R&D, knowledge spillover effects are required to keep the engine going. This condition is satisfied in a seminal publication of Gene Grossman and Elhanan Helpman (1991). The starting point is that consumers attach value to the number of variants that are on offer. Such a 'love for variety' makes the introduction of new varieties of a consumption good profitable. For, an expansion of the number of varieties yields additional utility and, thus, adds value. Firms or individuals may decide to develop 'blueprints' for new product variants and apply for a patent.[2] Monopolistic competition in the market for varieties generates the profit which enables firms to buy these blueprints. In this *expanding-product-varieties* model, there are no entry barriers regarding the R&D sector. Free entry implies the absence of excess profits in this sector. Endogenous growth is possible in the long run, owing to knowledge spill-over effects from past R&D. 'Standing on the shoulders of past giants' increases the productivity of scarce factors currently used in R&D. The growth rate in the market economy is lower than under a Pareto-optimal organization of the economy, because private firms do not take the intertemporal knowledge spill-overs into account.[3]

In the *expanding-product-varieties* model, direct competition between innovators (entrants) and incumbent producers is absent. However, if we assume that R&D-expenditures are aimed at realizing qualitative improvements of equipment used in the production of final goods, matters become different. In that case, an improved machine of a certain type will crowd out the existing machine, despite the latter still being profitable. This implies 'creative destruction' in the terminology of Joseph Schumpeter (1942). One might think that the incumbent himself aims at improving the equipment, in order to stay ahead of his competitor. However, one should be aware that it is not attractive for the incumbent to eliminate his own profit. 'Business stealing' is by definition an activity of others.

'Models of Schumpeterian growth' are available in different shapes and sizes. In some of these models, a constant growth rate of the economy emerges that is, however, once more, sub-optimal. In these models, growth in the market economy (private sector) may be either higher or lower than under a Pareto-optimal organization of the economy. The reason is that two disturbances, the 'appropriability effect' and the 'business-stealing effect', have different consequences. The appropriability effect states that even under imperfect competition the firm is not able to capture the full gain created by the innovation. As a consequence, the investment in R&D

will be lower than optimal from a social point of view. The business steal-ing effect leads to overinvestment as the impact of creative destruction is neglected by innovating firms. In the case of a substantial quality improve-ment resulting from R&D expenditure, creative destruction dominates and growth in the market economy turns out to be higher, as compared to the Pareto-optimal organization of the economy. This comes as no sur-prise, because major improvements of technology destroy many existing activities.

Schumpeterian models of economic growth are, therefore, more real-istic than, for example, *expanding-product-varieties* models, since the competition between incumbents and entrants makes clear that capitalist expansion may hurt. In these models, creative destruction simply boils down to the elimination of monopoly profits. In reality, the destruction of economic value may take on various shapes. In this context, Acemoglu (2009) points at (temporary) unemployment resulting from technological progress, as well as at the loss of firm-specific skills. No doubt, one could devise other examples, but the functioning of markets always takes place in the context of a given set of institutions, as we have already noticed in Chapter 1. Therefore, in reality, destruction of value is a far more com-plicated concept than the one which emerges in market theory. Acemoglu (2009, p. 489) seems to be aware of this, as he states in this context: 'A major insight of Schumpeterian models is that growth comes with potential conflicts of interest'.

3.2. GENERAL PURPOSE TECHNOLOGY (GPT)

In reality, technological development is not characterized by the relatively smooth progression as is usually assumed in Schumpeterian and other models of endogenous growth. Periods characterized by drastic changes in technology are succeeded by eras featuring gradual progress. Industrial or technological revolutions, which are related to important inventions, such as the steam engine, electricity and micro-chips, occur every now and then. In Chapter 5, we will take a closer look at economic history. Here, we confine ourselves mainly to the theoretical aspects of these phenomena.

Recently, the idea that the technological development exhibits irregu-larities has attracted attention in the economics literature. In this context, emphasis is put on breakthrough technologies or general purpose tech-nologies (GPTs). A GPT is a technological innovation, which makes numerous extensions and further applications possible. Examples of such technologies are given in Table 3.2. The introduction of GPTs has partly re-established the exogeneity of technological development. Totally new opportunities emerge, owing to such a breakthrough technology. However, this does not imply that we should think in terms of 'manna from heaven'. Obviously, technological progress is always the work of man. Inventors and innovators make use of scientific knowledge from the present and from the past. However, in the case of an exogenous breakthrough, technological progress is not directly related to economic variables, such as the size of the stock of physical capital or the level of expenditure on R&D.

The identification of GPTs requires assigning a number of essential features based on empirical observations. Elhanan Helpman and Manuel Trajtenberg (1998, p. 55) characterize GPTs by indicating three properties: '(1) They are extremely pervasive, that is they are used as inputs by a wide range of sectors in the economy. (2) Their potential for continual technical advances manifests itself *ex post* as sustained improvements in performance. (3) Complementarities with their user sectors arise in manufacturing or in the R&D technology'. Helpman and Trajtenberg (1998) emphasize the complementarity of inputs in the production process, when modelling technological progress based on GPTs.

The analysis relies on a model with 'expanding varieties'. For each GPT, there is a number of interrelating activities, which are in schematic form presented in Figure 3.2. The final goods are produced from a number of input components. These inputs are produced by applying labour. Aggregate productivity of all components in producing the final good is determined by the current GPT. Suppliers of input components hold property rights and earn a profit. Blueprints for new components can be developed by allocating labour to R&D. The costs of R&D can be recovered, because of the profits generated by producing input components. The engine of growth in the model is weak in comparison with most endogenous growth models. Accumulation of new variants leads to diminishing returns. There is no intertemporal spill-over effect in R&D. Thus, with the passage of time, developing additional variants will no longer be profitable. In the long run, a stationary equilibrium will result with a constant number of inputs. Before that stage is reached, a new GPT may enter the field with a higher aggregate productivity in the production function of final goods. To realize such a productivity increase, new input components must be produced.

As soon as a new GPT appears on the stage, all R&D-establishments will switch to the development of related input components. Initially, the new breakthrough technology will not be applied in the production of the final good, since too few specific inputs have been developed, as compared to the old GPT. However, at a certain stage, sufficient specific inputs for the new GPT will be available. Then, producers of the final good will switch to the new technology. Producing goods and services using a new

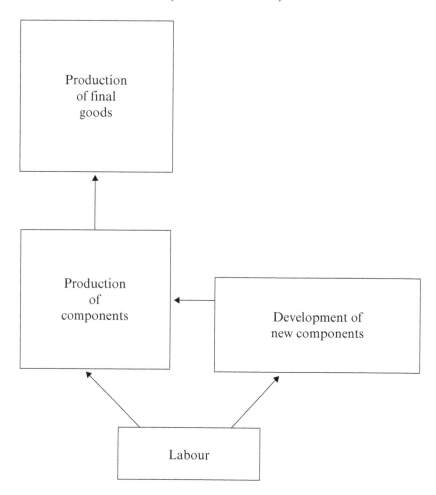

Figure 3.2   Scheme of the expanding varieties model

GPT requires that labour be previously employed to produce new specific components. At the outset, all R&D activities will be targeted at the development of components for the new technology, since the latter will yield higher profits in the long run. Investors exhibit 'perfect foresight', a traditional neoclassical assumption, so that they immediately put maximum effort into the new GPT. Patents are valuable since they will be a source of profit in the future, although the invention is currently not taken into operation.

   At the aggregate level, the model of Helpman and Trajtenberg (1998) generates a cyclical pattern. Immediately after the appearance of a new GPT, real GDP, consisting of wages plus profits on the input side, declines. Real GDP only starts to rise following the actual application of the new GPT in the production of final goods. This cyclical pattern can be demonstrated using a model simulation. The decline of real GDP during the first stage is caused by the re-allocation of labour from production of old components and from old R&D facilities towards the development of new components to be used later on. The decline of real GDP in the final stage is outweighed by the rise of real GDP during the second stage. If new GPTs appear with clock-like regularity, the economy grows in the long run, since output and total factor productivity rise during every complete cycle.

The model by Helpman and Trajtenberg (1998) is representative for the first generation of GPT-models. This type of theory has been inspired by the 'productivity slowdown' in the US, approximately between 1973 and 1990 (see, for example, Andrew Glyn, 2006, Chapter 1). However, labour productivity (output per hour) did not decline during this period, as is the case in the above-mentioned model, though productivity growth remained substandard in historical perspective. A similar outcome can be simulated with a modification of the Helpman-Trajtenberg model in which skilled labour is applied in R&D and unskilled labour is used in the production of components. In simulation results of the model, real GDP growth is substantially higher in the second phase of the cycle, which takes 20 years in the numerical example.

Richard Lipsey, Kenneth Carlaw and Clifford Bekar (2005) use historical data to determine the points of time at which GPTs were introduced in the US. They make use of the following definition: 'A GPT is a single generic technology, recognizable as such over its whole lifetime that initially has much scope for improvement and eventually comes to be widely used, to have many users, and to have many spill-over effects' (Lipsey et al., 2005, p.98). This definition does not differ significantly from the one used by Helpman and Trajtenberg (1998). However, Lipsey et al. (2005) insist that all four characteristics mentioned are necessary for the identification of a breakthrough technology. Table 3.2 shows the results of this research: a list of identified GPTs in the US. According to Lipsey et al. (2005), the economic history of the Western world started in 10 000 BC. For our purpose it is relevant to consider breakthrough technologies since the (first) Industrial Revolution. A distinction is made between process innovation (*Pr*), product innovation (*P*) and organizational breakthroughs (*O*).

Strikingly, biotechnology and nanotechnology are the only cases of process innovation in modern times. In fact, these are both GPTs that still have to prove themselves. Obviously, the distinction between process

Table 3.2   Introduction of General Purpose Technologies (GPTs)

No.	Name	Date	Classification
1	Domestication of plants	9000–8000 BC	Pr
2	Domestication of animals	8500–7500 BC	Pr
3	Smelting of ore	8000–7000 BC	Pr
4	Wheel	4000–3000 BC	P
5	Writing	3400–3200 BC	Pr
6	Bronze	2800 BC	P
7	Iron	1200 BC	P
8	Waterwheel	Early medieval period	P
9	Three-masted sailing ship	Fifteenth century	P
10	Printing	Sixteenth century	Pr
11	Steam engine	Late eighteenth to early nineteenth century	P
12	Factory system	Late eighteenth to early nineteenth century	O
13	Railway	Mid-nineteenth century	P
14	Iron steamship	Mid-nineteenth century	P
15	Internal combustion engine	Late nineteenth century	P
16	Electricity	Late nineteenth century	P
17	Motor vehicle	Twentieth century	P
18	Airplane	Twentieth century	P
19	Mass production	Twentieth century	O
20	Computer	Twentieth century	P
21	Lean production	Twentieth century	O
22	Internet	Twentieth century	P
23	Biotechnology	Twentieth century	Pr
24	Nanotechnology	Twenty-first century	Pr

Source: Lipsey et al. (2005). Reproduced with the permission of Oxford University Press.

innovations and product innovations is somewhat arbitrary. For, the introduction of new products may lead to cost-savings in production processes. In this respect, the application of the steam engine may serve as an example. Nevertheless, in Table 3.2, the steam engine is characterized as a product innovation. Moreover, three organizational breakthroughs are identified. One may have serious doubts whether these are really stand-alone breakthroughs. On the contrary, they may be part of a complex structure. We will return to these issues when we will discuss the notion of the techno-economic paradigm in the theory of Carlota Perez (2002) in section 3.3. The dating of GPTs in Table 3.2 is rather crude. This prohibits a thorough investigation of the influence that GPTs exert mutually.

According to Lipsey et al. (2005, p. 411), this mutual influence is an important part of the analysis: 'In every case that we have considered, the full effect of a new GPT (on productivity among other things) depends on the difference between the range of applications and the productivity of the new GPT on the one hand and the technologies it competes with and/or complements on the other hand'.

3.3. APPRECIATIVE THEORY

To understand the significance and impact of GPTs in the economy, Lipsey et al. (2005) apply two different methods. First, they rely on what is called in the economic literature 'appreciative theory'. This theory is not expressed in mathematical form, but is mainly descriptive. It is applied to get a broader picture of technological change and its implications for society in general. According to the authors, 'appreciative theory' is not a substitute for a formal mathematical analysis, but rather complementary in acquiring knowledge. Moreover, the authors apply a simple mathematical construct, the logistic curve, to give more structure to the description based on historical facts. In addition, rather complex mathematical models are developed to simulate the consequences of introducing GPTs. The numerical results are presented by showing the time-paths of the main variables. As the results are difficult to interpret, even in the case of the relatively less complex models, we only pay attention to the 'appreciative' part of the analysis.

The 'appreciative theory' of Lipsey et al. (2005) is based on what they call a structuralist-evolutionary decomposition, which is intended to break open the black box of the neoclassical production function. How this is accomplished is shown in Figure 3.3. The concepts applied in the decomposition are straightforward, but what is meant by the 'facilitating structure' needs clarification. The facilitating structure is defined as 'the set of realizations of technological knowledge, by which we mean the actual physical objects, people, and structures in which technological knowledge is embodied' (Lipsey et al., 2005, p. 60). There are two types of arrows in Figure 3.3. The broken arrows indicate (A) the flows of natural resources to the facilitating structures where goods are produced and (B) the flow of income and output called performance. The solid arrows indicate internal relationships. To understand what is meant in each case the authors mention the following examples (Lipsey et al., 2005, p. 56):

(i)   new technology is embodied in new machines;
(ii)   new technologies make previously useless materials valuable;

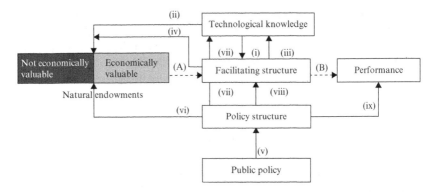

Source: Lipsey et al. (2005). Reproduced with the permission of Oxford University Press.

Figure 3.3   The structuralist-evolutionary decomposition

(iii)   new research laboratories increase the rate of R&D;

(iv)   a rise in population makes it economical to redeem waste land;

(v)   a new public policy requires creating a new government department;

(vi)   a new environmental protection law makes certain mineral deposits no longer profitable to extract;

(vii)   a new tax incentive policy increases the amount of R&D;

(viii)   a new anti-monopoly policy alters the concentration and location of industry;

(ix)   a new tax policy alters the distribution of income.

The appreciative theory of GPTs starts with placing the historical record into the structuralist-evolutionary classification system of technology, facilitating structure, policy, policy structure and performance. This gives rise to a great many observations, which are difficult to summarize. Therefore, here we will discuss the most salient points made by the authors. The effects of a new GPT on technology are to a large extent determined by the relationship with already existing GPTs. Lipsey et al. (2005) stress that new GPTs have arrived episodically in the course of time. As a consequence, a new GPT may compete with technologies that are not themselves already at the end of their development trajectory. For instance, the efficiency of water power was increased significantly when it came into competition with steam for powering factory plants. However, the reverse is also possible when a new technology cooperates with an existing technology. The combination of electricity and ICT provides an example.

With respect to the effects of GPTs on the facilitating structure, the authors make a distinction between transitional impacts and long-term changes. Transitional effects relate to decisions under uncertainty resulting in investment booms and adjustment lags. An example of the latter aspect is the long delay of electrifying the manufacturing sector in America and Europe, because it took decades before existing steam plants had operating costs above the full costs of electrically powered plants and had to be replaced. Long-lasting effects of GPTs on the facilitating structure are, for instance, the requirement of new skills of the labour force, new infrastructure, but also the destruction of existing sources of rent extraction, which lead to resistance by the groups that are hurt. In this connection, Lipsey et al. (2005, p. 417) note: 'When those with vested interests in the old sources of economic rent have substantial political power, a long period of conflict often occurs'.

Induced changes in policy and policy structure relate among other things to a different set-up of educational institutions. A failure to follow the right track may have severe consequences as the differences in educational policies between Germany and the US, on the one hand, and England, on the other hand, over the last 30 years of the nineteenth century show. The second Industrial Revolution required personnel trained in engineering skills. England failed to follow the changes made in the other countries and relied on its traditional system of part-time education and on-the-job training. This is seen as an important cause of the relative decline of the British industry. Another aspect under the heading of 'induced policy changes' is the observation that 'few if any modern GPTs have been developed without substantial public assistance in early stages of their development' (Lipsey et al., 2005, p. 418). The role of the Department of Defense in the US in this connection is well-known.

With respect to the effects of GPTs on performance two insights come to the fore (Lipsey et al., 2005, p. 425):

1) 'There are no necessary relations among the magnitudes of change in technology, in the facilitating and policy structures, and in performance'.
2) 'A second important insight that follows from S-E [structuralist-evolutionary] theory is that there is no necessary relation between the magnitudes of the change in technology and the changes it induces in the facilitating structure'.

To illustrate what is at stake the authors refer to the Industrial Revolution in Britain. During the first half, from 1780 to 1820, the factory system was installed, but this organizational GPT was not accompanied by increases in overall productivity. Then after 1820 the steam engine was

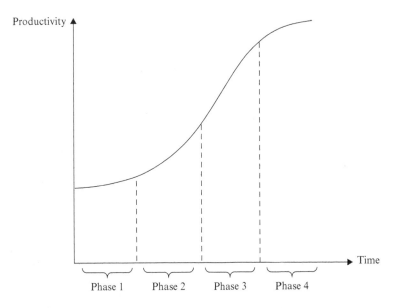

Figure 3.4   A logistic curve of technological change (GPT)

introduced in factories. This brought many changes in the facilitating structure as people moved to the new industrial cities, while significant increases were realized in productivity and real wages. This union of two already established technologies leads to the remarkable conclusion that 'a period when technological change was less fundamental than it had been from 1780 to 1820 was accompanied by larger increases in productivity and larger changes in the facilitating structure than occurred from 1780 to 1820' (Lipsey et al., 2005, p.426). In this context, it will come as no surprise that the authors reject the idea, discussed in section 3.2, that the introduction of a GPT always causes a productivity slowdown.

The appreciative theory based on a structuralist-evolutionary decomposition is rather eclectic and, therefore, difficult to deal with. However, at a 'second level of abstraction', the logistic curve is introduced to give more structure to the theory. The logistic curve is characterized by a slow take-off and, next, a rapid development, which, subsequently, weakens gradually. Lipsey et al. (2005) distinguish between four sub-periods, as indicated in Figure 3.4. One should note that the vertical axis of Figure 3.4 depicts the efficiency or productivity of the GPT. As the authors rightly observe: 'the full description of a single GPT requires several attributes' (Lipsey et al., 2005, p.434). To simplify, it is assumed that performance is adequately measured by the unit cost of services that the technology produces. In practice, this implies that a number of conventions must be applied. For instance, valuing durability may require adjusting depreciation costs. Here, we will not elaborate on these issues as our concern is mainly theoretical. However, there is another way of looking at the impact of GPTs. The evolution of a GPT and its derivative technologies leads to many applications in the form of new products, processes and organizations. It is usually assumed that the cumulative applications of GPTs also follow a logistic curve. In this case the variable 'applications' is measured along the vertical axis. Measurement problems aside, this can be considered as an alternative way to depict the time-paths of GPTs. Lipsey et al. (2005) simplify things further by using one generic version for both the efficiency and the applications curve.

In phase 1, the new GPT is introduced into the facilitating and the policy structure, which are, at that time, still adapted to the preceding GPT. Investments in the new GPT are fairly small. The ascent of the steam engine provides a nice example. Starting from around 1700, initially the machine was solely used to remove water from the coal mines. In this connection, Lipsey et al. (2005, p. 184) note: 'It was typical of GPTs that it began as a relatively inefficient machine with only a few users but increased over time in efficiency and range and number of applications'.

In phase 2, the facilitating structure is reshaped. This entails an era of turmoil, which may last many years, involving a high degree of uncertainty all the time. As emphasized by Nathan Rosenberg (1994) and reiterated by Lipsey et al. (2005) technological innovation is an activity fraught with many uncertainties. Technological change is a complex process and even Marx did not grasp its full implications as Rosenberg (1994, p. 97) notes:

> Looking back on Marx, it is apparent that, although he had a profound appreciation for the technical dynamism of capitalism, he did not appreciate the extent to which this was due to such institutional measures that reduced risk and by reducing risk, encouraged the experimentation that made innovation so commonplace under capitalism.

In a world characterized by experimentation there are of course winners and losers. Around 1850, the steam engine was utilized on a large scale, in the textile sector, in the (beer) breweries, in the production of iron (steel) and in the railways. The replacement of sailing ships by steamships turned out to be a sluggish process, as competition boosted efficiency in the (sailing) shipping industry. As we have seen, the steamship is a separate GPT in the classification of Lipsey et al. (2005) (see Table 3.2).

Selection and creative destruction play an important role in phase 2. These issues do not only refer to the crowding out of existing economic activities, but also to the winning of the race at the introduction of new products. In this context, the distinction between Schumpeter Mark I and Mark II competition is of importance (see, for example, Wersching, 2010).

Joseph Schumpeter published his diverging views on the process of competition and technological progress with an intervening period of three decades. Schumpeter Mark I stems from his path-breaking work in the area of economic development (Schumpeter, 1912). However, Schumpeter Mark II is based on his view on capitalism, which he developed in a later stage of his career (Schumpeter, 1942). Both the location and time of publication are different. Therefore, both views may be correct, as reality is subject to major changes under the impact of emerging GPTs.

In phase 2 with Schumpeter Mark I competition, there are many sellers in the market. A strong entrepreneurial spirit and easy entry into the market feature during this stage. The knowledge required to produce new goods is external to the firm; in other words, it is public knowledge. Obviously, it is also thinkable that producers imitate their predecessors in the market. In that case, external spill-over effects are important. However, the way in which knowledge is acquired is of minor importance. Many firms enter the market and price-competition is intensive. Those who cannot keep pace with the pack will drop out. In the end, a limited number of firms survive that are capable of exploiting the economies of scale, either concerning the organization or concerning technology. We present a few examples to illustrate this point. In the American (US) automotive sector, the number of firms increased substantially between 1895 and 1909. In the peak-year 1909, the total number of firms amounted to 272. After that, the number of firms decreased to only nine in 1941, despite continuous growth of sector output. Another example concerns the production of radios, not a GPT itself, but the consequence of the introduction of electricity. Lipsey et al. (2005, p. 43) summarize the development concisely: 'Over 600 radio-producing firms were established during the period 1923–26, but only 18 survived until 1934. By 1934, the evolutionary hand had done what no individual could have done in 1923, to sort out those who had what it took to survive from those who did not'.

In the case of Schumpeter Mark II competition, large firms that possess long-term patents dominate the market. Thus, barriers for potential entrants are high. Competition is more or less a routine action; it is aimed at sustaining or expanding the market share. This type of competition fits in phase 3 of the logistic curve. The opportunities for the application of the GPT are numerous and the structure of the economy is totally geared for the new situation. As a consequence, the productivity of the new GPT is high: 'For example, the technological knowledge for the mass-produced automobile had to be embodied in factories and cars. Large investments in

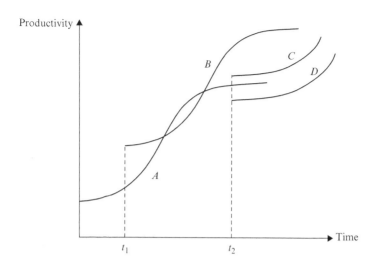

Productivity

Time

t_1 t_2

Source: Lipsey et al. (2005). Reproduced with the permission of Oxford University Press.

Figure 3.5   Productivity curves for different patterns of two successive GPTs

infrastructure, such as roads and petroleum production and distribution, were required to give them value' (Lipsey et al., 2005, p. 411).

During phase 4, the opportunities to create new products, processes and organizational improvements by means of the GPT decline. A type of diminishing returns sets in. Evidently, the opportunities for improvements within the framework of the GPT in force get exhausted. The economy grows at a slower pace during the maturity phase of a GPT. The introduction of a new GPT could solve this problem. The stagnation of the economy increases the pressure to innovate. This opinion is shared by Lipsey et al. (2005, p. 439): 'But as one GPT begins to traverse the flattening part of its logistic trajectory, the pressure for the invention of a replacement builds up'. Nevertheless, according to the authors, the emergence of GPTs does not exhibit a fixed pattern. It is hard to predict the arrival of new GPTs. As observed above, breakthrough technologies may overlap and influence one another.

Figure 3.5 depicts some possibilities. The current curve A may be replaced, in the course of time, by one of the alternative curves (B, C or D). Under which conditions the alternatives will be introduced, if at all, partly depends on the forward-looking vision of profit-maximizing entrepreneurs. The switch from A to B and to D entails a temporarily lower productivity, although to a different degree. These variants correspond with the state of affairs in the model of Helpman and Trajtenberg (1998). In their model, the productivity of the new GPT initially falls short of the productivity of the old GPT. However, forward-looking entrepreneurs invest in the development of components for future use. Nevertheless, in the model of Helpman and Trajtenberg the final good is produced using just one GPT. In contrast, Lipsey et al. (2005) emphasize that, in practice, GPTs do not only overlap, but also may reinforce one another, although this is not visible in Figure 3.5.

The authors assign special importance to three overlapping GPTs in the history of the American economy: 'By the early 1940s, the facilitating and policy structures of the US economy had been altered drastically to fit the needs of electricity, mass production, and the automobile' (Lipsey et al., 2005, p. 201). These GPTs resulted in a 'secular boom' from 1945 until the early 1970s, during which technological progress remained steady and the facilitating structure was fine-tuned to the needs of the underlying technologies. In this context, the authors note that electricity was the most important breakthrough technology, by far: 'Electricity has transformed the structure of the economy in ways that few, if any, other GPTs in history have ever done in the 10,000 years since the neolithic agricultural revolution' (Lipsey et al., 2005, p. 201).

Economic history can be structured in a more comprehensive way if one assumes that cycles occur with a frequency of approximately half a century. Such a view is supported by Carlota Perez (2002) who focuses attention on the concept of a technological revolution. According to Perez (2002, p. 8) a technological revolution may be understood 'as a powerful and highly visible cluster of new and dynamic technologies, products and industries, capable of bringing about an upheaval in the whole fabric of the economy and of propelling a long-term upsurge of development'. Every technological revolution is characterized by a life-cycle, which can also be depicted using a logistic curve, in her opinion. Similar to Lipsey et al. (2005), Perez divides the cycle into four phases. The basic idea is the same, but with one important difference. The transition between phases 2 and 3 is indicated as a 'turning point', at which the exuberant developments that correspond with major structural changes are corrected, so that afterwards the economy reaches a more balanced growth path. In the vision of Perez, such changes are often accompanied by a financial crisis that forces both firms and the government to put things in order. A new technological revolution only comes into being when the existing technologies have reached the stage of maturity and both the pressure and the opportunities to innovate are large. Figure 3.6 illustrates this process, showing two symmetric cycles. Both cycles, one from 0 until t_1 and the other from t_1 until t_2, encompass about fifty

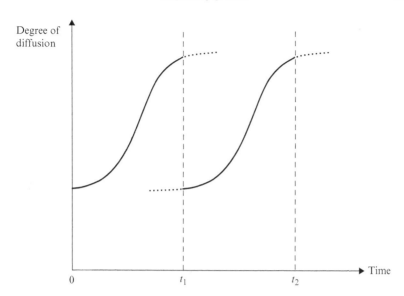

Figure 3.6   Consecutive curves of GPTs

years. Figures 3.5 and 3.6 differ substantially. Perez (2002) measures the cumulative applications, or what she calls the degree of diffusion, on the vertical axis of Figure 3.6. In this case it seems reasonable to assume that there is no 'quantum leap' when a GPT is introduced, in contrast with the examples presented in Figure 3.5, where productivity is measured along the vertical axis.

A technological revolution does not only include the introduction of a single GPT. Rather, it concerns a coherent entity consisting of new technological developments. Apart from new products and new production processes, changes regarding, first, exploitation of energy and raw materials, second, transportation- and communication-systems and, third, infrastructure, need to be considered. Emphasis is put on the synergy between the technologies that are distinguished in the context of a new GPT. Moreover, Perez also pays attention to the necessity of transforming 'the way of doing things' following a technological revolution. Therefore, every technological revolution is accompanied by a techno-economic paradigm, which Perez (2002, p. 15) describes as: 'a best-practice model made up of a set of all-pervasive generic technological principles, which represent the most effective way of applying a particular technological revolution and of using it for modernizing and rejuvenating the whole of the economy'. The similarity with the manner in which Lipsey et al. (2005) describe the appearance of GPTs is obvious. However, the methodological stance of both authors is clearly different. We come back to this issue in the closing section.

3.4. EVALUATION

Studying technological development requires a specific context. If changes occur, one needs to specify which items are subject to these changes. In the neoclassical growth theory the aggregate production function plays this role. Capital accumulation with a given labour supply leads to diminishing returns and, ultimately, to stagnation. Population growth offers a solution for this problem, but it does not explain the long-run growth of per capita output. However, technological progress, in the form of an exogenous trend, warrants a continuous expansion of per capita income.

The hypothesis of autonomous technological progress has been considered as inadequate from the very start. Accumulation of capital often goes hand-in-hand with the improvement of equipment. Technological opportunities induce creative entrepreneurs to innovate. Scientific progress yields the possibility to invest in innovation in the form of research and development expenditure (R&D). On the basis of these principles, endogenous growth models have been developed that fully explain technological progress. Thus, the theory has gone from one extreme to the other. In practice, technological progress is far more volatile than in the models featured by balanced growth in the long run. This insight opens the door for a combination of both rather extreme theoretical positions.

The introduction of GPTs sheds new light on the process of economic growth. The combination of an exogenous impulse, in the form of an emerging GPT, and the resulting endogenous R&D leads to growth that exhibits a more or less cyclical pattern. To sustain long-run economic growth, new breakthrough technologies need to come to the fore quite frequently. Despite the more realistic outcome, models with GPTs based on the Walrasian paradigm exhibit a number of limitations. The economic agents with perfect foresight, who populate these models, are excellently fit to serve their own interests, while equilibrium prevails, as markets always clear. However, this does not seem to be the way the real world works.

Lipsey, Carlaw and Bekar (2005) change the scene by the introduction of an 'appreciative theory', which is defined by contrasting the prevalent mathematical method of practicing economics with a mainly verbal approach. Here, we will not answer the question whether their analysis of GPTs is sufficiently rigorous. It is clear that the authors identify a number of GPTs in the history of the Western world using their definition. Next, they investigate the common properties of the GPTs that they distinguish.

Starting point for their deliberations is an evolutionary method, which takes account of uncertainty of investors, the path-dependency of certain developments, as well as the possibility of conflicts instead of perfect harmony. This vision is, obviously, closer to reality than Walrasian equilibrium theory. However, Lipsey et al. (2005) want to go further along the evolutionary path than appreciative theorizing alone makes possible. They construct rather complicated simulation models to illustrate the impact of GPTs. But, as is often the case in the economic literature simulation models turn out to be a blind alley. The resulting simulations yield cycles in all shapes and sizes, but a clear conclusion is lacking. The reassurance, that the models 'are intended to capture an increasing amount of the rich detail contained in the historical fact set' (Lipsey et al., 2005, p. 495) does not take science one step further. It is difficult to acquire scientific knowledge without a certain degree of generalization.

From a methodological perspective, it seems fruitful to seek alliance with Joseph Schumpeter who pleads for a kind of appreciative theory coined 'histoire raisonnée' (reasoned history), referred to in our 'Introduction'. In this context, Schumpeter (1942, p. 44) states, while discussing the work of Karl Marx: 'He was the first economist of top rank to see and to teach systematically how economic theory may be turned into historical analysis and how the historical narrative may be turned into histoire raisonnée'. Such an approach is essential to understand the development of capitalism. In an extensive discussion on the methodological view of Schumpeter and his struggle with the notion of innovation Chris Freeman and Francisco Louçã (2001, p. 63) come to the heart of the matter: 'innovation is historical by nature, and can be understood only as a historical process: its clustering and non-random distribution, and its relation to the changes in organizational and institutional structure, are part of the organic functioning of modern capitalism'. The theory of the long wave, as elaborated by Carlota Perez (2002), fits better in this tradition than the open-ended approach of Lipsey, Carlaw and Bekar (2005). In Chapter 5 we will dwell at length on her work as well as on that of others on the significance of long waves in economic development.

NOTES

1. It may be slightly confusing using the same symbol A in defining labour potential and in the AK-model, but this is not unusual. See, for instance, Acemoglu (2009).
2. Sjak Smulders and Theo van de Klundert (1995) choose a different approach. In their contribution, firms opt for in-house R&D in order to develop less expensive production methods. Monopolistic competition in the market for final products gives the opportunity to finance this R&D. The number of firms and, consequently, the number

of product variants is constant in this model. In Smulders and Van de Klundert (2004), both models are combined and entrepreneurs choose between process-innovation and product-innovation on the basis of a comparison of returns.

3. In the one-sector model of Grossman and Helpman (1991), monopolistic competition as such does not lead to a distortion, because the mark-up over costs is the same for all product varieties.

4. Follow the leader

4.1. COPYING TECHNOLOGY

As already noted in Chapter 3, in the neoclassical growth theory technological progress is considered as an exogenous variable. Thus, the technological knowledge is publicly accessible. It is as if every firm can look up in
the book of blueprints how it can produce specific goods. This assumption
is still valid in the case where more countries are distinguished. In every
country firms are able to make use of the technological possibilities of the
more advanced countries. Differences in welfare between countries may
be caused by several other factors, such as saving behaviour, population
growth and the given initial situation. The question then arises whether
the backward countries are able to catch up with the more advanced
economies. If the production per worker in poor countries grows faster
than the production per worker in rich countries, then we indicate this as
convergence. In this case, countries grow towards each other, but it is not
warranted that the levels of per capita production will be equal when the
growth rates are the same. Structural differences may be present, which
cause welfare levels to diverge, even though the process of convergence has
been finished. Convergence is then incomplete.

In the growth theory, the process of convergence is viewed in various
ways. In the neoclassical theory, convergence depends on the relative scarcity of capital. Assume that two countries are perfectly identical, except
for the available stock of physical capital. The relatively poor country
disposes of less capital in the initial situation than the comparatively rich
country. This relative shortage of capital implies that both the marginal
and the average capital productivity in the poor country are higher than
in the rich country, due to the assumed diminishing returns in the neoclassical model. In the poor country, saving will therefore lead to a higher
growth rate of output. As a result, both economies will converge, so that
they will realize the same growth rate of output and the same level of
output per worker. Differences with respect to the production level may
be sustained in the long run, if countries are characterized by mutually
diverging values of the structural parameters. For example, in the long
run, characterized by a situation of balanced growth, a country with a

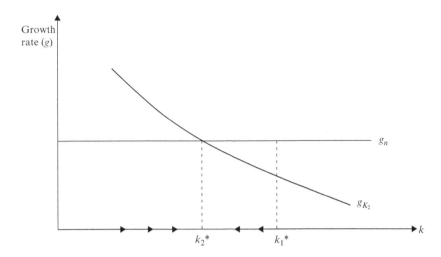

Figure 4.1   Convergence according to the neoclassical growth theory

lower saving and investment ratio will be featured by a lower volume of capital per worker and, therefore, a lower production per worker than a country with a higher saving ratio. The long-run growth rate is the same in both countries, and is determined by the population growth and by technological progress.

This possibility is illustrated in Figure 4.1, which corresponds to Figure 3.1, but now there are two countries with different savings rates. In the 'leading country', country 1, the rate of growth is equal to the natural rate of growth (g_n). The long-run equilibrium level of the effective capital-labour ratio is indicated by k_1^*. In the backward country, country 2, with a lower savings rate the growth rate of capital will be higher as long as $k_2 < k_2^*$. Therefore, this country is in a process of convergence to the leader, but ultimately convergence will be incomplete. The long-run equilibrium level of the effective capital-labour ratio in the backward country will be smaller than that of the rich economy: $k_2^* < k_1^*$.

In the theory of endogenous growth, it is not as easy for countries to realize technological progress. Some effort needs to be made, for example, in the form of expenditure on research and development (R&D). Obviously, one may also copy from other countries that are closer to the top of the technological ladder. However, it seems reasonable to assume that copying entails costs as well. To clarify these issues, we start from a simple two-country model, as discussed in David Weil (2005).[1] The two countries have the same labour supply at their disposal. Goods are produced using labour only. Notably, physical capital is absent in this model.

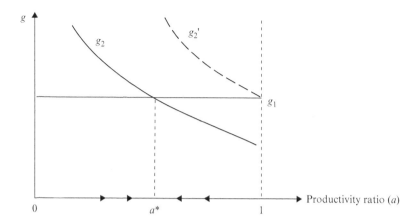

Figure 4.2   Convergence according to endogenous growth theory

The labour productivity in the leading country (A_1) may be increased by allocating a higher share of the labour volume to R&D activities. The higher the share of labour dedicated to R&D is, the faster the economy will grow. If the share of R&D efforts is fixed, then the growth rate is constant. In Figure 4.2, this is illustrated by the horizontal line g_1. Country 1 is the technological leader and g denotes the growth rate of output. The growth rate of the production per worker is also equal to g_1, because the labour volume is fixed. The productivity ratio of country 2, the follower, as compared to country 1, the leader, is measured on the horizontal axis ($a = A_2/A_1$). If this ratio equals unity, then convergence is complete. It is assumed that the costs of copying fall short of the costs of innovating, since a technological spill-over effect is present. One could say that firms in the follower country receive a *productivity bonus*, because they can copy leading technologies. The magnitude of the productivity bonus depends on the intensity of knowledge spill-overs across countries. The closer a country gets to the technological frontier, the higher the costs of copying become. The less there is left to be imitated, the more difficult imitation becomes. Thus, the growth rate of the follower is a decreasing function of the productivity ratio ($a = A_2/A_1$), as the curve g_2 in Figure 4.2 shows. Both growth rates are equal at the ratio a^*. This equilibrium is the outcome of the convergence process, as the arrows on the horizontal axis of Figure 4.2 demonstrate. To the left of a^* the follower grows faster than the leader. The reverse is true to the right of a^*.

In this case, the catching-up process leads to a solution, in which the productivity level in the backward country (country 2) remains permanently lower than the productivity level in the leading country

(country 1). Of course, this result has to do with the assumptions on which the analysis is based. For, it is assumed that imitation requires less expenditure on R&D than innovation. The rapid growth of country 2 is to a large extent based on technological spill-overs. If both countries grow equally rapidly, the backwardness of country 2 becomes a permanent phenomenon. Country 2 spends less on R&D than country 1, but country 2 grows at the same pace, owing to the spill-over effect. By devoting more labour to R&D efforts, the relatively poor country 2 can realize a relatively high productivity (a). If the amount of labour dedicated to R&D is equally large in both countries, as illustrated by the dotted curve g_2', complete convergence results ($a = 1$). By definition, the costs of imitation are then equal to the costs of innovation. The result that a country that spends less on R&D will reach a lower level of productivity, corresponds with the result in the neoclassical model that less investment in physical capital leads to a lower long-run level of labour productivity.

It seems plausible that imitation is fraught with difficulties. Nevertheless, it needs to be argued why international technology transfers are not self-evident, in contrast with the neoclassical assumptions. A first aspect to be noted is that 'technologies developed in the richest countries will not be appropriate to the poorer countries' (Weil, 2005, p. 225). Poor countries apply technologies that require less physical and human capital per worker in comparison with rich countries. If the innovations in the rich countries are adapted to capital-intensive production methods, they are of little use for the poor countries. Weil (2005) gives the example of the magnetic levitation train, which does not affect the productivity level of countries in which the transportation system is dominated by bicycles and battered buses. Application of new technologies is tied to the absorption capacity of countries. This absorption capacity is dependent upon the economic structure, which differs in relation to the wealth of a country. We will return to this issue in section 4.3.

A second aspect that stands in the way of an unlimited transfer of technology concerns the role of 'tacit knowledge'. A substantial part of the knowledge that is applied in the production of goods is not codified, either in manuals or in alternative ways. This knowledge resides in the brains of engineers and managers and is passed on from one person to another in an informal way. Even if it is known in theory how something should be done, then one does not always succeed in executing this. Practical experience is indispensable. Accumulation of experience takes both time and effort.

Finally, one may point out the role of patents. Poor countries have to wait until patents expire or they must innovate 'around' these patents. The latter strategy requires much effort. On the other hand, it is not always true that patent rights can be easily enforced in all countries.

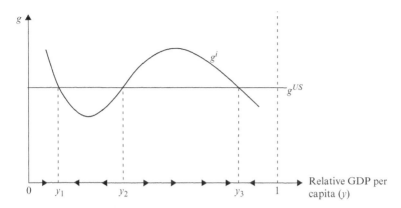

Figure 4.3   Convergence and divergence according to empirical analysis

In order to be able to follow the technological leader, a number of obstacles need to be removed. Therefore, it is not surprising that the process of catching-up is far from linear. Empirical research characterizes the relationship between the per capita growth rate of countries (g) and the level of per capita GDP relative to the US in the initial situation (y) by using a polynomial (see Monojit Chatterji, 1992, and Ton van Schaik and Henri de Groot, 1996). Figure 4.3 depicts such a relation. Although on the horizontal axis the ratio of per capita GDP of country i relative to that of the technological leader is measured, one may make a comparison between Figure 4.3 and Figure 4.2. In this connection, it does not make a significant difference whether per capita income or productivity is depicted on the horizontal axis. For, in the model that underlies Figure 4.2, the labour volume is the same in both countries. In this case differences in productivity are equal to differences in output per capita. The curve g^{US} in Figure 4.3 represents the (constant) growth rate in the US, while the curve g^i refers to the growth rate of other countries, given their relative GDP per capita. The empirical relation behind Figure 4.3 is based on a large sample of countries. In Chatterji (1992), the sample consists of 109 countries, while the sample of Van Schaik and De Groot (1996) contains 104 countries.

Figure 4.3 may also be interpreted as a theoretical relationship, which sketches the growth of country i (g^i) as a function of relative per capita GDP in the initial situation (y^i). It appears that the curves intersect three times. In all these cases, the countries grow at the same rate, viz. the growth rate of the technological leader, the US. However, as a thorough inspection of Figure 4.3 makes clear, the equilibria corresponding with the ratios y_1 and y_3 are stable ones. In contrast, the equilibrium that corresponds with ratio y_2 is an unstable one. As a consequence, countries with a relative per capita GDP that falls short of y_2 are on their way to a low-level equilibrium-trap. For countries with an initial situation $y_1 < y < y_2$ the growth rate of per capita GDP is even lower that the growth rate of per capita GDP in the US. One may refer to this case as divergence. Convergence only occurs at initial positions $y > y_2$. The equilibrium corresponding with y_3 does not imply complete convergence in Figure 4.3. However, in Chatterji (1992), countries with an initial level $y^i > y_2$ converge to a high equilibrium level with output per capita equal to that in the leading country ($y^i = 1$). The institutional factors that determine whether or not complete convergence will be realized are to be discussed in the next section. The existence of multiple equilibria may be associated with convergence clubs, groups of countries that are moving towards either the low equilibrium or the high equilibrium.

As remarked earlier, the y^i-curve can be interpreted as a theoretical relationship. The question then arises what explains the capricious way in which the curve runs. One may assume that it is easier for countries that are at a large distance from the technology frontier to imitate specific things from rich countries, but that this potential declines the further they grow. Low-hanging fruit can be plucked easily. Next, there is a phase in which countries are sufficiently congruent with more advanced countries, which again makes catching-up an option. To understand what this means the convergence hypothesis has to be qualified in the sense that catching-up is not only a question of technological backwardness but also of having the required social capability. As Moses Abramovitz (1986, p. 387) puts it: 'Tenacious societal characteristics normally account for a position, perhaps a substantial position, of a country's past failure to achieve as high a level of productivity as economically more advanced countries'. Nevertheless, social capability and technological opportunity interact. The technological opportunities press for adaption and change. This implies that 'the constraints imposed by social capability on the successful adoption of more advanced technology gradually weaken and permit its fuller exploitation' (Abramovitz, 1986, pp. 388–9). Furthermore, it should be noted that the catching-up process is self-limiting. The more the process of catching-up approaches its completion, the more the productivity bonus decreases, despite the fact that catching-up becomes easier (see Van Schaik and De Groot, 1996). Then the growth rate of the lagging country decreases. At a certain point (y_3 in Figure 4.3) the growth rates of the leader and the follower are equal. In a number of somewhat complicated empirical and theoretical approaches, convergence clubs result from extensions of the neoclassical model (see, for example, Fabio Canova 2004). However, it seems realistic to take into account endogenous growth and technology transfers across countries, as in Chatterji (1992) and Van Schaik and De Groot (1996).

4.2.   CATCHING-UP AND INSTITUTIONS

In his well-known essay on economic backwardness, Alexander Gerschenkron (1962) lists a number of features of the industrialization process. Briefly summarized, this process boils down to the following. The greater the backwardness of an economy:

1) the greater the discontinuity with the preceding development will be;
2) the more emphasis will be put on bigness of both plant and enterprise;
3) the larger the focus will be on producers' rather than consumers' good industries;
4) the larger the reliance will be on technological borrowing and financial assistance from abroad;
5) the more intense the downward pressure on living standards will be;
6) the greater the role of institutional agencies will be, for example, banks and the state.

Gerschenkron (1962) especially emphasizes that industrialization is accompanied by large-scale investments across a broad spectre of activities. In this connection, it should be emphasized that economic agents are not reluctant to apply advanced technological opportunities. Relatively labour-intensive production methods due to low wage costs are not an option: 'The overriding fact to consider is that industrial labour, in the sense of a stable, reliable, and disciplined group that has cut the umbilical cord connecting it with the land and has become suitable for utilization in factories, is not abundant but extremely scarce in a backward country' (Gerschenkron, 1962, p. 9). In manufacturing, mutually reinforcing developments matter: 'Fruits of industrial progress in certain lines are received as external economies by other branches of industry whose progress in turn accords benefits to the former' (Gerschenkron, 1962, pp. 10–11). For investments at such a large scale, much capital is required. In some cases, for example in Germany in the past, banks that maintain close relations with companies may finance the industrial expansion. In other cases, the government has to give a helping hand by either subsidizing firms or by restricting competition. The situation in the backward economies differs from the situation in England at the eve of the Industrial Revolution. First, the industrial development in England was a more gradual one. As will be discussed in Chapter 5, the first Industrial Revolution was

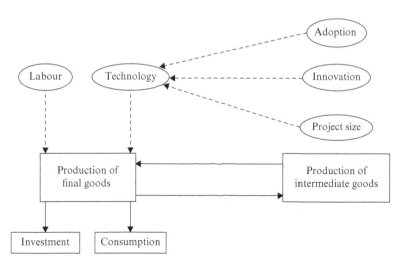

*Figure 4.4   Schematic presentation of the main relationships in the model
by Acemoglu et al. (2006)*

characterized by a relatively small-scale water-powered mechanization of
industry, with a prominent place for cotton spinning and iron products.
Moreover, in England capital had been accumulated via profitable trade
activities. Thus, after the property rights had been ensured, industrial
development could proceed without direct government support.

The description of Gerschenkron (1962) makes clear that institutions
are of vital importance in the process of industrialization of backward
countries. However, institutions that foster the industrialization may
have a perverse effect the closer the economy approaches the technological frontier and innovation, instead of imitation, is required. This is the
central theme in Daron Acemoglu, Philippe Aghion and Fabrizio Zilibotti
(2006). The authors analyze the growth opportunities of a country that
operates below the technological frontier. The model of Acemoglu et al.
(2006) is presented in schematic form in Figure 4.4. Solid arrows indicate
flows of goods, whereas broken arrows stand for the driving forces in the
model.

Final goods are produced under perfect competition applying labour
and intermediate goods as inputs according to the existing technology.
Labour supply is fixed. The production of intermediate goods is performed
on 'production sites' owned by capitalists. The economy is populated by
overlapping generations of agents, who live for two periods. Capitalists
have property rights on 'production sites' and workers are endowed with
skills. At each site there is a leading firm with some monopoly power.

Entry restrictions allow firms to set a limit price. Capitalists hire managers to operate the firm. The production of an intermediate good requires one unit of the final good. Managers set intermediate goods prices, which determine profits. Profits are distributed between capitalists and managers. Managers get a share of profits to solve the moral hazard problem caused by the opportunity of managers to divert profits for their own use without being prosecuted. Technological progress depends on three components. First, managers adopt existing technologies by benefiting from the state-of-the-art in the world in the previous period. Second, high-skilled managers are able to innovate relying on the state of local knowledge in the previous period. There are two types of managers (or entrepreneurs), low-skilled or high-skilled. Capitalists do not know the skill level of the managers they hire. The capability of managers is revealed *ex post*. Third, the project size in the generation of new technological knowledge is chosen by capitalists, who have to bear the investment costs. Investment costs consist of an amount of final goods.

Capitalists maximize the volume of the firm. In each period, they have to decide on two issues: (1) the size of the investment project; (2) whether or not to retain low-skilled managers, who are not capable of innovation. Despite this characteristic it may be profitable to retain old unskilled managers, because they may contribute to investment costs by reinvesting their profits in the firm. These retained earnings make it attractive for capitalists to invest in large projects and to retain old unskilled managers. The option of retaining old unskilled managers has to be compared to the alternative of replacing the old unskilled by new managers with unknown skills. To make the trade-off possible the capitalist has to know the probability that a new hired manager is high-skilled and therefore able to innovate. Finally, it should be observed that old high-skilled managers are never replaced. The decision to replace low-skilled managers depends among other things on the level of labour productivity (A) relative to the level of the technological leader ($\bar{A}$). The ratio $a = A/\bar{A}$ is, similar to section 4.1, a measure for the proximity to the technological frontier, i.e. an inverse measure of the countries' distance to this frontier. If the ratio a is low, then it pays to retain low-skilled managers, since investing in large projects, in which the leader is imitated, is highly profitable. In the proximity of the technological frontier this is no longer the case. To maximize profits, efforts have to be directed towards innovation. Somewhere between these two cases, a ratio a_s exists. For ratios $a < a_s$, low-skilled old managers are retained (regime: $R = 1$), but above this threshold, thus for $a > a_s$, they are terminated (regime: $R = 0$).

The results of this somewhat complicated analysis can be clarified, making use of some figures. Thereby, we choose for a set-up different

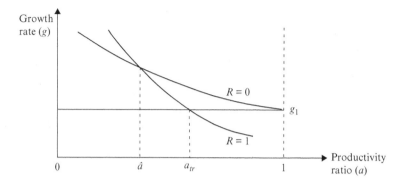

Figure 4.5   Catching-up under different regimes

from the one in Acemoglu et al. (2006). We follow a different approach to assure comparability with the figures presented in section 4.1. As shown in Figure 4.5 we measure the rate of growth of productivity (A) of the follower country as a function of the productivity ratio ($a = A/\bar{A}$). The growth rate of A equals the growth rate of final output, because of a linear relation between aggregate output and the level of productivity. Once more, the growth rate of the technological leader (g_1) is constant.

The growth rate of the follower country (g_i) depends on the regime chosen with respect to the selection of managers. In the regime $R = 1$ of retaining low-skilled managers, the growth rate declines when getting closer to the technological frontier – as a increases. Initially, the growth rate in this regime may be higher than the growth rate in the regime $R = 0$, in which low-skilled managers are replaced by younger ones. At a productivity ratio $\hat{a}$, the growth rate is equal in both regimes. The growth rate (g_i) in the regime $R = 0$ also declines, but the decrease is smaller than in the regime $R = 1$, since an additional engine of growth in the form of innovation by high-skilled managers is in operation. This additional source of economic growth also warrants that, in the end, full convergence is realized in this model: $g_i = g_1$ at $a = 1$. In contrast, if the regime $R = 1$ is maintained throughout, full convergence does not occur. A long-run equilibrium with $g_i = g_1$ is then reached at $a = a_{tr}$. Acemoglu et al. (2006) refer to this situation as the non-convergence trap. Full convergence is not realized, since the economy is not sufficiently innovative.

Whether the follower ends up in the convergence trap, depends upon the point of regime switch. Obviously, the productivity ratio at which this happens, say a_s, depends on the the trade-off made by capitalists who are maximizing their profits. The threshold level a_s is reached when the value

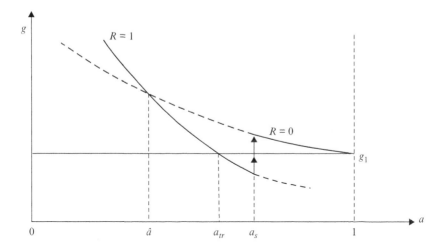

Figure 4.6   Catching-up in case of a regime-switch failure

of the firm retaining low-skilled old managers is lower than the expected value of the firm that hires a young manager.

For the outcome of the process of catching-up, it is important whether a_s lies to either the left of a_{tr}, or to the right of a_{tr}. In the former case, the economy switches in time in order to be able to converge completely. In the latter case the economy ends up in the low equilibrium trap, as illustrated in Figure 4.6. As argued before, capitalists switch at the productivity ratio a_s, but now this will not occur. The economy gets trapped in the point a_{tr}, the non-convergence trap. This low-level equilibrium is stable, as a close inspection of Figure 4.6 teaches. An economy featured by a substantial backwardness may rely for too long on what the authors characterize as an *investment-based strategy*. In order to attain complete convergence, a timely switch towards an *innovation-based strategy* is necessary.

What has this all to do with institutions? In the model of Acemoglu et al. (2006, p. 64) institutions mainly concern anti-competitive policies in the backward country: 'When the government chooses a less competitive environment in a backward economy in order to encourage long-term relationships, greater investment, and faster technological convergence the situation is reminiscent of Gerschenkron's analysis'. Restrictions on the opportunities to enter the markets for intermediate goods raise the profits of incumbent firms. A higher return makes investment projects more attractive. A consequence of this so-called 'appropriability effect' is that low-skilled managers will be retained longer. Firms have the financial resources and the connections to keep off challengers. This aspect

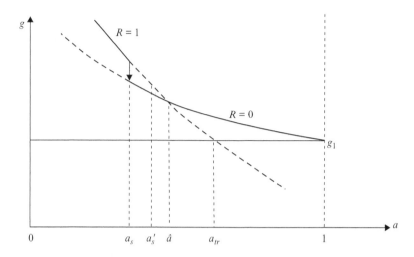

Figure 4.7 Catching-up in case of too early a regime switch

is referred to in the literature as the 'rent-shield' effect. Ultimately, the impact of restricting competition is that the economy remains longer in the regime of the *investment-based strategy*. To assess the implication of this result from a social point of view we need a criterion. For welfare comparisons the usual norm is the present value of the consumption stream. In the main text of the paper Acemoglu et al. (2006) discuss institutional changes from the vantage point of growth maximization. The authors note that comparing welfare-maximizing strategies to the equilibrium 'is very similar to the comparison of the growth-maximizing strategies to the equilibrium' (Acemoglu et al., 2006, p. 61).

Institutional changes that extend the period in which the investment-based strategy is followed may be advantageous from the growth-maximizing point of view. In Figure 4.7 such a case is illustrated. In the figure the switching point in the equilibrium situation (a_s) lies to the left of the point of intersection ($\hat{a}$) of the regime curves $R = 0$ and $R = 1$. As a result of this the economy may switch to the innovation-based strategy too early. Whether this actually happens depends upon the initial position with respect to the productivity ratio (a_{t-1}). One can say that switching is inappropriate from a growth-maximizing strategy for values of the productivity ratio: $a_s \leq a_{t-1} < \hat{a}$.

Restriction of competition results in a_s in Figure 4.7 shifting to the right, for example to the point a'_s. If this shift is sufficiently large, i.e. $a_{t-1} \leq a'_s$, then the economy finds itself in the *investment-based regime*. The anti-competition policy then leads, completely in line with the view of

Gerschenkron (1962), to a higher growth rate of the backward economy. For the case $\hat{a} < a_s$, as illustrated in Figure 4.6, restriction of competition also leads to a shift of a_s to the right. The result is then that the switch to the innovation-based strategy ($R = 0$) occurs later than would be desirable from a growth-maximizing strategy. This means that the growth rate will be lower than without the change in institutions (competition policy in this case). If such a situation holds on long there is the danger that the economy moves towards the non-convergence trap. Therefore, as the economy approaches the technological frontier competition should not be too restrictive. More competition induces more innovation and therefore higher growth if countries become richer. Acemoglu et al. (2006, p. 65) summarize the situation in the following way: 'Institutions that are appropriate for early stages of development therefore become inappropriate close to the frontier. An economy that adopts such institutions must later abandon them'.

We close this analysis with a couple of remarks. The first remark concerns the possibility of fostering the *investment-based strategy* with investment subsidies. If the government accounts for a part of the costs of investment then a_s in Figure 4.7 will shift to the right. One may calculate the level of the subsidy that is necessary in order to let a_s coincide with $\hat{a}$. The second remark concerns the possibility that an economy ends up in a *political economy trap*. As already established in Chapter 2, economic power, if desired, can be transformed into *de facto* political power. Acemoglu et al. (2006) assume that capitalists, who have made profits in the previous period, may bribe politicians to limit competition as much as possible. Less competition leads to higher profits. The investment-based strategy thus remains the preferable strategy for a longer period of time. Possibly, this may result in an economy that ends up in the non-convergence trap, as illustrated in Figure 4.6.

As we have seen, one of the issues at which Gerschenkron (1962) points in his analysis of backwardness and growth is the focus on producer goods industries rather than on consumer goods industries. Industrialization is accompanied by changes in the sectoral pattern of the economy. We will pay attention to these issues in the next section.

4.3. STRUCTURAL TRANSFORMATIONS

Catching-up does not only imply that rapid growth is realized via imitation of existing technologies. The structure of the economy needs to be adapted, too, and this process takes time. Catching-up requires a structural transformation of the economy. The sector structure of an economy depends upon the level of development. Structural change raises its own problems, especially in developing countries. Therefore, it is useful to pay some attention to this phenomenon.

Using a cross-section of a large number of countries, it can be demonstrated that the sectoral structure of the economy at different levels of disaggregation follows a normal pattern (see, for example, Hollis Chenery and Moshe Syrquin, 1975). This means that the shares of the value added of the distinguished sectors in total value added are a function of per capita GDP. Other explanatory variables, such as population size and the export/GDP ratio, may be taken into account to improve the statistical relationship. The cross-country model of Chenery and Syrquin (1975) covers the period 1950–70 and consists of 101 countries. In Henk van Gemert (1987), the normal pattern is estimated using a pooled cross-section time-series analysis, in which autonomous changes in the course of time may be taken into account. However, Van Gemert limits the sample to data for 19 OECD-countries for the period 1962–80, so that the process of industrialization in developing countries remains unseen. Leandro Prados de la Escosura (2005) studies the structural transformation in 18 European countries for the period 1850–1990 (as far as data are available for the individual countries). Thereby, the emphasis lies on the differences in the pattern of industrialization between early starters and latecomers. Based on the differences in the sectoral pattern in the period prior to the Great War in comparison with the normal pattern, the author concludes: 'in the case of the latecomers, the relative size of industrial output grew faster within the same income range, supporting Gerschenkron's contention of a more intensive industrial growth in the case of latecomers' (Prados de la Escosura, 2005, p. 15).

Inspection of the normal pattern learns that the share of the primary sector (predominantly agriculture) in value added declines when per capita GNP increases, whereas the share of services rises. The share of manufacturing initially goes up, but falls at a relatively high income level. A similar result holds for the share of manufacturing employment in total employment, although the turning point is reached at a lower level of per capita GNP.[2] Reflecting on the decline in the share of manufacturing in output and factor use at higher income levels Syrquin (1988, p. 239) notes: 'Such a decline has taken place in the last 20 years in virtually all industrial countries, and has become known as de-industrialization'.

According to Robert Rowthorn and Ramana Ramaswamy (1999) deindustrialization is a phenomenon related to the decline in the share of manufacturing employment. To explain this phenomenon the authors insist that the share of manufacturing output should be measured in real terms, because changes in the real output share show the impact of changes in the income elasticity of demand for manufactures. A decline in the share

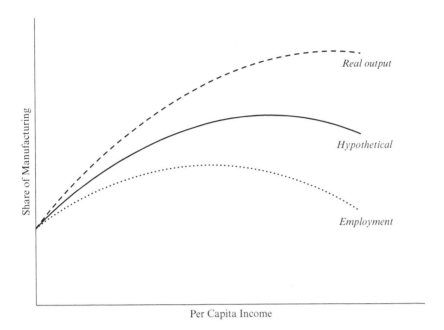

Source: Rowthorn and Ramaswamy (1999).

Figure 4.8 Output and employment shares of the manufacturing sector

of real output of the manufacturing sector as such leads to a fall in the share of manufacturing employment. However, this is not the whole story because account must be taken of diverging productivity changes. The productivity increase in manufacturing is higher than that in other sectors, so that less labour is needed to produce a given volume of output. Apart from this supply effect there is a demand effect, because the difference in productivity growth translates into a relative price effect. Manufactures become relatively cheaper and this stimulates the demand for these goods.

Rowthorn and Ramaswamy (1999) illustrate in Figure 4.8 what happens to the manufacturing sector in a schematic way by showing how the actual shares in output and employment (dotted curves) evolve in comparison with a 'hypothetical' pattern. For convenience, units are chosen to have initially the same value for the shares in real output and employment. The hypothetical curve shows the uniform share of output and employment if productivity growth were the same in all sectors. The shape of the hypothetical curve reflects the changes in the income elasticity with respect to manufacturing, which is high initially but declines at higher income levels. The actual shares of output and employment differ from the hypothetical values as a result of the relatively fast productivity growth in manufacturing, whereby the supply effect (less labour needed for production) and the demand effect (more demand on impact of lower prices) are taken into account. Empirical research reveals that deindustrialization is mainly caused by factors that are internal to advanced economies. According to Rowthorn and Ramaswamy the impact of north-south trade on deindustrialization has been mainly through stimulating labour productivity in the manufacturing sector of developed economies.

Further disaggregation reveals other interesting characteristics of normal patterns. It turns out that, as a country becomes more developed, light manufacturing loses terrain vis-à-vis heavy industry, in terms of the share in total value added. Thereby, it is striking that the sector 'metal products, machinery' exhibits the most pronounced rise. This result confirms the view of Gerschenkron (1962) that industrialization is accompanied by a strong expansion of the producers' goods industries.

The analysis of the structural transformation on the basis of a normal pattern is in static terms. In a dynamic version of the transformation process, the contribution of the different sectors to the growth of the economy forms the starting point of the analysis. In Figure 4.9, derived from Chenery, Robinson and Syrquin (1986), such an imputation is sketched for a division of the economy into three sectors. The contribution of every sector is determined by the product of the share in GNP according to the normal pattern (ρ_j) and the growth rate of the value added of the sector (G_j). If the growth rates of all sectors were equal, then the sectors' contribution to the aggregate growth rate would be equal to the sector shares in GNP. However, this is not the case in Figure 4.9, since the contribution of the most rapidly growing sector, manufacturing, is greater than the value of its static share, whereas the reverse holds for the sector primary production.

On the basis of the pattern in Figure 4.9, Syrquin (1988) distinguishes between three stages of transformation:

Stage 1: *Primary production*. In this stage, the predominance of primary activities is the major source of the economic expansion. Admittedly, the growth rate of primary production falls short of the growth rate of manufacturing, but the share of the former sector is so large that the contribution of primary production still dominates the contribution of manufacturing. However, the large weight of the primary production sector keeps the aggregate growth rate low.

Stage 2: *Industrialization*. The focus in the economy shifts from primary production to manufacturing. The contribution of the growth of manufacturing exceeds the contribution of the agricultural sector by far.

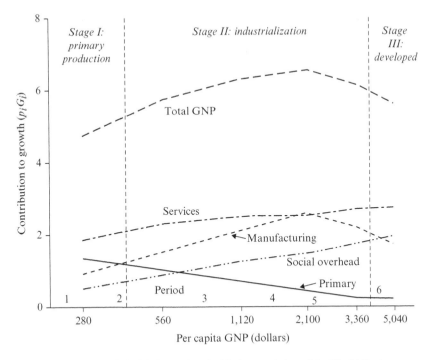

Source: Chenery et al. (1986). Reproduced with the permission of the World Bank.

Figure 4.9   Sectoral sources of growth

Stage 3: *The developed economy.* The transition to this stage is determined by a decrease in the demand for manufacturing products, due to low income elasticity. Initially, the continuous growth of exports balances this development, but, ultimately, the contribution of manufacturing to growth goes down. The service sector becomes increasingly important: 'In industrial countries, services account for half of total GDP growth' (Syrquin, 1988, p. 247).

The analysis of normal patterns yields 'stylized facts', but it is not very informative with respect to the underlying causes. Additional research, based on accounting procedures, offers further information, but to obtain a more elaborate picture of the determinants of the transformation process advanced models are required. A couple of supplementary studies, discussed in Syrquin (1988), are important for our reflections in Chapter 7 on catching-up in the world at large.

The first supplementary research concerns the effect of export expansion and import substitution on the growth of manufacturing output. In this context, a distinction is made between large and small countries. In large countries, in terms of GDP, as expected the exports play a less important role, especially in an early stage of industrialization. However, during this phase, import substitution makes a significant contribution to the growth of the manufacturing sector. For a number of smaller countries, from an economic viewpoint (including Korea, Taiwan and Japan), in the period 1950–70 the calculation has been carried out for two subsequent periods. Thereby, periods characterized by a significant export expansion turn out to be preceded by periods featured by a strong import substitution. This sequence points at the significance of infant industry arguments. Syrquin (1988, p. 254) summarizes the implications concisely: 'The results suggest that an economy may have to develop an industrial base and acquire a certain technological mastery before it can pursue manufactured exports on a significant scale'. In this connection, a warning is appropriate in line with the considerations of Acemoglu et al. (2006), discussed in section 4.2: 'The crucial question is then not one of export promotion versus import substitution, but rather one of designing the latter to avoid inefficient production and delays in shifting out of it' (Syrquin, 1988, p. 254).

The second supplementary research concerns the existing inefficiency in developing countries, resulting from the limited mobility of production factors. If the marginal product of a production factor, for example, labour in manufacturing exceeds the marginal product of labour in agriculture, then the allocation is inefficient. The expansion of the economy may then be fostered by redirecting labour from the agricultural sector to the manufacturing sector, so that the marginal products are equalized. The measurement of marginal productivities is difficult, but the relative labour productivity (sector's share in value added divided by the sector's share in employment) may serve as a partial indicator for the returns across sectors. In Figure 4.10, this index is depicted based on the results of the research with regard to the normal pattern. The productivity gap between manufacturing and primary production is at its maximum in the middle income range. Therefore, in this range, resource shifts may make the largest contribution to aggregate growth.

Weil (2005) mentions the following causes for the lack of factor mobility: (1) geographical isolation, due to the costs attached to relocations; (2) a minimum wage in the high-wage sector. As a consequence, hiring additional workers in this sector leads to a marginal productivity of labour that is below the minimum wage, thus preventing reallocation from the low-wage to the high-wage sector; (3) hidden unemployment in the agricultural sector, whereby the workers' remuneration exceeds the marginal product of labour.

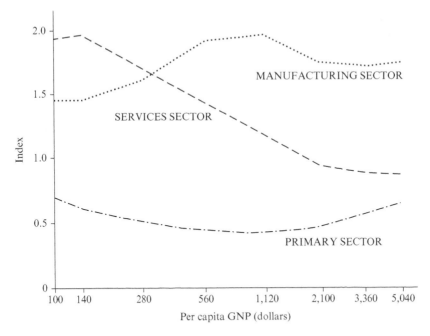

Notes: Index signifies labour productivity in a sector relative to labour productivity for the whole economy.

Source: Chenery et al. (1986). Reproduced with the permission of the World Bank.

Figure 4.10   Relative labour productivity

Syrquin (1988) also presents calculations, which show the contribution of resource allocation to economic growth. This factor appears to make a substantial actual contribution, particularly in the industrializing stage. However, in the high-income range the effect is practically zero. The positive effects of the reallocation of labour peter out: 'If productivity gains continue to decline at income levels beyond those in the simulation, however, it will no longer be attributable, even partially, to the reduced shift out of agriculture. A different – and probably negative – allocation effect may become important as labour continues to shift into services' (Syrquin, 1988, pp. 257–8). In Chapter 7, in which the expansion of countries in more recent periods will be studied, this matter will be raised again.

4.4.   EVALUATION

According to Gerschenkron (1962), the industrialization process starts with 'The Great Spurt'. Discontinuity is characteristic for the economic development of countries. As long as fundamental obstacles exist, growth stagnates and the distance of countries vis-à-vis the technological leader becomes larger and larger. With 'The Great Spurt' a catching-up process is set in motion that leads to a partial or eventually to a complete convergence towards the productivity level of the leader.

Different approaches exist to explain the economic expansion of the follower country. In the neoclassical theory, the state of the technological knowledge is not the variable that determines the backwardness. Technological knowledge is freely available in this theory. Developing countries lag behind developed countries, due to the existence of capital scarcity. The volume of capital goods per unit of labour is comparatively low. This implies that the marginal productivity of capital is relatively high. If sufficient savings are invested in the domestic economy, then the pace of economic growth is high and the backwardness vis-à-vis the leader is reduced (catching-up).

In the endogenous growth theory, efforts must be made in order to innovate. Economic growth depends on the expenditure on R&D. In this view, the idea fits in that copying knowledge by the follower country entails costs. Additional expenditure on R&D is necessary to fine-tune the copied technologies to local circumstances. As a result, it takes time to equal the level of the leader. However, there is a knowledge spill-over effect, so that less needs to be invested in R&D in comparison with richer countries in order to grow, nevertheless, at a higher rate. The more the backwardness in terms of productivity diminishes, the lower the growth rate will be. It becomes increasingly difficult to imitate the technological leader. Alternatively formulated, the costs of imitation become higher the closer a country gets to the technological frontier. At a certain moment, the growth rate of the following country has fallen down to the growth rate of the leading country, so that both countries expand at the same pace. The convergence process stops, but there is no complete convergence in terms of productivity levels, if the following country does not raise its R&D expenditure as a percentage of GDP up to the level of the leading country. At the moment that a country has become as rich as the leader, the country must innovate just as much as the leader to hang on to the latter. The other side of the coin is that partial convergence is based on a difference with respect to the structure of both countries. However, this conclusion also applies in the neoclassical model. In this model, a lower saving rate in the following country will lead to convergence that is only partial, too. The capital stock and the production per worker are permanently lower than the levels in the leading country.

One may assume that the catching-up process proceeds less monotonically than is supposed in the above consideration. Let us assume that the costs of imitation initially increase. If more and more low hanging fruits have been picked, one has to try to find one's luck at a greater height. Because this is difficult, the growth rate of the follower falls. Meanwhile, countervailing powers are put into operation. The social capability to apply technological improvements improves. One learns from the learning process and the costs of imitation decrease at a certain level of relative per capita GDP. The growth rate of the follower increases. When the expansion continues, there will be a moment that this process has expired. The costs of imitation definitely go up if the convergence becomes successful. It can be shown that, under these assumptions, three equilibria do exist, at which the growth rate of the leader and the follower are equal. The middle equilibrium turns out to be unstable. In order to converge to a higher level of welfare, the relative per capita GDP needs to be higher than the level that corresponds with the unstable equilibrium. If not, then the economy converges to the low equilibrium. The economy is trapped and 'The Great Spurt' in the sense of Gerschenkron remains absent.

The study of Gerschenkron (1962) contains yet another important message. Institutions play a significant role in the catching-up process. Network relations and long-term contracts between firms, including banks, are advantageous for the trust that is required for large-scale investments. A project such as catching-up with the leader requires an approach in which bigness and finance opportunities are of vital importance. Profitability and re-investing profits foster economic growth when a country is lagging behind. Possibly, the government may give a helping hand by restricting competition thus increasing the profitability of investments. In this case, too, it is true that incomplete convergence is unavoidable, if countries stick too long to a strategy of imitating. Switching to an *innovation-based strategy* in time is necessary to realize complete convergence. In this context, this means that other institutions might be required to reach the desired target.

Acemoglu, Aghion and Zilibotti (2006) have modelled these ideas in an elegant way. In the model, two regimes are distinguished. In the investment-based strategy, the emphasis is on imitation. High investment leads to a high growth rate, if the technological frontier is at a far distance. The incumbent entrepreneurs run the show. In the case of an innovation-based strategy, many new things need to be done. This implies that it pays to replace older, less competent managers or entrepreneurs by young and dynamic entrepreneurs. Thus, the high rate of growth of the economy can be maintained. Switching from an investment-based strategy to an innovation-based strategy is accomplished by capitalists who maximize the value of the firm. If the switch is made relatively late, the economy may end up in a non-convergence trap. Whether this really happens, depends on the values of the structural parameters. Thereby, the government may play a role by affecting the competition in the goods market, for example by raising entry barriers. Wherever institutions matter, the insights from the political economy ought to be taken into account, as elaborated upon in Chapter 2. In the present case, this means that the capitalists who benefit from limited competition may bribe politicians to repulse competitors. This may lead to partial convergence, i.e. in the words of Acemoglu et al. (2006, p. 67) to a 'political economy trap'.

Backward countries do not only have to catch up with the technological leader, but they also must transform the sector structure of the economy in the course of time. Empirical research shows that a normal pattern exists, in which the share of the value added of sectors in the total value added is a function of per capita GDP or GNP. On the basis of this research, Syrquin (1988) distinguishes between three stages of transformation. In Stage 1, the emphasis is on primary production. As a consequence, growth is rather modest. In Stage 2, industrialization occurs, so that the focus shifts towards manufacturing. In Stage 3, the economy is more fully developed and a process of de-industrialization definitely takes place. The share of manufacturing in total value added decreases. Similar phenomena may be observed at a more disaggregated level. Stylized facts of a different order complete the picture presented above. For example, Syrquin (1988) points at the fact, that, in a number of countries, the process of industrialization is accompanied by a change in the international pattern of specialization. In this context, periods featured by significant exports expansion are preceded by periods characterized by strong import substitution. Such a sequence indicates the relevance of the infant industry argument. Local industries benefit from a certain degree of protection against competitors in the world market if they are under way to absorb specific technologies. Once more, the conclusion is that institutions need to be revised when they are no longer efficient.

Another *stylized fact* of a different order concerns the inefficient allocation of factors of production, which is usually observed in developing countries. Such an allocation is inefficient, if the difference between the marginal productivities of factors of production in the distinguished sectors appears to be substantial. The data concerning the average productivity of labour points in the direction of inefficiency. Besides, the reallocation of resources turns out to make a substantial contribution to economic growth at low income levels. Labour moves from agriculture to manufacturing, but, at a high level of income, this well has dried up. It is interesting that Syrquin (1988) foresees a negative effect of re-allocation during a continuing expansion if more and more labour moves to the services sector. For a re-allocation of resources, the prevailing institutions are also important.

The process of catching-up in all its aspects is important for the analysis in subsequent chapters. Europe's position vis-à-vis the US will be scrutinized in Chapter 6. Catching-up by developing countries and the developments in the People's Republic of China will be the central issues in Chapter 7.

NOTES

1. In the two-sector, two-country model by Theo van de Klundert and Sjak Smulders (1996), international specialization of the countries concerned in the course of time is taken account of, apart from the spill-over effects between the leader and the follower.
2. The three-sector model of structural development is pioneered in a study by Jean Fourastié (1949). Although the author analyzes changes in the patterns of output and employment shares in terms of demand and supply his work has not received the credits it deserves in the economic literature.

PART II

Historical developments in a theoretical
perspective

5. The long wave

5.1. MEASUREMENT, DATING, EXPLANATION

The idea that economic developments are characterized by a superimposition of cycles of a different length and amplitude appeals to one's imagination. In this context, a special fascination proceeds from the possible existence of a dominant long wave, featured by a length of approximately 50 years. Several authors are of the opinion to have detected such a long wave. Nikolai Kondratieff (1892–1938) is considered the pioneer in this area. This Russian economist was executed by the Stalinist regime in 1938. Kondratieff (1926) showed that economic indicators, such as prices, interest rates, international trade and coal production exhibit a long wave. Others had preceded him in this respect, such as, for example, the Dutch scientists Jacob van Gelderen (1913) and Salomon de Wolff (1924). Kondratieff, who did not possess any knowledge of the work of his predecessors, took the credit, owing to the appreciation of the famous economist Joseph Schumpeter (1939). Therefore, waves of approximately 50 years in time series of economic variables are known as Kondratieff waves (or, simply, K-waves).

The question whether K-waves really exist is continuously under debate, and so are the causes of K-waves. In the past, the emphasis was on the analysis of monetary variables, due to a lack of statistics with regard to the real sector of the economy – because, in the past, monetary statistics were easier to collect. However, times change. In a recent study Andrey Korotayev and Sergey Tsirel (2010) investigate, using spectral analysis, whether time series with respect to the growth rate of world GDP exhibit long waves. Spectral analysis offers the opportunity to decompose time series into waves of different shapes and sizes. The possibility to establish statistical significance is an additional advantage. The times series with respect to world GDP growth exhibit large outliers during the First World War (1914–18) and the Second World War (1939–45) as well as during the Interbellum. This forces the authors to adjust some observations, after which they find an acceptable pattern of waves. The Kondratieff-wave is part of this pattern. Moreover, the K-wave is statistically significant. Therefore, the authors conclude: 'we have some grounds to maintain

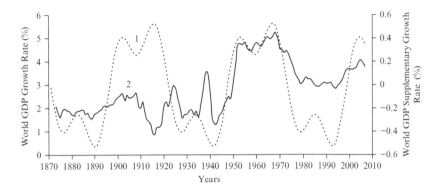

Source: Korotayev and Tsirel (2010).

Figure 5.1   *Comparison between the constructed K-wave (curve 1) and the smoothed series of world GDP growth rates (curve 2)*

that our spectral analysis has supported the hypothesis of the presence of Kondratieff waves in world GDP dynamics' (Korotayev and Tsirel, 2010, p. 14). In addition, the authors find sufficient indications for the existence of the Juglar-cycle (with a length of seven to nine years) and the Kitchin-cycle (with a length of three to four years). Furthermore, a Kuznets-cycle, with a length of 17 to 18 years, can also be detected in the spectrum. The authors conclude that the 'Kuznets swing should be regarded as the third harmonic of the Kondratieff wave' (Korotayev and Tsirel, 2010, abstract).

Figure 5.1 makes clear what a K-wave constructed on the basis of spectral analysis looks like. The constructed K-wave (curve 1, according to the vertical axis to the right) is compared to the 11-year moving average with respect to the world real GDP growth rate thus eliminating cycles of shorter duration in the series (curve 2, according to the vertical axis to the left).[1] From this comparison, it follows that a relationship exists between both curves for the period 1870–1914 and for the period after 1946. The connection is less clear for the period prior to the First World War. Really significant differences occur for the World War years and for the interwar years, which have been eliminated in the spectral analysis. However, the authors are able to provide an explanation: 'if we suppose that the 1st World War moved to the 1920s the second part of the upswing phase of the 3rd K-wave, whereas in the 1930s and 1940s the return to the original "phase timetable" took place, then the deviation from the pattern in question observed in those years can be also interpreted' (Korotayev and Tsirel, 2010, p. 17). It just depends on what one defines as interpretation. The distinction between the impact of shocks, on the one hand, and

Table 5.1   Dating according to Korotayev and Tsirel (2010)

Kondratieff wave number	Variant 1 Phase A/Phase B	Variant 2 Phase A/Phase B
I	.............../1820–50	.............../1820–50
II	1851–75/1876–94	1851–75/1876–94
III	1895–1913/1914–46	1895–1929/1930–46
IV	1947–73/1974–91	1947–73/1974–83
V	1992–2007/.............	1984–2007/.............

endogenous mechanisms, on the other hand, is complicated, as is more often the case when analyzing time series.

Using the obtained results, a dating of K-waves can be constructed. Given the problems mentioned above, as well as the uncertainties surrounding more recent developments, the authors present two variants, which differ with respect to the datings chosen. In both variants, the average annual growth rate of world GDP in Phase A systematically exceeds this growth rate in Phase B. Table 5.1 compares both variants of Korotayev and Tsirel. Five Kondratieff-waves are distinguished, while figures for Phase A of K1 and Phase B of K5 are missing, because the data are not available. Moreover, one should note that the data for the period 1820–70 exclusively concern the West (12 important European countries and four 'Western offshoots').

The analysis of Korotayev and Tsirel (2010) supports the hypothesis of the long wave. However, the question arises whether this hypothesis should be investigated at the level of world output. The economic development of countries is anything but synchronous. As discussed in Chapter 4, technological backward countries may catch up with the leader. Moreover, a leading country may fall back in the order of ranking if the wrong strategies are pursued. The hegemony of England after the Industrial Revolution, both in the domains of the economy and technology, provides an appealing example. In the course of time, it appeared to be impossible to maintain this lead vis-à-vis other countries. In fact, around 1900, the US started to dominate England in the economic domain. In the next chapter we will return to this topic.

Some researchers argue that even if a long wave exists, it cannot be proven using macroeconomic data. These authors refer to the process of creative destruction that accompanies technological development. In this view, long waves are caused by technological breakthroughs that occur at a certain frequency. We have already discussed these technological breakthroughs in Chapter 3. If the waves are overlapping to some extent, then winners and losers necessarily coexist. New sectors emerge, whereas incumbent firms languish and may eventually have to shut down. The economy is then in the *downswing phase*. In the analysis of Korotayev and Tsirel, this is indicated as Phase B. As soon as the new technology is fully implemented, things settle down and a boom or upswing occurs (Phase A). This does not necessarily mean that economic growth in the downswing falls short of economic growth in the upswing. Chris Freeman and Francisco Louçã (2001, p. 257) lucidly observe what really matters in this view:

> For us, the 'downswing' of a long wave is not just a slower rate of growth in aggregate production, although this may well occur: it is a period of structural adjustment to the very rapid rise of a new constellation of technologies. It is the sharp contrast between the surging growth of the new industries and the slow-down, stagnation, or even contraction of the old ones, that is the main feature of the 'downswing', not the combined aggregate of all industries.

Carlota Perez (2002) shares this opinion, while adding yet another argument. The large volatility of relative prices during the structural adjustments in the downswing complicates the construction of time series for certain variables at the aggregate level: 'How do you compare one computer in the 1960s with one in the 1970s, in the 1980s and now?' (Perez, 2002, p. 62). Apart from that, the relevant variables are the increase in labour productivity or the change of total factor productivity, when one wants to explain long waves as a result of technological progress.

As observed in Chapter 3, the explanation of long waves based on technological development not only concerns the introduction of a break-through technology (GPT). A technological revolution, as defined by Perez (2002) needs to take place, in which new technologies, products and sectors, in mutual cohesion, shake up the economy and lead the development into other grooves. Freeman and Louçã (2001), as well as Perez (2002), distinguish between five technological revolutions, corresponding with the five Kondratieff waves. In all cases, path-breaking innovations are the foundation of a comprehensive development. Freeman and Louçã (2001, p. 141) refer to 'examples of highly visible, technically successful, and profitable innovations'. Perez (2002) speaks of the 'big-bang of the revolution', when referring to the start of a fundamental breakthrough.

The first technological revolution in England may be associated with the opening of Arkwright's Cromford Mill in 1771, which was the starting point of mechanization and cost-saving in the textile sector. Sixty years later, the 'Rocket steam engine for the Liverpool-Manchester railway' marked the rise of steam power and the great significance of the railways for the second technological revolution. During the third technological revolution, England was overtaken by the US. The initiating big-bang was the opening of 'the Cargenie Bessemer steel plant in Pittsburgh' in 1875. The introduction of the Ford-T model, produced in Detroit, was the catalyst of the fourth technological revolution. The most recent technological revolution goes back to Intel's first microprocessor in 1971, the original and simplest 'computer on a chip'.

The big-bang heralds the start of a technological revolution. However, such a technological revolution is first of all a coherent whole, a 'constellation of technical and organizational innovations'. The most important elements of such a constellation include:

- carrier branches or leading sectors in the economy;
- core and other key inputs;
- infrastructural systems of transport and communication;
- management and organizational changes.

Table 5.2 presents the characteristic factors for the distinguished technological revolutions. The dating of the corresponding long waves is depicted in Table 5.3.

A technological revolution is accompanied by numerous imbalances. Perez (2002, p. 39) enumerates the areas of tension. These areas regard the tension between:

- the new industries and the mature ones;
- modern firms and the firms attached to the old ways;
- the regional strongholds of old industries and spaces occupied by the new industries;
- the capabilities of those trained in the new technologies and those whose skills become increasingly obsolete;
- the working population in the modern firms or dynamic regions and those that remain in stagnant ones and may be threatened with unemployment and income uncertainty;
- the thriving new industries and the old regulatory system.

As we have discussed in Chapter 3, in the theory of Perez (2002, 2009, 2010) every technological revolution advances through four phases, which are parts of a logistic curve. Figure 5.2 shows what happens in the subperiods distinguished. However, this is not the whole story. In the view of Perez, the transition from phase 2 to phase 3 is accompanied by a derailment of the economy. Phase 2 is the Frenzy phase, in which speculative

Table 5.2   Technological revolutions

Constellation of technical and organizational innovations	Carrier branch and other leading branches of the economy	Core input and other key inputs	Transport and communication infrastructure	Managerial and organizational changes
1. Waterpowered mechanization of industry	Cotton spinning, iron products, water wheels, bleach	Iron, raw cotton, coal	Canals, turnpike roads, sailing ships	Factory systems, entrepreneurs, partnerships
2. Steampowered mechanization of industry and transport	Railways and railway equipment, steam engines, machine tools, alkali industry	Iron, coal	Railways, telegraph, steam ships	Joint stock companies, subcontracting to responsible craft workers
3. Electrification of industry, transport, and the home	Electrical equipment, heavy engineering, heavy chemicals, steel products	Steel, copper, metal alloys	Steel railways, steel ships, telephone	Specialized professional management systems, 'Taylorism', giant firms
4. Motorization of transport, civil economy, and war	Automobiles, trucks, tractors, diesel engines, aircraft, refineries	Oil, gas, synthetic materials	Radio, motor-ways, airports, airlines	Mass production and consumption, 'Fordism', hierarchies
5. Computerization of entire economy	Computers, software, telecommunication equipment, bio-technology	'Chips' (integrated circuits)	'Information highways' (Internet)	Networks; internal, local, and global

Source: Freeman and Louçã (2001, p. 141). Reproduced by permission of Oxford University Press.

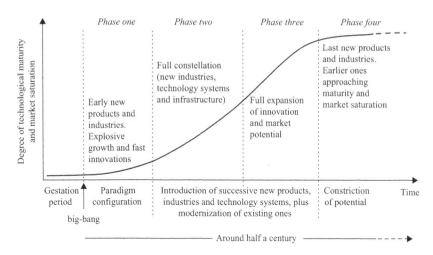

Source: Perez (2002).

Figure 5.2   The life-cycle of a technological revolution

behaviour, based on new opportunities, leads to an overheated economy as well as to financial bubbles. After the dust has been cleared and the bubbles have burst, the economy reaches smooth waters and economic growth is more or less balanced. Thus, the transition from phase 2 to phase 3 involves a turning point, which is, for that matter, not a point at all, but a period of crisis that may be shorter or longer. Not enough data are available to test a theory that has been elaborated according to these lines. Perez (2002) roughly follows the set-up of Freeman and Louçã (2001), as presented in Table 5.2, when moving over to a historical interpretation of the technological revolutions (or great surges) that have occurred. This implies that, initially, the long wave is split into two parts, the installation period and the deployment period.

The hypothesis that a specific turning point characterizes the transition between these periods is a central theme in the works of Perez. The question arises whether this is justified. For example, Papenhausen (2007) does not share this point of view, although he also starts from the thought that there are four phases of economic development. The author combines Perez's phases 1 and 2 into one and considers the turning point as a part of a new phase 'which encompasses a structural crisis era where conflicts erupt between the economic and the lagging social institutions' (Papenhausen, 2007, p. 19). Anyhow, the role of crises in the dynamics of long waves deserves further consideration. Section 5.2 will be devoted to the role of financial crises in the theory of the long wave.

Table 5.3   Comparison of datings

Rank	Perez (great surges) Installation/Deployment	Freeman Louçã (K-waves) Upswing/Downswing
1.	1771–1793/1798–1829	1780s–1815/1815–1848
2.	1829–1848/1857–1873	1848–1873/1873–1895
3.	1875–1893/1895–1918*	1895–1918/1918–1940
4.	1908*–1929/1943–1974*	1941–1973/1973–?
5.	1971*–2001/2008–?	?

It is instructive to compare the dating of long waves of Perez (2002), on the one hand, and Freeman and Louçã (2001), on the other hand, even though in both cases the years chosen are only an approximation of what happens in reality. Table 5.3 shows the comparison of these datings. The most important differences between both approaches that can be derived from Table 5.3 are:

1) In the work of Perez, the sub-periods are not strictly connected, since room is left for the turning point already indicated above.
2) The periods of Deployment in the view of Perez and the Upswing in the work of Freeman and Louçã broadly correspond. These periods are characterized by a relatively high growth rate. In the common theory of K-waves, it is usual to start from there. Perez reverses the sequence, for which arguments can certainly be put forward. This change also implies that Perez's installation period roughly corresponds with the traditional downswing.
3) Most differences concern the dating of the first wave. At the beginning of the Industrial Revolution, the distance between Installation and Upswing is shorter, as may be expected. Perez considers the 'canal mania' of 1793 as the start of the transition from installation to deployment. According to Freeman and Louçã, this phenomenon is part of the upswing: 'These bandwagon and bubble phenomena were to become typical of the very-fast-growing sectors in each successive Kondratieff Wave' (Freeman and Louçã, 2001, p. 168).
4) When dating the waves, Perez takes account of overlapping waves. The relevant years indicating some overlap are marked with an '*'. The fourth and fifth surges start, even prior to the completion of the preceding surges. This follows from the hypothesis that every surge starts with a previously selected *big-bang*. In contrast, Freeman and

Louçã are more alert to the fact that technological revolutions are featured by a long prehistory. For example, the authors observe, that 'the new industries and technologies that characterized the upswing of the second Kondratieff wave, had already come together in an interdependent constellation in the 1820s and 1830s' (Freeman and Louçã, 2001, p. 188). Further investigation of the developments indeed often reveals a certain degree of overlap.

The question arises whether the datings in Table 5.3 correspond with the results of Korotayev and Tsirel (2010). A comparison of the data in Tables 5.1 and 5.3 makes it clear that a certain degree of similarity is observable, at least as far as the period 1820–1974 is concerned. The datings are not exactly equal, but one may assume that economic growth in the periods considered was high during the Upswing and the Deployment.

As observed above when technological change is at stake one should consider changes in factor productivity as in Alexander Field (2003). The author compares the increase in total factor productivity (TFP) for different periods of the US economy. Changes in TFP are obtained by growth accounting, which is based on neoclassical theory. The decomposition method first attributes growth to changes in capital and labour inputs. The residual is the part of growth that stems from increases in the productivity of these inputs. The residual is a measure for the increase in total factor productivity (TFP). The accounting method will be explained in greater detail in Chapter 7. Using figures of TFP from different sources Field (2003, p. 1399) comes to the surprising statement that 'the years 1929–41 were, in the aggregate, the most technological progressive of any comparable period in US economic history'. At first sight, one would not expect the economy to be so productive during the years of a severe depression. Different explanations can be ventured for this remarkable result. Some of these explanations are related to measurement problems such as the years chosen to mark the beginning and end of periods or adjustments to the capital input series. After a careful inspection of the arguments in question Field (2003, p. 1410) comes to the conclusion that the rate of technological change is high during the depression years partly as a result of serendipity: 'Technical advances do not necessarily arrive in a steady stream, and the 1930s were characterized by progressive programs in a remarkably large number of industries and sectors'. The Great Depression certainly had some impact on productivity as a process of Darwinian selection eliminated inefficient firms. Moreover, as Field also observes the downturn with low levels of capital utilization fostered the search for organizational improvements. If it is accepted that technological change as such is remarkably high during the Great Depression, how does this fact relate to the dating of long waves? In the analysis of Perez (2002) the period considered by Field (2003) is marked as a turning point (see Table 5.3). It is a period of rerouting the system, implying reform, enrichment and consolidation of the institutional structure. There is no indication whatsoever that productivity growth should be exceptionally fast in such periods of transition. The result obtained by Field remains puzzling, although Michael Perlman (2011) suggests that it is caused by eliminating so-called X-inefficiency. However, the empirical evidence for this argument is rather thin as appears from the following citation: 'Presumably, a previous laxity in cost cutting played a role' (Perlman, 2011, p. 213).

Figures may not tell the whole story. A very important reason for the existence of an upswing and a downswing in the economy is the fact that every technological revolution involves a generic learning process as well. In the terminology of Perez, every revolution is accompanied by a new techno-economic paradigm. This paradigm has to do with learning new technological and organizational principles: 'But this learning must overcome the forces of inertia that stem from the success of the previous paradigm. Its prevalence is the main obstacle for the diffusion of the next revolution. These counteracting forces, these battles between the new and the old, are the core of the whole interpretation presented here' (Perez, 2002, p. 19). We will discuss the political implications of this conflict in section 5.3.

5.2.   THE FINANCIAL INSTABILITY HYPOTHESIS

An alternative explanation for the occurrence of long waves is based on the financial instability hypothesis of Hyman Minsky (1964, 1995). In essence, this hypothesis boils down to the following. During the upswing of the economy, optimism grows, while, gradually, more and more risks are taken. Besides, financial intermediation increases. New financial assets and instruments for debt financing are developed. A deterioration of the relative debt position of the private sector results from these financial innovations. The ratio of the debts to GNP continuously increases. During mild recessions, which hit the economy, this need not be disastrous. However, if the rise in debt continues then, at a certain point, things become untenable. Income is too low to meet all obligations. Panic breaks out and the owners of financial assets try to sell these in the capital market. Consequently, asset prices collapse, while many firms go bankrupt, both in the financial sector and in the real sector of the economy. This marks the end of a longer period of economic expansion.

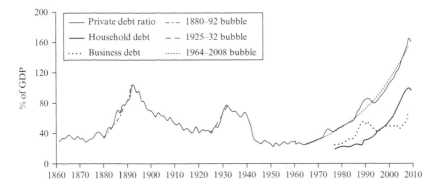

Source: Keen (2009a).

Figure 5.3   Australian long-term debt-to-GDP ratios

Newly developed time series of public debt over a long period are discussed in Carmen Reinhart and Kenneth Rogoff (2011). Here we restrict ourselves to an interpretation of time series of the Australian economy presented in Steve Keen (2009a). As Figure 5.3 makes clear, three debt bubbles may be distinguished in the period 1860–2010. The length of the third bubble, from 1964 to 2008, is much larger than the duration of the preceding bubbles. The question arises whether this interpretation of the figures is realistic. Keen (2009a, p. 350) only observes that the third bubble, also the most recent one, is the biggest. In this context, he argues: 'Just as the bursting of the two earlier debt bubbles ushered in depressions, I expect the same will result from the bursting of this bubble and for the same reason'. To appreciate this statement, it is useful to further investigate the financial instability hypothesis of Minsky.

The theory of Minsky fits in the Post-Keynesian tradition, in which money is not neutral and expectations may be out of step. It is essential that investment is financed, to a large extent, by bank loans. Money creation affects the real economy, so that 'money matters'. This sharply contrasts with neoclassical theory, in which an increase of the money supply leads to a rise in the price level, while investment is fully determined by savings. The Post-Keynesian theory assumes that production capacity is not fully utilized. In this theory, the investment function plays a pivotal role. Entrepreneurs determine the level of investment. Consumers decide on the level of consumption. The level of production (actual output) is determined by aggregate demand. Production capacity may deviate from this level. The ratio between the actual level of production and the productive capacity indicates the rate of capacity utilization. One may assume that this capacity utilization rate influences the behaviour of entrepreneurs. Minsky (1995, p. 83) states that his starting point is 'the simple Hansen-Samuelson interaction between the accelerator and the consumption propensity'. In his view, constraints such as the relative inelasticity of finance or an inelastic labour supply also need to be taken into account. However, this is not sufficient, because in a Post-Keynesian approach the rate of capacity utilization has to be introduced as an additional constraint. The impact of the constraints on the supply side of the economy remains somewhat obscure as Minsky does not formalize his ideas.

Financial asset prices play a prominent role in Minsky's view. However, in the neoclassical theory with perfect foresight of economic agents these prices reflect future asset returns. Minsky reserves room for overoptimistic expectations and speculation: 'There is no "correct" price for a future income stream. The market price of an asset depends upon the time-path the income it yields is expected to follow as well as the certainty with which these expectations are held' (Minsky, 1964, p. 331). If financial asset prices increase, a new actor may appear on the scene, viz. the Ponzi financier.[2] This entrepreneur buys various financial assets with borrowed funds. The income from these assets is not always sufficient to pay the interest, but the Ponzi financier speculates that the price increase of financial assets will be sufficient to meet all obligations and even to make a profit. Ponzi debtors increase the fragility of the financial system. Similar forms of speculation frequently occur in real estate markets.

In the theory of the long wave based on the financial instability hypothesis, five distinct phases may be distinguished:

1) The starting point is a period of relatively stable growth during which firms and banks maintain a conservative course with respect to investing and financing. The risk premium is high, as economic agents have learnt their lessons from past failures.

2) Under the circumstances sketched above, most projects are successful. Debts can easily be repaid and it pays to incur more debt. Leveraging results in higher profits. Consequently, entrepreneurs and banks become less careful. The risk premium falls, while the economic expansion accelerates.

3) However, this development is not free from danger: 'Stability – or tranquility – in a world with a cyclical past and capitalist financial institutions is destabilizing' (Minsky, 1982, p. 101). The economy then goes into a phase that is characterized by Minsky as 'the euphoric economy', in which everyone thinks that the sky is the limit. Several new forms of finance and investment products are eagerly accepted. The fact that economic agents do not learn from past mistakes is

confirmed by Carmen Reinhart and Kenneth Rogoff (2008). It seems to be hard to erase the 'this time is different syndrome'.

4) The asset price inflation attracts Ponzi financiers, who skate on thin ice. Debt positions rise, while the interest rate goes up.

5) When the boom reaches its end, major problems arise. The profitability of projects turns out to be disappointing. Lower profits and higher interest rates reduce the demand for capital goods. It becomes more difficult to sell goods. The burden of the debt on the shoulders of the entrepreneurs is heavier than previously expected. Some entrepreneurs go bankrupt. All economic agents want to get rid of their debts. Financial asset prices collapse, due to massive sales. Liquid positions are taken. Ponzi financiers are wiped out. The asset price deflation causes aggregate demand to decrease, since wealth co-determines aggregate spending. Henceforth, more firms get into trouble. The economy slides into a depression.

As noted in Hans Visser (2010) Minsky owes much to Irving Fisher. However, Minsky is considered to be more pessimistic than Fisher, because according to the latter a Schumpeterian innovation-wave is needed to start a cyclical process dominated by myopic investment behaviour. In the view of Minsky quiet times carry the seed of their own decline, as people become over-optimistic if things go well for some time. Another difference is that for Minsky a downturn does not have to be accompanied by a fall in the price level of goods, though a decline of asset prices is an essential element in the theory. If prices of goods fall real debt will not decline. As a result debtors are forced to cut spending even more. Creditors who gain by deflation may not increase their spending. Therefore the economy faces a more protracted period of low spending and high unemployment. Because of this phenomenon it could be maintained that contrary to Visser (2010), Fisher is the more pessimistic scholar of the two.

The theory of Minsky is rather complicated. Modelling this theory is anything but simple. Moreover, one may expect that results can only be traced by running simulations. Minsky (1995, p. 86) considers the computer-based simulations of complex systems using dynamic, non-linear equations as scientific progress: 'these developments have freed economists from the need to force their theorizing into a strait-jacket determined by mathematical tractability'. Keen (1995, 2009a) formalizes some of Minsky's ideas by means of an extension of the Goodwin growth cycle model. In Goodwin's model, workers consume all of their income, while investment is determined by the profits of firms. Production capacity depends upon the stock of physical capital. Total output equals production capacity, the circular flow is closed. Labour demand depends on output and labour productivity, which increases at a constant percentage annually. Labour supply is exogenous. The internal dynamics of the system is determined by capital accumulation and a Phillips-curve mechanism that determines wage formation. Robert Goodwin (1967) shows that the interaction of the process of capital accumulation with that of wage formation will lead to a cyclical pattern. If employment rises as firms invest more, the share of labour in national income will increase. As a result, profits decline and investment decreases. This affects employment negatively. Thus, the increase of wages slows down and funds available for investment rise. The circle is then closed. It should be noted that the economy grows, owing to the exogenous increase in labour productivity, but the process as such exhibits a cyclical pattern.

In accordance with the Post-Keynesian tradition, Keen (1995, 2009a) introduces an investment function in the Goodwin model. Net investment is a function of the profit rate times the level of output minus depreciation. If investments exceed realized profits, then the resulting discrepancy is financed by bank loans. Obviously, firms must pay interest on these loans. The interest rate is a linear function of debt to output ratio. Interest payments come at the expense of net profits. In the model, bankers do not make profits and have nothing to spend. In a more recent version of his Goodwin-Minsky model, Keen (2009a) also introduces Ponzi speculation by firms. The rate of change of Ponzi speculation is a non-linear function of the rate of economic growth. Ponzi investments are completely financed by borrowing funds. This means a higher burden of interest payments for firms, without any productive revenues.

It should be noted that, in the analysis of Keen, consumption is a residual variable, which sharply contrasts with the original model of Goodwin. In the model of Goodwin, workers consume all of their income, while firms invest all of their profit. Thus, the circular flow is closed. In the model by Keen, the propensity to invest function replaces the assumption that all profits are invested. The level of consumption is then equal to the discrepancy between the level of production, which depends on the size of the physical capital stock and the fixed capital-output ratio, and the number of investment goods bought by entrepreneurs. Thus, consumption is a residual variable. This does not correspond with the Post-Keynesian paradigm, in which a consumption function is usually assumed. The elimination of the consumption decision makes the model less realistic because consumption is less sensitive to the business cycle than investment. The question about the strength of this objection will be left unanswered here.

The model of Keen (2009a) can be reduced to a system of six differential equations. As depicted in Figure 5.4, numerical simulations based on more or less reasonable parameter values generate a cyclical growth pattern. The introduction of Ponzi-loans implies that the recovery of growth will

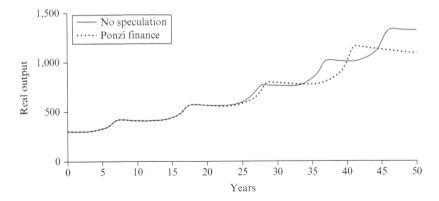

Source: Keen (2009a).

Figure 5.4   Simulation results for real output in the model by Keen (2009a)

take longer and longer, since profits are, to a diminishing extent, allocated to productive goals. This continues 'until, ultimately, the debt incurred in the final cycle overwhelms the economy's debt-servicing capacity and a depression ensues' (Keen, 2009a, p. 353). This way, it can be shown that an economic expansion, financed by both productive and speculative loans, may run into trouble. It should be remarked that debt deflation remains absent, which contrasts with the analysis of Minsky. In the model of Keen, an increasing burden of the debt leads to a crowding-out of productive investments, which eventually results in a stagnation of the economy.

In case the threat of deflation caused by debt reduction becomes real, this can be prevented by an adequate government policy. Assistance to financial institutions, government budget deficits and a policy of 'cheap money' may keep up the circular flow. In this context, the question arises whether the portfolios of firms, households and financial institutions will be sufficiently cleaned up during such an adjustment process. Minsky is moderately optimistic with regard to this issue. In contrast, Steve Keen (2009b) and Peter Temin (2010) doubt whether political solutions offer enough solace in the recent great recession. For example, Temin (2010, p. 16) concludes: 'Recent policy initiatives appear to have done little to reduce the underlying risk of another financial crisis'. The message from Keen (2009b, p. 12) is even more dismal:

The scale of private debt in the USA means (a) that the deleverage process already underway in the USA will swamp government attempts to stimulate

Table 5.4   Typology of capitalist expansions

	Supercapitalism	Balanced capitalism
England	First industrial revolution 1770–1795	Great British leap 1795–1834
	Second industrial revolution 1834–1848	Victorian boom 1848–1873
America	Gilded Age 1875 – 1890	Progressive era 1890–1917
	Roaring twenties 1920–1929	New Deal 1930–1970
	Neo-liberalism 1980–2007	Reform? 2010 –

demand; and (b) that it is most unlikely that another 'Ponzi' rescue of the American economy can be affected via stimulating private borrowing; and (c) the collapse in credit creation will easily outweigh Bernanke's dramatic attempt to boost the money supply. A Depression is therefore highly likely.

5.3.   PERIODIZING CAPITALISM

As we have noticed in Chapter 1, capitalism in the view of Polanyi (1944) is characterized by a double movement. On the one hand, it is necessary to decouple economic activity from social relationships in order to allow markets to function optimally. On the other hand, interventions are frequently necessary to limit the excesses of the capitalist expansion. This inherent contrast leads to an alternation of periods of great economic freedom for economic agents and periods in which regulation imposed by the public sector plays a predominant role. In Chapter 2 we have elaborated upon this, based on the history of the US economy. In Table 2.1, we have summarized this dynamic interaction between the economy and politics.

Table 5.4 presents the earlier findings for the American economy, supplemented with data for England in the period 1770–1873, in a slightly different way. The supplementary data for England enable a comparison of the typology of the capitalist expansion based on political constellations with the dating of long waves by Freeman and Louçã (2001) and by Perez (2002). Robert Reich (2007) introduces the notion of 'supercapitalism', implying a form of unrestrained and relentless capitalist expansion. Reich indicates a more balanced growth that is controlled by regulation as 'democratic capitalism'. From a historical point of view, we prefer the expression 'balanced capitalism'. Moreover, it should be noted that democracy functions on the basis of different political institutions at the beginning of the period considered compared to the situation in modern times.

The periodization in terms of supercapitalism and balanced capitalism with respect to England requires some elucidation. One of the main characteristics of the First Industrial Revolution concerned investments in profitable projects by both new entrepreneurs as well as by the old oligarchy of landed aristocrats. This meant that 'manufacturing interests could often determine government policy' (Freeman and Louçã, 2001, p. 166). This was very opportune in the struggle about issues, such as the number of working hours, obtaining permits for the building of canals and overcoming the resistance against the introduction of factory production. According to Perez (2002), the transition to a more balanced development during the Great British leap was heralded by the canal mania of 1793, which led to the panic of 1798. Regulation to prevent overinvestment took the economy into smooth water. Another characteristic of this era concerns the income distribution. Under the Speenhamland Law, an allowance system was introduced, according to which workers who earned a wage that was too low got compensated, according to a scale based on the price of bread.

In course of time, the Speenhamland system appeared to be too expensive, while it did not foster the efficiency of the labour market. The power of the class of manufacturers and merchants steadily increased and the Speenhamland system was replaced by the *New Poor Law* of 1834, which offered little direct benefits to the unemployed. Anyway, a real labour market came into existence following this change in the turbulent era of the second great surge in the terminology of Perez (2002). Times were hard for workers, as prominent novelists like Charles Dickens and Elizabeth Gaskell document. The repeal of the *Corn Laws* in 1846 meant that food prices declined putting a downward pressure on nominal wages. Therefore, workers did not benefit from the lower prices. In the case where labour is abundant the real wage in equilibrium is fixed at the minimum level.

The period of the Second Industrial Revolution was coloured by heavy social unrest and resistance from the workers. Referring to the 1830s and 1840s, Freeman and Louçã (2001, p. 186) note: 'This was the only period in the nineteenth century when Britain came close to a social revolution'. A real revolution never took place and the Victorian boom, which followed after a period of huge turmoil, was the first that was accompanied by a rise in real wages (see Gregory Clark, 2005). In the theory of Perez (2002) the transition to the Victorian boom is related to the railway mania of 1847 and the subsequent recession. However, in this theory there is little or no attention for developments in the labour market.

In Table 5.4, the emphasis lies on the double movement from a dynamic perspective, as has been elaborated upon in Van de Klundert (2010). Periods of unlimited capitalist expansion lead to excesses, which trigger resistance. If it is possible to translate this resistance into political action, then this changes the character of the capitalist expansion. Adequate regulation subsequently leads to a more balanced development. However, such a development may cause stagnation of the economy after a lapse of time. New reforms are then in order, but in this case in the opposite direction, giving entrepreneurs more freedom to invest and to innovate. Examples are the abolishment of the Speenhamland Act in England in 1934 and the deregulation in the US in the 1980s.

Technological development is an important factor with regard to the changes in the political climate. A comparison of the data in Tables 5.3 and 5.4 teaches that periods of supercapitalism *grosso modo* correspond with the notion of Installation in the analysis of Perez (2002). A similar correspondence exists between the periods of balanced capitalism and Deployment in the terminology of the author. However, the coherence between the periods distinguished in Tables 5.3 and 5.4 is not perfect. On the one hand, this is the inevitable consequence of the arbitrary character of all such classifications. On the other hand, one should be careful not to get caught by a kind of technological determinism. As explained in Chapter 2, political processes are characterized by their own dynamics. In this context, Freeman and Louçã (2001, p. 255) emphasize: 'the necessity to take full account of the "semi-autonomous" developments in the political and cultural subsystems, as well as in technology and the economy'. Besides endogenous developments in the domain of the interaction between economics and politics exogenous factors, such as wars, play an important role, as we have seen in Chapter 2.

From Table 5.3, it also appears that the classification of long waves of Freeman and Louçã (2001) differs from that of Perez (2002). This has partly to do with a difference in vision regarding the double movement. Perez puts the emphasis on the transition (turning point) of exuberant developments with speculative crises to a more balanced growth based on enforced reforms. In Freeman and Louçã (2001), every wave consists of an upswing (boom), followed by a downswing (crisis of adjustment). During the downswing room needs to be created for the emergence of new industries that are to replace the stagnating sectors. Vested interests then must be overruled. This implies that support for liberalization and deregulation must be gained. Such a process often elapses in a more complicated way than adaptations in the opposite direction (regulation), certainly if the latter adjustments result from evident derailments within capitalism. In this context, the response to the Gilded Age and the Great Depression in the 1930s provide appealing examples.

5.4. EVALUATION

In reflections on long waves, alternatively referred to as K-waves (named after Nikolai Kondratieff, a pioneer in this respect), the following questions take a central place. Does a long wave in the economy really exist? And if so, what is the duration of a single wave? Is it possible to measure these waves applying scientific methods? If K-waves do exist, how can they be explained? One should note that these questions cannot be answered separately.

When determining whether K-waves really exist, one often starts from time series with respect to real GDP growth in the countries distinguished. In this context, the line of reasoning is that economic growth during the so-called upswing exceeds economic growth during the so-called downswing. When exploring time series, again, a number of questions arise. Which countries ought to be taken account of in the research? Which statistical methods are the most appropriate to detect K-waves? In general, the results of empirical research are not very satisfactory. The existence of K-waves is not beyond reasonable doubt, but the debate continues. Recently, Korotayev and Tsirel (2010) have shown that the existence of long waves can be proven statistically. Although the methods they use are very sophisticated, their approach is also debatable. The authors make use of aggregate data, but are not able to do so consistently, due to the limited availability of data for the period 1820–70. Furthermore, they are forced to adjust the data with respect to both World Wars and with regard to the Interbellum, due to the excessive developments during these periods.

However, according to Freeman and Louçã (2001), supported by Perez (2002), one may not assume right away that the economic growth during the upswing exceeds the economic growth during the downswing. In both publications, the explanation of K-waves is the first matter of importance, not the statistical measurement of these cycles. The starting point is the occurrence of technological revolutions, which succeed one another in the course of time, and for that reason, cause a discontinuous path of technological development. Technological revolutions involve a large number of connected phenomena. Apart from the introduction of one or more breakthrough technologies, these phenomena include leading sectors featured by fast growth, the application of specific or core inputs, the necessity to adjust the infrastructure to the new developments, as well as various organizational changes. At the start of a technological revolution, changes are fierce. Old sectors with limited growth opportunities must make way for new, expansionary sectors. In brief, the situation is then characterized by a high degree of creative destruction. The effect of these developments on the growth rate of GDP is ambiguous. Therefore, Freeman and Louçã (2001) demonstrate the existence of long waves based on an extensive description of technological revolutions. Perez (2002) also follows this approach, but emphasizes a more theoretical explanation of the long wave using a logistic curve, as discussed in Chapter 3.

Alternative explanations for the existence of long waves are available. The financial instability hypothesis of Minsky (1964, 1995) provides an interesting example. This hypothesis can be briefly summarized as follows. If the economy prospers, optimism steadily rises and entrepreneurs are readily willing to invest. These investment outlays stimulate the expansion even further. A climate of self-fulfilling prophecies prevails. Investors do not consider debt accumulation as a real problem. Innovations in the financial sector stimulate these developments in the goods producing sectors of the economy. In such a world of exuberance, the Ponzi-investor appears on stage, a person who does not pay much attention to the direct return on investment, but fine-tunes his behaviour to expected capital gains. This cannot simply go on forever. A bubble is created, that has to burst eventually. If so, a depression may result, as the deleveraging by firms and households does have major consequences. The question then arises whether the government will be able to turn the tide, either via fiscal policy or via supporting financial institutions, the latter in cooperation with the Central Bank, which may also provide 'cheap money'.

Minsky himself has not elaborated on the duration of such overinvestment cycles. Keen (2009a, 2009b) hints at the parallels between developments in the 1930s and the recent financial crisis. Thus, he suggests that Minsky's financial instability hypothesis underpins the existence of K-waves. Perez (2002) also reserves room for financial instability, apart from the technological explanation of long waves. At the end of the installation phase of a technological revolution, the level of investment in new, profitable sectors is too high (examples include the canal mania in 1793, the railway mania in 1847 and the internet bubble of 2000). In this period speculation also increases in the finance sector, due to the introduction of new financial products. Eventually, the bubbles burst and the economy reaches smoother waters, the period of deployment, in Perez's terminology. Coupling technological and financial developments seems to be a fruitful approach although the emergence of financial bubbles requires no immediate cause in the work of Minsky, as emphasized in Visser (2010). However, Perez (2002) does not fully succeed in clarifying the role of the financial sector in the transitions from installation to deployment around the years 1793, 1847 and 1893.

To present a complete picture of long-term developments, one should take into account 'semi-autonomous developments in the political and cultural subsystems' (Freeman and Louçã, 2001, p. 255). The double movement as defined by Polanyi (1944), which we discussed in Chapter 1, completes the description of long waves. To correct the excesses of a capitalist expansion, in a democracy a political majority is required. The same holds true in the opposite case, when necessary freedom needs to be created to facilitate technological breakthroughs. As has been explained in Chapter 2, the economy and politics exert a mutual influence. This complication, too, contributes to a reasonable amount of doubt with respect to the existence of a more or less regular pattern of long waves.

However, the regularity in the pattern of waves is only important if one is eager to present forecasts. The existence of systematic K-waves is not a prerequisite for understanding complicated economic, technological and political developments. However, one may conclude that the hypothesis as such has led to seminal research. Traditional ideas such as 'this time is different', 'capital markets function efficiently' and 'the technology exhibits continuous progress' have to be adapted, partly owing to considerations with regard to the long wave.

The obtained insights are therefore useful to understand recent changes. The financial crisis of 2007/2008 shows parallels with the developments in the 1930s. However, despite the double bubble at the turn of the century (Perez, 2009), the consequences are now not that far-reaching, owing to government interventions. The question then arises whether these government measures always will be sufficient, because with or without a stereotype long wave, capitalist dynamics are inherently unstable. Peter Temin (2010, p. 16) summarizes the lines of reasoning in the form of two lessons:

> The first is that the open American economy is prone to collapse every once and a while. Favorable conditions . . . can eliminate 'great' economic contractions for a generation or so, but American exuberance appears to chafe under these conditions. The second lesson is that there are strong pressures for unregulated capitalism that only abate in the face of sharp economic downturns like the 'Great Depression'.

NOTES

1. The constructed K-wave concerns supplementary growth rates, that is to say 'a series of increments (or decreases) of the annual world GDP growth rates that are accounted for by Kondratieff waves' (Korotayev and Tsirel, 2010, p. 16). The pattern with a so-called double peak shows resemblance with a well-known idealized scheme of the wholesale price oscillations in the course of K-waves for the US.
2. Named after Charles Ponzi, an Italian who migrated to the US and made a living out of swindle. His name is attached to a pyramid-construction with which he 'separated fools from their money' in the 1920s.

6. A tale of two continents

6.1. FORGING AHEAD AND CATCHING-UP

In the preceding chapters, we have indicated that the (first) Industrial Revolution occurred in England in the final quarter of the eighteenth century. The question arises as to why this revolution took place in this specific country and why the countries on the European continent lagged behind. England, in turn, lost its lead in the economic domain to the US around 1900. Again, the question arises what caused these diverging developments. Nowadays, the economic positions of the US and Europe (EU-15) are comparable. Has this already been the case for a long time, or has Europe only succeeded in bridging the gap after the Second World War? What are the consequences for Europe if this process of catching-up has been completed? How must Europe then proceed? One should not expect that unambiguous answers can be given to all of these questions, but there is a lot to say about the issues of 'forging ahead' and 'catching-up'.

No macroeconomic data are available for the first great surge (1771–1829), according to the classification of Perez (2002). Starting from 1820, data are available for per capita production in a number of countries. Table 6.1 depicts GDP per capita in the US and in some European countries in the period 1820–1913. These figures are index numbers. The index for the leading country, in this case England, has been set equal to 100. In 1820, the other European countries and the US had fallen behind substantially. Remarkably, the Netherlands was doing quite well in comparison with other followers. Just like England, the Netherlands was a commercial nation with a relatively high level of welfare at the eve of the Industrial Revolution.

The question why England took the lead vis-à-vis the European continent has been heavily debated. North and Thomas (1973, p. 156) characterize the initial conditions as follows: 'England by 1700 was experiencing sustained growth. It had developed an efficient set of property rights embedded in common law. Besides the removal of hindrances to the allocation of resources both in the factor and product markets, England had begun to protect private property in knowledge with its patent law. The stage was now set for the Industrial Revolution'.

Table 6.1 GDP per capita 1820–1913 (index numbers)

Country	Year			
	1820	1870	1900	1913
England	100	100	100	100
Belgium	74	81	80	82
Germany	63	59	68	76
France	69	57	62	68
The Netherlands	89	81	77	78
Italy	62	45	38	50
United States	73	75	89	105

Source: Maddison (1995).

Joel Mokyr (1990) adds that England disposed of a relatively large number of skilled workers, as compared to the European continent. Moreover, the transportation system was excellent, partly owing to the multitude of canals. The exact importance of the above-mentioned factors is hard to assess. However, one is, in general, convinced that the 'Glorious Revolution' of 1688 was important for the further developments. As discussed in Chapter 1, this revolution meant that the parliament obtained an important and independent role, which paved the way for a greater political power of the emerging rich middle-class. Thus, the foundation had been laid for the technological revolution, while the resistance of the losers from technological progress, the victims of the creative destruction, got hardly any chance. Mokyr (1990) describes how unsuccessful the various attempts to block the progress actually were. Riots were violently suppressed by the government: 'During the Luddite outbreaks in 1811–1813, the British government deployed 12,000 men against rioters, a force greater in size than Wellington's original peninsular army in 1808' (Mokyr, 1990, p. 257). Legal attempts to block the introduction of machinery also failed, because employees had the political power to suppress regulations inimical to the introduction of new technologies.

Robert Allen (2011) presents an original explanation for the occurrence of the Industrial Revolution in England. The author assumes a technological development that is both endogenous and directed. A directed technological development implies that savings on the input of a certain factor of production are targeted. In this case, the intended changes concern the input of labour and the use of coal. In comparison with other European countries, real wages were high in England at the end of the eighteenth century. Moreover, as coal was abundant, the price of energy was low.

Therefore, the introduction of labour-saving and energy-using technologies offered huge advantages. Obviously, this induced inventors to focus on these types of new technologies. This resulted in the mechanization of leading industrial branches (cotton), in the application of steam engines in the pumping of water out of mines, in the production of iron and in the rise of the railways. Subsequently, learning-by-doing led to further technological improvements.

In the countries of continental Europe, the industrialization only got going in a later stage. The power of the traditional crafts remained large in France, even after the abolishment of the guilds, with the following consequence: 'the industrial France that emerged in the nineteenth century thus continued to be based on skilled small-scale handicrafts producing for relatively local markets' (Mokyr, 1990, p. 260). Furthermore, the continent was the stage for great political unrest. The French Revolution (1789) and the Napoleonic wars exerted a negative influence on economic development. David Landes (1998, p. 257) summarizes this impact as follows: 'Twenty-five years of revolution and war from 1789 to 1815 diverted continental resources from building to destruction, played havoc with enterprise and trade, generated some invention but delayed much application, inspired projects but then inhibited them – in effect, delayed industrial emulation of Britain an extra generation'.

The figures in Table 6.1 make clear that the second great surge (1829–73), according to the classification of Carlota Perez (2002), has also not been accompanied by large-scale catching-up effects. Even stronger, with the exception of Belgium and the US, the other countries lose ground vis-à-vis England. In Belgium the industrialization got under way at a relatively early stage, probably owing to the abundant availability of coal.

To give an impression of the further developments in Europe and in the US, we turn to figures with respect to the labour productivity (production per hour), which are available starting from 1870. These data give a more decisive answer to the question about the state of the technology than the data with respect to the level of per capita output. The difference between both indicators is determined by the number of hours worked per capita, the participation rate. This ratio depends upon the demographic composition of the population and the realized leisure time, which both differ per country. The calculation of the index numbers now starts from the number for the US being equal to 100. As observed earlier, the technological leadership went over from England to the US after 1900. The figures in Tables 6.1 and 6.2 confirm this observation.

During the third great surge (1875–1918), investments in England in the new industrial sectors, such as electricity, steel and chemistry, were low compared with those in the US and Germany. In contrast, investments

Table 6.2   Labour productivity 1870–1992 (index numbers)

Country	Year						
	1870	1913	1929	1938	1950	1973	1992
United States	100	100	100	100	100	100	100
Belgium	94	70	64	61	48	70	98
Germany	70	68	58	56	35	71	95
England	115	86	74	69	62	68	82
France	60	56	55	62	45	76	102
The Netherlands	103	78	84	72	51	81	99
Italy	46	41	38	44	34	66	85

Source: Maddison (1995).

in profitable projects abroad, in the domains of mining, plantations and infrastructure (railways) were relatively high. This came at the expense of growth in the domestic economy. The financial sector dominated the allocation of investment funds. Chris Freeman and Francisco Louçã (2001, p. 254) emphasize that the existing power relationships lie at the bottom of these developments: 'the enormous strength of the City of London in financial services meant that financial capital and overseas portfolio investment increasingly dominated in economic policymaking, rather than manufacturing'. The power of the financial sector was not the only obstacle that hampered the search for congruity with new technological developments. Other institutional factors contributed to this relative stagnation as well. In the US, but also in Germany, institutes for higher education were established, aimed at the training of engineers, for whom the demand was high in the new industries. In this respect England lagged behind. The same held true for the education and training of secondary and low-skilled technical workers. Once more, Freeman and Louçã (2001, p. 252) put their finger on an important issue: 'The British tradition of part-time training and education "on the job" may have been appropriate for the techniques based on mechanical ingenuity and learning by doing in the early stages of the Industrial Revolution, but they were increasingly inappropriate for the skills associated with the new technologies'. In addition to the above-mentioned differences in institutions, Karl Gunnar Persson (2010) points at the typical British union structure. Unions were based on skills, instead of on the sectors, in which the members worked. As a consequence, the employers were often confronted with 'multiple-unions' during negotiations. Every union stood up for its own members, which made it often more difficult for firms to introduce new technologies: 'in a multiple-union context a particular union can acquire "hold-up" power both in wage negotiations and in negotiations over the introduction of a new technology' (Persson, 2010, p. 120).

As discussed extensively in Chapter 4, backward countries may catch-up with the leader from a technological viewpoint, because much can be imitated or copied. This implies that countries with a relatively low per capita GDP grow at a comparatively fast rate. Alternatively formulated, there is a negative relationship between the level of per capita GDP and the growth rate of this variable. Statistical research shows that no catching-up occurred in the 1870–1913 period (see Theo van de Klundert and Ton van Schaik, 1996). Catching-up is difficult if the leader is on a fast track. In that case, keeping pace with the leader is already a major achievement. The German manufacturing sector succeeded in doing so after the political reforms of the 1870s. However, the macroeconomic figures in Table 6.2 do not make this sufficiently clear, since the developments in the agricultural sector and in the services sector are taken into account in these figures. Differences with respect to the shares of these sectors in the aggregate economy affect changes in macroeconomic indicators. In the period considered Germany had a relatively large agricultural sector with a modest growth of labour productivity. For empirical evidence see Stephen Broadberry, Giovanni Federica and Alexander Klein (2010).

The events during the period 1913–29 are dominated by the consequences of the First World War. Except for the Netherlands (not involved in the war, owing to its neutrality) the backwardness of Europe vis-à-vis the technological leader increases. The divergence is reinforced during the period of the Great Depression (1929–38) and, of course, to an even stronger degree by the consequences of the Second World War, which become clear in Table 6.2 when comparing the outcomes for the years 1938 and 1950. After 1950, the time is ripe for a catching-up spurt that is also significant from a statistical point of view, as demonstrated in Van de Klundert and Van Schaik (1996). In 1992, all Western European countries, with the exception of England, have more or less caught up with the technological leader, the US. Therefore, some authors refer to the period 1950–73 as the Golden Age of European Growth. After 1973, any catching-up effect in terms of per capita GDP is absent. However, the figures in Table 6.2 make clear that the catching-up in terms of labour productivity does continue after 1973. The difference is explained by the decrease of the participation rate (number of hours worked related to total population) in the European countries compared to the US (see, for example, Van Schaik and Van de Klundert, 2013).

As discussed in Chapter 4, catching-up means imitation of the technology of the leader. This implies relatively less focus on innovation. For the realization of economic growth, the emphasis must be put on investing. In their study on the selection of entrepreneurs and innovative economic growth Daron Acemoglu, Philippe Aghion and Fabrizio Zilibotti (2006) argue that a country in such a situation may benefit from an investment-based strategy. Following Gerschenkron (1962), the authors assume that specific institutions are favourable for fostering the catching-up process. In this context, one may think of long-term relationships between firms and banks, large-scale enterprises and government support, either in the form of subsidies or in the form of policies that restrict competition. In section 4.2 the model of Acemoglu et al. (2006) is discussed in more detail. It appears there that measures limiting competition foster investment. For, entrepreneurs or managers (the functions are interchangeable in the model) are then better capable of reaping the fruits of their investments in technological innovation. In the economic literature, this is known as the 'appropriability effect'. When catching-up is far advanced, however, an innovation-based strategy is more adequate. The less imitation is possible, the more one has to invent oneself. This requires a change in institutions, since the selection of entrepreneurs capable of innovating becomes more important. Newcomers ought to get their chances, but this is complicated if the incumbents enjoy a certain protection under the prevailing institutions. Retained earnings of incumbents protect them against dismissal by capitalists. This so-called 'rent-shield' effect implies that restricting competition hampers innovation. Therefore, an innovation-based strategy will be introduced in due time if the institutional setting allows sufficient competition.

In an extensive study on the European economy since 1945, Barry Eichengreen (2007) reaches a similar conclusion, although the terminology used is different and the approach is descriptive rather than analytical as in Acemoglu et al. (2006). In this sense the contribution of Eichengreen is supplementary to Acemoglu and coauthors. Both studies agree that growth based on catching-up is grounded on massive investments and the set-up of mass production. Complementary sectors are necessary to foster the coordination of the process of economic growth. In this respect Eichengreen (2007, p. 4) notes: 'As industrial production grew more complex and industrial sectors grew increasingly interdependent, it became more pressing to get a range of industries up and running simultaneously'. To mobilize the required savings and finance large-scale investments patient banks with long-lasting relationship with their clients contributed to the economic expansion. As the author notes, such a way to foster growth through heavy capital accumulation and the acquisition of well-known technologies can be characterized as extensive growth. This stands in contrast with intensive growth, which is based on different forms of innovation and selection of workers and managers.

Extensive growth requires adequate institutions. Apart from long-standing relationships between financial and industrial firms, as emphasized in Acemoglu et al. (2006), extensive growth requires in the view of Eichengreen (2007) other institutions to stimulate economic development. The problem of running industrial firms simultaneously was solved in Europe by government planning and state holding companies. The free play of market forces was kept in check by a set of norms, formal as well as informal. It was a prerequisite for the coordination of the economic activities of social partners and contributed to what Eichengreen (2007) typifies as 'coordinated capitalism'. What this means is summarized in the following statement: 'Catch-up was facilitated by solidaristic trade unions, cohesive employers' associations, and growth-minded governments working together to mobilize savings, finance investments, and stabilize wages at levels consistent with full employment' (Eichengreen, 2007, p. 3).

As catching-up nears completion things had to change, because intensive growth requires different institutions. According to Eichengreen such a switch was necessary from the 1970s onwards. However, this timing of the transition seems premature. As observed above, in terms of productivity (production per hour) the catching-up process was still under way in the 1970s and 1980s. In the more recent period the European integration has led to a more intensive competition in product markets, which may be beneficial for an innovation-based growth. Capital markets became more integrated, but labour markets and redistributive policies were not reformed as may be necessary for intensive growth. The question remains whether countries have a choice. Is there a trade-off between more material welfare and other aspects of social welfare?

Europe differs from America, as far as institutions are concerned. This has to do with the role that socialism has played in these two regions. The Industrial Revolution was coupled with the rise of an industrial proletariat, which inspired Marx and other authors to analyze capitalism critically. Workers unified and socialist parties were established in order to improve the situation of workers; quite often, there was a class struggle even in a literal sense. However, in the US, socialism was suppressed in a violent manner time and again. In Europe, the power of the ruling class was substantially weakened by the turmoil of the First World War. This led to the introduction of proportional representation as an electoral rule in a large number of European countries between 1917 and 1920, as Alberto Alesina and Edward Glaeser (2004) demonstrate. This laid the foundation for a significant influence of social-democratic parties and of the working class.

The importance of this development for the arrangements made in the context of the welfare state will be discussed in the next section.

6.2. THE WELFARE STATE

The concept of the welfare state concerns redistribution from the rich to the poor. Prior to 1880, public support of the poor was virtually absent. In most European countries, poor-relief expenditure fell short of 0.5 per cent of the national product. In the US, this percentage was even lower than 0.2 in the years before 1930. At the aggregate level, private charity was of minor importance, too. England formed a notable exception, especially in the heyday of England's *Old Poor Law*. In Chapter 5, we have referred to the Speenhamland system that arranged the support for the workers in the English countryside. As a result of this system and similar provisions in other places in England, expenditure on support for the poor rose above two per cent of the national product in the period 1795–1834. This development is striking, since accomplishing redistribution requires political power, as we argued in Chapter 2. An alternative explanation may be that the land-owners, who practised political power, worried about the ups and downs of their workers. However, such a paternalistic explanation of the remarkably large support to the poor under the *Old Poor Law* seems hardly convincing. The true reason for the support was the fear of the land-owners that the workers would otherwise migrate to the cities. By offering the workers a dignified existence, during bad seasons as well, this migration could be prevented. As we have already noted in Chapter 4, the power of the land-owners ceased to exist, at least in this respect, after 1834. The *New Poor Law* then marked a substantial decrease of poor-relief.

Starting from 1880, the share of the population with a political voice gradually increases. The elite democracies of the nineteenth century, in which property requirements kept most men from voting, make way for fuller democracies. This has important consequences for the redistribution, as Peter Lindert (2004, vol. I, p. 179) rightfully observes: 'Fuller democracies spent much more of taxpayers' money on social transfers than did those elite democracies'. However, universal suffrage is not a guarantee for a proportional representation of the population in the political arena. Other political institutions, such as, for example, a district system, determine the extent to which minorities are represented. Although the historical developments differ much between countries, proportionate representation is nowadays an acquired right on the European continent. Alberto Alesina and Edward Glaeser (2004, pp. 98–99) summarize the developments towards more democracy in Europe as follows:

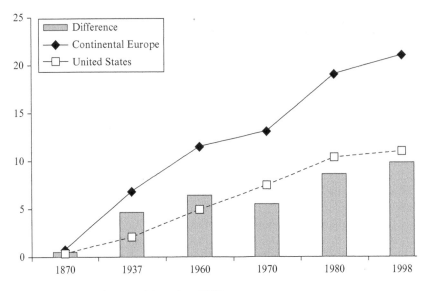

Source: Alesina, Glaeser and Sacerdote (2001).

Figure 6.1   Government expenditures on subsidies and transfers (per cent of GDP), 1870–1998

Proportional representation is a relatively recent phenomenon. In 1890, no European country had proportional representation and only Belgium, Finland, Portugal, and Sweden had this institution at the start of World War I. In the rest of Europe, the conversion to proportional representation happened mainly between 1917 and 1920 when Austria, Denmark, France, Germany, Italy, the Netherlands, Norway and Switzerland all adopted proportional representation.

Despite these differences in timing, a further inspection of the developments leads to the conclusion that labour unions and socialist parties have played an essential role in obtaining political power for the population as a whole. The workers' revolt and the strikes in Belgium from 1886 to 1893 and the unsuccessful Spartacus revolution in 1919 in Germany make clear that matters were sometimes dealt with in a violent way. In the Netherlands, the development was fairly moderate; the general suffrage for males was introduced in 1917 as a compromise between various political parties. This compromise, in which the religious parties stipulated public funding of their schools, in exchange for support of proportional representation, is known as the Pacification of 1917.

Figure 6.1 makes clear that subsidies and transfers increased after 1870. The values on the vertical axis concern government expenditure on subsidies and transfers as a percentage of GDP. The figures for continental Europe relate to 10 countries (Austria, Belgium, France, Germany, Greece, Ireland, Italy, the Netherlands, Spain and the UK).[1] The outlays consist of both direct support measures and social insurance expenditures. Consequently, not in all cases is redistribution from rich to poor at stake. In this context, Lindert (2004, Vol. I, p. 6) notes: 'Programs drifted from being help-the-poor programs to being broad social safety nets that gave many benefits back to the income classes who paid the taxes. Still, there is a definite redistributive element to all social spending, and this is what makes it so controversial'.

The rise of social expenditure in the Western world since 1870 is not the only lesson that can be learnt from Figure 6.1. The structurally large discrepancy between the figures for continental Europe and the US is remarkable. In America, outlays on subsidies and transfers are considerably lower than in Europe, which gives rise to the notion of *American exceptionalism*. One should note that Americans are more involved in charity than Europeans, but this does not compensate for the huge discrepancy with regard to public transfers. The difference between the continents asks for a further explanation, since the income inequality prior to redistribution in the US exceeded that in Europe. Apart from that, the continued rise in social outlays, relative to GDP, on both continents, even after democratization has been accomplished needs to be explained as well. Especially in the 1960s and the 1970s, many authors signal an explosion of the welfare state. Before answering the implicit questions raised above, it seems useful, following the exposition on the political economy in Chapter 2, to put the theory of redistribution under scrutiny.

In the simple case that everybody puts her/his own self-interest first, while a 'one person, one vote' rule applies, redistribution only takes place if the income of the median voter falls short of the average income – for, a majority of the voters then have an interest in income redistribution. Of course, one needs to take account of the costs of redistribution. The latter consist of both administrative expenditure and efficiency losses (deadweight loss), resulting from the distortions of the marginal trade-offs made by economic agents. These concern both the decision-making of the tax-payer and the decision-making of the recipient of transfer income. If total costs are not prohibitive, the median voter opts for redistribution. However, this theorem does not give a clear lead to explain *American exceptionalism*. As observed above, the primary income distribution is more unequal in the US than in Europe. The costs of redistribution do not seem to differ that much between these two regions. Based on the median voter theorem, redistribution should therefore be higher in the US compared to Europe. One possibility to retain this pure economic theory is to

Capitalism and democracy

take account of the expectations of the median voter. If the chance is not mere hypothetical that this voter will reach a higher income echelon in the not-too-distant future, voting for redistribution becomes less opportune. To determine whether this argument is relevant empirically, one needs to investigate whether the mobility among the income ranks is higher in the US as compared with Europe. Research has made clear that the differences are rather small. Alesina and Glaeser (2004, p. 63) notice: 'The middle class in the United States seems only very slightly more upwardly mobile than its counterpart in Germany'. Additional research seems to point in the same direction.

The above observations entail that the simple starting points of economic theory ought to be given up. Economic agents are not only motivated by self-interest, but they do pay attention to the welfare of other economic agents. Therefore, room needs to be reserved for certain forms of altruism. Moreover, the complications in the political domain are plenty. Despite the democratization of Western societies, important differences continue to exist in the area of proportional representation in parliament. The US has a district system with one representative of the majority in each district in the national parliament. With a little good will, one may even construct an index for the degree of proportional representation in various countries.

Alesina and Glaeser (2004) show that a positive statistical relationship exists between such an index, on the one hand, and government transfers as a percentage of GDP in the OECD-countries, on the other hand. Added control variables, such as per capita income and the share of people over 65 in the total population turn out not to be significant. Figure 6.2 shows the observed relationship. The variable on the vertical axis is Transfers/GDP. In the US and other Anglo-Saxon countries, the index for proportional representation is low and the same holds true for the degree of income redistribution. According to Alesina and Glaeser (2004), the variable proportional representation explains approximately half of the difference in social outlays (as a share of GDP) between Europe and the US. Other political institutions, such as federalism in the US and checks and balances, incorporated in the constitution, contribute to a lesser extent to the explanation of *American exceptionalism.*

Yet another argument may be put forward regarding why the poor may only play a relatively minor role in the political arena. Lindert (2004, Vol. II, p. 5), following Gary Becker, starts from the hypothesis that 'the ultimate size of the transfer depends on the pressures exerted by the competing pressure groups'. The input of more resources may generate more *de facto* political power for a specific group, but this input is determined by the income that needs to be sacrificed. By definition, the income of the

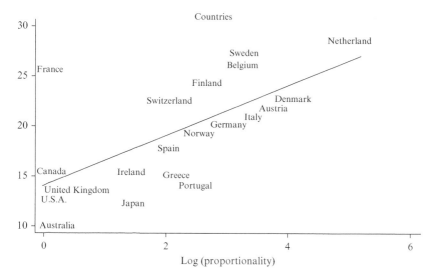

Alesina, Glaeser and Sacerdote (2001).

Figure 6.2 Transfers/GDP versus Log (proportionality) for OECD countries

poor is low. They will allocate little or no resources to the political struggle. Therefore, they hardly exert any influence on the ultimate macroeconomic equilibrium. If the degree of income inequality is rather high, as is the case in the US, this is a factor that one needs to take into account. With regard to this issue, Lindert (2004, Vol. II, p. 8) is extraordinarily outspoken: 'A main reason why greater inequality fails to tax the rich more is that the inequality discourages the poor from joining the fight for progressive redistributions'.

Behavioural explanations are also important with respect to *American exceptionalism*. Altruism does exist, though compassion is lower the further away the other person is, either from a social or an ethnical viewpoint. In the US racial conflicts form an important barrier for redistribution. The black minority is predominantly poor and the white majority is less inclined to get their wallets out for this group of poor people. Furthermore, in the US, according to the *communis opinio*, people dependent on a benefit are generally lazy. According to this view the fact that they are in trouble is their own fault. In Europe, according to the World Value Survey (1995), there is greater understanding for those poor who are not to blame for the fact that they are currently at the bottom of society. Empirical research, based on a sample of 53 countries, indicates a negative relationship between social welfare spending and racial fractionalization (see Alesina and Glaeser, 2004, Chapter 6). The variable racial fractionalization is an index number, which indicates the probability that, when drawing randomly two people from a population, these people are from different races.

All in all, the empirical research of Alesina and Glaeser (2004) is rather fragmented. They do not make use of a comprehensive sample in order to establish the significance and impact of all relevant variables in regression analysis. Nevertheless, the authors draw a fairly definite conclusion: 'We believe that about one-half of the US-Europe gap can be explained by European homogeneity. As such American racial heterogeneity stands, along with political institutions, as one of the two critical factors explaining the absence of a welfare state in America' (Alesina and Glaeser, 2004, p. 146).

The difference with regard to beliefs between the US and Europe is not considered as a separate cause when attempting to explain the magnitude of the redistribution. According to Alesina and Glaeser, ideological differences have resulted from brainwashing, alternatively indicated as indoctrination. As we have noted in section 6.1, American capitalism differs from European capitalism, since socialism has never come to grips with US society. Owing to all kinds of political developments, the labour movement and the socialist parties in Europe have been able to put their mark on both the political and the economic institutions. Moreover, alternative societal systems go along with different opinions with respect to inter-human relationships. The ruling elite dominates the prevailing ideology. In the view of Alesina and Glaeser (2004, p. 198) this has to do with: 'top-down belief formation through the school systems, but also through political campaigns and the media'. Besides, the observed discrepancies in beliefs may be self-fulfilling, as demonstrated in Roland Bénabou and Jean Tirole (2006).

The thought that capitalism is shaped differently on the two continents is a challenging one, but then the question arises regarding why things have gone this way. Why has socialism never got a foothold in the US? Being a country of immigrants, America is different. Immigrants are individualistic rather than collectivistic. Racial contrasts also hampered the formation of class consciousness among workers. Europe was exposed to a greater political and military turmoil. The First World War weakened vested interests and provided socialism with the opportunity to grab a certain amount of power.

A thorough explanation of the discrepancies in the area of redistribution does not answer the question why transfers as a percentage of GDP kept rising on both continents after the Second World War (see

Figure 6.1). Lindert (2004, Vol I, p. 188) ascribes both the rise of total transfer outlays as a percentage of GDP and the relative increase of its separate components to the following factors:

- the ageing of populations;
- globalization;
- the rise of income per capita;
- social affinities felt by middle-income voters.

Ageing leads to an increase of outlays on pensions based on the pay-as-you-go system. Globalization implies higher income uncertainty. Economic agents may want to cover the risk of exposure to shocks from abroad. However, empirical research frequently demonstrates that there is no significant relationship between total social outlays and the degree of openness of an economy. It seems plausible that per capita income has a positive effect on social outlays, but, in this case, too, the relation is not unambiguous from a statistical point of view. Lindert (2004) attaches a great significance to a certain form of social affinity. If people are aware that their fate is always uncertain, they will be more willing to opt for a social security system: 'In particular, the Great Depression and the Second World War gave middle income voters new reasons to believe that they and their families might sink economically and might need a safety net' (Lindert, 2004, Vol. I, p. 189). Furthermore, the author notices that the Roman-Catholic Church dropped its conservative attitude and supported the expansion of the welfare state. Such a vision seems rather blunt, in light of the papal encyclicals *Rerum Novarum* (1891) and *Quadragesimo Anno* (1931), which were published long before the Second World War.

At the end of section 6.1 we argued that the economic institutions in Europe need to be adapted after the catching-up movement vis-à-vis the US has been completed. Intensive growth, in the terminology of Eichengreen (2007), requires a high degree of labour market flexibility. The social security system may block such flexibility. However, the debate about the merits of the system of social security is anything but new, as Lindert (2004, Vol I, p. 3) emphasizes: 'Any reading of the social history of early modern Europe turns up all the arguments we hear today'. Every time again the key issue is to reconcile the 'three social goals: helping people in a given state, giving them an incentive to avoid that state, and keeping down the program budget' (Lindert, 2004, p. 4). According to Lindert, the expansion of the welfare state has not come at the cost of economic growth, as his own empirical research makes clear. This raises the question: 'Is the welfare state a free lunch?' In a sense, it is, according to the author, since the European countries have succeeded in both opting for the right mix of taxes and in taking measures 'for minimizing young adults' incentives to avoid work and training' (Lindert, 2004, p. 227). Moreover, some elements of the social security system enhance productivity. Of course one should be aware that not everybody agrees with the views of Lindert (see, for example, Persson, 2010, p. 204).

The debate about the organization of the economic system goes further than the social security system only. The way in which, under capitalism, the efforts of firms and other economic agents are coordinated, is subject to discussion. The next section will be devoted to these issues.

6.3.   VARIETIES OF CAPITALISM

The literature on the varieties of capitalism starts with the influential work of Michel Albert (1991), introducing a contrast between the Rhineland model and the Anglo-Saxon model. Peter Hall and David Soskice (2001) provide a theoretical base for the difference between both varieties. In their study, the focus is on the modern enterprise. Firms have to deal with their employees with respect to issues such as wages, terms of employment and training; with financial markets to acquire funds for their activities; with buyers of their products concerning price and delivery; with other firms from which they get their inputs; and so on. These relationships require coordination between the parties that are involved. For simplicity the varieties approach is characterized by the confrontation of two variants with respect to the coordination problem: liberal market economies (LMEs) and coordinated market economies (CMEs). This way, the Western countries can be divided into two main groups. In order to clarify the differences, we quote the authors extensively to show what they have in mind: in LMEs 'firms coordinate their activities primarily via hierarchies and competitive market arrangements. (. . .) Market relationships are characterized by the arms-length exchange of goods or services in a context of competition and formal contracting. In response to the price signals generated by such markets, the actors adjust their willingness to supply and demand goods or services' (Hall and Soskice, 2001, p. 8). However, in CMEs, 'firms depend more heavily on non-market relationships to coordinate their endeavours with other actors. (. . .) These non-market modes of coordination generally entail more extensive relational or incomplete contracting, network monitoring based on the exchange of private information inside networks, and more reliance on collaborative, as opposed to competitive, relationships to build the competencies of the firm' (Hall and Soskice, 2001, p. 8). In the case of CMEs the focus is on strategic interaction, whereas markets hold a key position in LMEs.

In order to investigate whether such a division is meaningful, one has to examine whether the Western countries exhibit systematic differences with respect to the coordination of the activities of firms. Alternatively formulated, does institutional complementarity exist as far as relationships among economic agents are concerned? Peter Hall and Daniel Gingerich (2004) investigate whether such complementarity with regard to relationships indeed exists, using six constructed variables:

- *Shareholder Power*: legal power of ordinary shareholders.
- *Dispersion of Control*: the number of companies with a multitude of shareholders in comparison with companies with controlling shareholders.
- *Size of Stock Market*: market valuation of the stock exchange as a percentage of GDP.
- *Level of Wage Coordination*: level at which wage negotiations take place.
- *Degree of Wage Coordination*: degree of coordination between employers and employees.
- *Labour Turnover*: short-term jobs (less than one year) as a percentage of all jobs.

For every variable, an index is constructed, with a value between zero and one. The closer the index number is to unity, the more important strategic interaction is compared to the operation of markets. The first three variables refer to coordination in the domain of corporate governance, while the last three variables relate to the degree of coordination of labour relations. All data used apply to the early 1990s. Factor analysis can reveal whether the statistical material contains a dominant factor. This turns out to be the case, and it is self-evident to identify this factor as the coordination index.

Analogously, one may construct separate indices for corporate governance and labour relations. The index for corporate governance is derived from the first three variables in the list given above, whereas the index for labour relations is based on the last three variables. In Figure 6.3 these indices are set against each other. It follows from this figure that the institutions in both domains are strongly complementary. Moreover, Figure 6.3 makes clear which countries can be classified as LME and which countries can be classified as CME. LMEs with a low score in both areas include: Australia, Canada, New Zealand, the Republic of Ireland, the UK and the US. However, one should note, that in the first four countries market forces in the domain of corporate governance are not fully developed. The group of CME-countries with high scores consists

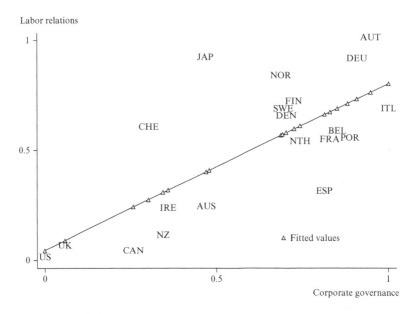

Source: Hall and Gingerich (2004).

*Figure 6.3   Institutional complementarities between coordination in labour
relations and corporate governance*

of: Austria, Belgium, Denmark, Finland, Germany, Iceland, Japan, the
Netherlands, Norway, Sweden and Switzerland. These countries are characterized by high levels of strategic coordination in both their labour and
financial markets. In addition, there are four ambiguous cases: France,
Italy, Portugal and Spain. In these countries the strategic coordination
in the labour market is less important than in the CMEs. Therefore, this
group of countries is indicated as MMEs (mixed market economies) by the
authors. From Figure 6.3 it becomes clear, however, that these countries
may also be classified as CMEs.

In section 6.2, we have seen that important differences exist between
the organization of the welfare state in Europe and in the US. In the view
of Hall and Gingerich (2004), these discrepancies are part of a broader
spectre of complementarities across sub-spheres of the political economy.
This is in accordance with the findings as depicted in Figure 6.3. Countries
in the south-western area of this figure, with relatively low transfer
outlays, can be identified as LMEs.

Hall and Gingerich (2004) further elaborate on the phenomenon
of institutional complementarity, making use of seven variables. In

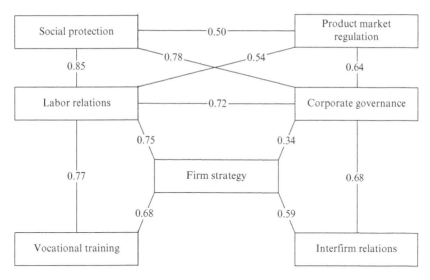

Source: Hall and Gingerich (2004).

Figure 6.4 Complementarities across sub-spheres of the political economy

Figure 6.4, these variables are presented in a rectangle. Labour relations and corporate governance are part of the analysis that we discussed earlier. The meaning of the variables social protection, product market regulation and vocational training is self-evident, although measurement, if desirable, requires further specification. The variable interfirm relations refers to the annual number of mergers and acquisitions in a country expressed as a ratio of its population. At stake is the cooperation between firms when obtaining access to new technologies and new markets, in comparison with purely relying on market forces for such purposes. The variable firm strategy is a composite in which various core practices of the firm are taken together. One may think of items such as the use of participatory work teams, alliances with other firms, long-term relations with investors and so on. The numbers on the lines that connect the variables in Figure 6.4 are the calculated correlation coefficients. These coefficients indicate the extent to which these variables are interdependent, in the context of distinguishing varieties of capitalism. According to Hall and Gingerich (2004, pp. 21–22) the results are satisfactory, since these coefficients suggest 'that corporate strategy varies systematically with the institutional support available for different types of coordination in the political economy, as varieties of capitalism theory predicts'.

If such clear differences can be observed between capitalist systems, does the same then hold true for their economic performance? This important question has been at the heart of the varieties literature ever since the beginning. According to Hall and Soskice (2001, p.41), both variants perform equally well, but in a different way: 'The institutional frameworks of liberal market economies provide companies with better capacities for radical innovations, while those of coordinated market economies provide superior capacities for incremental innovations'. Radical innovations include, for example, substantial shifts in product lines, development of new goods and major changes of production processes. The authors attempt to validate their hypothesis by comparing patent statistics per sector in the US (LME) and in Germany (CME). In the US, many patents have been granted in dynamic sectors, such as bio-technology, medical engineering and semiconductors. In contrast, in Germany patent-specialization is focused on traditional sectors, such as, for example, agricultural machines, engines and mechanical elements. However, the analysis of Hall and Soskice (2001) is not fully convincing. It is not difficult to raise objections against the applied method. First, the comparison only concerns two countries. Second, patent statistics are not a reliable source to determine the nature and the size of the technological development (for an extensive criticism, see: Dirk Akkermans, Carolina Castaldi and Bart Los, 2009).

Hall and Gingerich (2004) take a different road. Using panel data for OECD-countries in the period 1971–97, the authors examine the following two hypotheses with respect to economic growth:

Hypothesis 1:   In the case where there exist higher levels of market (strategic) coordination in the sphere of labour relations *or* corporate governance, the rate of economic growth increases as the level of market (strategic) coordination in the other sphere increases.

This hypothesis is tested by introducing an interaction term in the regression equation explaining per capita annual growth. As required, a number of control variables are introduced to condition the relation. The interaction term in the form of the product of the indices for coordination in labour relations and for coordination in corporate governance is positive, of considerable magnitude and statistically significant. This result confirms the relevance of complementaries between both spheres of coordination.

Hypothesis 2:   Economic growth is higher in the case where levels of market or strategic coordination are consistently high or low across spheres and lower in the case where there is more variation in the types of coordination in the political economy.

This hypothesis is tested by introducing the general coordination index and its square in the regression equation explaining economic growth. The resulting U-shaped relation between growth and coordination shows that growth is higher if a consequent strategy is applied. Therefore, both varieties of capitalism perform more or less equally well in terms of general efficiency.

This conclusion contrasts with the view of Eichengreen (2007) and other authors, discussed in section 6.1, that the institutions that are adequate in the case of catching-up need to be adjusted as soon as the economy approaches the technological frontier. Generally, CMEs are countries in the phase of catching-up, certainly in the period that Hall and Gingerich investigate. Nevertheless as time goes by things may change as the authors are also aware. Therefore, additional research is performed by testing of the following hypothesis: 'Secular economic developments over the past two decades have not altered the efficiency of institutional complementarities posited by the varieties of capitalism perspective between labour relations and corporate governance' (Hall and Gingerich, 2004, p. 31). The above-mentioned past two decades refer to the period 1985–1997. Remarkably, the results of the statistical research for the more recent period are disappointing. The impact of institutional complementarity on growth weakens and it is even not significant according to standard statistical criteria. This forces Hall and Gingerich (2004, p. 32) to acknowledge that: 'these results lend some credence to the view that secular economic changes may be diminishing the effectiveness of existing institutions, which should increase pressures for institutional change'.

It is evident that the economic pressures in the recent past have led to a partial convergence of CMEs into the direction of LMEs. This is in accordance with the now familiar idea that strengthening of the innovative power of the economy requires a high degree of market flexibility. But this comes at a cost. The financial instability in the LMEs may be greater than in CMEs, as unchecked market forces foster speculative behaviour. Obviously, the emphasis on shareholders' value advances behaviour aimed at short-term successes and may even be accompanied by the destruction of value. Furthermore, the income distribution is more unequal in LMEs as compared with CMEs, which may corrode social cohesion. To put it briefly, one needs to take account of various factors and developments. When dealing with the theories with respect to the long wave in Chapter 5, we discussed similar problems. Therefore, convergence of institutions is certainly not a matter of one-way-traffic. Moreover, the divergence in opinions with respect to the organization of capitalism between the two continents is deeply rooted, as we have concluded in section 6.2. Thus, there is something to say for the conclusion of Hall and Gingerich (2004, p. 36): 'the absence of wholesale convergence in the face of the substantial economic pressures experienced during the 1980s and 1990s suggests that the distinctions drawn by the varieties of capitalism literature between different types of political economies are likely to be relevant for some time to come'.

6.4. EVALUATION

The history of Europe differs from the history of the US both from an economic and a political point of view. In this chapter, the discussion of economic history starts in 1750 at the onset of the Industrial Revolution in England. The countries on the European continent were not able to follow the technological leader, England, immediately. Even after the industrialization of continental Europe was realized, productivity levels did not converge completely to that of the British economy in the period prior to the Second World War.

Meanwhile, the US had overtaken England, in terms of GDP per capita, during the upswing of the third Kondratieff wave (according to the classification of Freeman and Louçã, 2001), or the deployment phase of the third technological revolution, alternatively indicated as the 'great surge' (according to the classification of Perez, 2002). One might state that the well-known law of the 'advantage of backwardness' is applicable in this case. The accumulation of capital was accompanied in England by a growing power of the financial sector, which invested savings abroad rather than in new, emerging sectors within the English borders. At first, Germany was quite capable of following the third technological revolution, but, starting from the First World War, Germany fell more and more behind the US. Both World Wars and the Great Depression put Europe as a whole at a great distance from the US.

This situation changed after 1950. The Western European countries then succeeded in catching up with the US, i.e. the leader from the perspective of technology. In the early 1990s labour productivity (production per hour) had nearly been levelled. Per capita output remained higher in the US, since Europeans devote comparatively less hours to work. The preferences towards leisure seem stronger than in the US. The catching-up process after the Second World War was favoured by adequate institutions, in which trust, networks of companies and cooperation between employers and workers dominated the picture.

With respect to the redistribution of income and the design of the welfare state there remain important differences between the continents, as shown in section 6.2. Subsidies and transfers as a percentage of GDP are much lower in the US than in the West-European countries. The expression 'American exceptionalism' has been introduced to mark this difference. These differences between the US and Europe cannot be explained by the median voter theorem. On the contrary, on the basis of this theorem redistribution should be higher in the US than in Europe. According to Alesina and Glaeser (2004) the difference with respect to the redistribution is caused by two factors. First, in Europe labour unions and socialist parties gained political power after the political turmoil following the First World War. Second, racial heterogeneity undermines the solidarity among people. The authors believe that American racial heterogeneity and political institutions are the two factors explaining the US-Europe gap in the field of redistribution. Apart from this, it should be stressed that social outlays as a percentage of GDP increased substantially on both continents following the Great Depression and the Second World War.

The political climate has a more far-reaching impact on the institutional design of the economy. In countries with left-wing influences the coordination of economic activities is not left exclusively to market forces. Strategic interaction, in which reputation and commitment are important, supplements the coordination through markets. Hall and Soskice (2001) elaborate on this idea by distinguishing varieties of capitalism.

Liberal market economies (LMEs), which heavily rely on market forces, are confronted with coordinated market economies (CMEs), with a strong emphasis on non-market relationships to coordinate their endeavours. LMEs include the Anglo-Saxon countries (apart from the US and the UK, also Australia, Canada, New Zealand and the Republic of Ireland), while the group of CMEs consists of countries on the European continent, as well as Iceland and Japan. 'A tale of two continents' thus gets a somewhat broader interpretation, but this only enriches the content of the story. American exceptionalism, as discussed in Alesina and Glaeser (2004), is a designation that is too limited, given the more fundamental differences in the context of the literature on varieties of capitalism. An examination of the indices with which the significance of institutions can be quantified, reveals that England and the US, but also Australia, Canada, New Zealand and the Republic of Ireland, are close to one another, as also appears from Figures 6.2 and 6.3. Is it perhaps possible to persist in the opinion that the individualism of the islanders has been kept alive along with the move of migrants from England to other continents? Besides, the contrast between these forms of capitalism has been noticed before. Michel Albert (1991) sets the Anglo-Saxon model against the Rhineland model. This classification is more or less in line with the division into

LMEs and CMEs, but the terminology of Albert has reached a broader audience.

An important question is whether both variants of capitalism converge under the impact of economic developments. Eichengreen (2007) is a proponent of the hypothesis that the institutions in Europe require adjustment now that the process of catching-up has been completed. At the technological frontier, an innovation-based strategy, in the terminology of Acemoglu et al. (2006), is desirable. In this respect, free markets, labour market flexibility and creative destruction are necessary. The latter concept emphasizes that those economic activities that are out of date need to be given up. As a consequence of these developments the question arises: will Europe show a closer resemblance to the US in the near future?

However, the Great Recession of 2007/2008 and its aftermath put matters in a somewhat different perspective. Firms in the Anglo-Saxon model fine-tuned their policies prior to the financial crisis too much to the short-run wishes of the shareholders. Banks and insurance companies took too many risks and, ultimately, the government had to intervene in order to rescue a number of important players. After the recession, the call for measures to prevent financial catastrophes in the future is loud. However, it remains to be seen whether enough will be done in the area of regulation in all economies concerned.

Institutional changes are associated with political power relations, as we have argued many times before. The question arises whether the Great Recession has led to a major change in this respect. In this context, the situation differs from the Great Depression in the previous century, as Temin (2010) stresses, for example. Anyway, the welfare state in Europe is under severe pressure. Phenomena such as the ageing of the population and changes in the ethnical composition of the population undermine the solidarity, which is a factor of vital importance in the context of redistribution and social insurance. Under impact of the crisis the debate about the negative consequences of the welfare state is revitalized. Adjustments will certainly take place. Therefore, the answer to the question posed above is affirmative. Europe will become more similar to the US, but as stated in Hall and Gingerich (2004), a wholesale convergence does not seem likely.

NOTE

1. Including the figures for the UK makes the indication 'continental' somewhat misleading.

7.   The world economy at large

7.1.   CONDITIONAL CONVERGENCE

In the preceding chapter, we discussed the differences between the capitalist systems in Western countries. It is necessary to take a look at the world as a whole, in order to obtain a picture of future developments with respect to capitalism. The level of welfare highly differs across countries. A large inequality exists in terms of per capita GDP. The other side of the coin is the availability of a large potential for growth at the global level. For developing countries may grow at a high pace by imitation of technologies of the rich countries and by adjustment to these technologies. If such a catching-up process takes place, radical changes will occur on the world stage as the balance of power shifts, with major consequences for the cooperation at the global level. We will elaborate on these issues in the next chapter. If the catching-up of developing countries turns out to be disappointing, the question arises of how this can be explained. For some economists, a disappointing catching-up process is incomprehensible, as Steve Dowrick and J. Bradford DeLong (2003, p. 194) observe: 'That the pattern of economic growth over the twentieth century is one of striking divergence is surprising to economists, for economists expect convergence'.

Indeed, as shown in Chapter 4, most theoretical models of economic growth of backward countries rely on catching-up. However, convergence is often incomplete, because local circumstances or institutions differ from those in developed economies. Divergence at low levels of per capita GDP is a possibility in case catching-up is not only a matter of exploiting knowledge spill-overs, but is related to the social capability to do so. Despite this qualification Dowrick and DeLong (2003) have a point. Our knowledge of the expansion of capitalism in the world is unsatisfactory. Reason enough to analyze the issue from a different angle. Therefore, in this chapter the potential convergence of backward countries in the world economy is studied mainly from an empirical perspective.

There are several ways to proceed. First, one may investigate in the context of a historical narrative, whether individual countries succeed in imitating the technological leaders. Second, in a statistical approach of the problem, one may search for general insights with respect to the convergence of countries. After a brief characterization of the descriptive method, we will discuss the statistical approach in more detail.

In section 6.1 we have concluded that the Western European countries initially did not succeed in keeping up with the technological leader, England, let alone in catching-up with this leader. In the period 1820–70, the Industrial Revolution took off with great difficulty on the European continent. The period 1870–1950 is characterized by great turmoil and by the transition of the technological leadership from England to the US. Only after 1950 did catching-up to the US economy gather momentum in Western Europe. However, again and again, convergence only takes place on a limited scale. Dowrick and DeLong (2003) discuss these developments in a broader perspective. The notion of a convergence club, which the authors have derived from William Baumol and Edward Wolff (1988), is at the heart of their analysis. A convergence club is a collection of countries where the 'forces of technology transfer, increased international trade and investment, and the spread of education were powerful enough to drive productivity levels and industrial structures to (or at least toward) those of the industrial core' (Dowrick and DeLong, 2003, p. 195).

Dowrick and DeLong identify such convergence clubs in the world as a whole for the sub-periods 1820–70, 1870–1913, 1913–50 and 1950–2000. The authors demonstrate which countries joined the club and which countries dropped out. In this respect, the membership of the convergence club in the sub-period 1950–2000 is illustrative. In Latin-America, countries such as Venezuela, Peru, Argentina, Chili and Uruguay were no longer members of this club. In Africa many countries also dropped out in comparison with the preceding sub-periods. However, the 'East Asian miracle' led to the entry of a large number of countries: Japan, South Korea, Taiwan, Hong Kong, Singapore, Thailand, Malaysia, Indonesia (after 1965) and China (after 1978). In Latin America, Colombia and Mexico entered, while India experienced a rapid development after 1980. The narrative method contains a wealth of details, but it hardly offers any general insight. On the contrary, questions arise that are not easy to answer, as Dowrick and DeLong (2003, p. 203) have to acknowledge: 'In the second (1950–2000) era of globalization, the implications of globalization for the size of the convergence club are less clear. Why has it been such a friend to East Asia but not to Latin America? Why has the eastern Mediterranean done so well and the south-western Mediterranean so badly?' Thus, the question is justified whether general insights might be obtained by applying the statistical method.

As stated in Chapter 4, catching-up implies that the growth of GDP per worker, as a measure for labour productivity, is higher the lower the

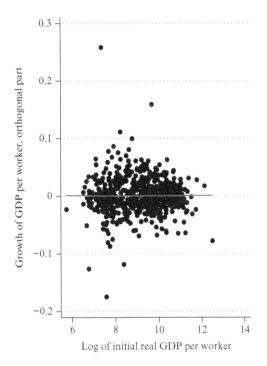

Source: Rodrik (2011b).

Figure 7.1 *Unconditional growth regression (decadal regression for 1970–2008)*

level of GDP per worker is in the initial situation. A low level of GDP per worker, in comparison with other countries and, especially, compared to the most advanced economies, entails that a country can learn many things from other countries in the domain of technology. Imitation of the existing technology may lead to rapid growth, even though adaptation to local circumstances is necessary. Statistical testing of this hypothesis, using a sample of countries, systematically yields a negative result. There is no negative and statistically significant relationship between the growth rate of GDP per worker and the initial level of this variable. Figure 7.1, derived from Dani Rodrik (2011b) illustrates this conclusion. As a matter of fact, production per hour worked, instead of GDP per worker, ought to be taken as a measure for labour productivity, but this variable is not available in the Penn World Tables, on which the author bases his analysis. The number of countries in the dataset is large, although the author does not indicate how many countries are included. One may increase the number of observations by distinguishing sub-periods. Rodrik (2011b) starts from the period 1970–2008 and then makes a distinction between four sub-periods. Every observation in Figure 7.1 thus corresponds with the development of one country during one decade. The scatter plot of observations in Figure 7.1 shows the absence of any relationship between these variables. Thus, there is no convergence at all in the world economy at large. The picture is changed if countries in the sample are weighted by their population size. As shown in Xavier Sala-i-Martin (2006, p. 354) there is then a negative relation between growth and the initial income level, because 'the few countries in Asia that have converged to income levels of the OECD are large and populous, while many of the countries that have diverged (chiefly African countries) are not'. This approach is relevant if one wants to study changes in the world distribution of income. In case one is interested in analyzing catching-up growth, weighting countries by population size does not make sense, because growth depends on national factors as Sala-i-Martin agrees.

The conclusion that unconditional convergence does not occur can be maintained, but conditional convergence may still be an option. This implies that convergence may take place, but that a large number of other factors need to be taken into account, which might disturb the direct relation between the growth rate of labour productivity and the initial position. It is not difficult to think of a large number of conditional factors, which may exert influence on the process of convergence. This has led to an extended literature in which conditional convergence is tested using regression analysis. The results differ substantially, which has led to a considerable amount of scepticism. Barry Bosworth and Susan Collins (2003) present an update, in which they examine a large number of possibilities using a sample of 84 countries, together representing 95 per cent of gross world product and 84 per cent of the total world population. The authors insist on standardization, which should remove an important reason for varying results in empirical studies. This means that regression results should be obtained by using a standard set of countries, standard time periods and a standard set of conditioning variables. Conditioning variables are determinants of economic growth that appear to be significant in many other studies. The dependent variable is the growth rate of output per worker in the period 1960–2000. In contrast with Rodrik (2011b), no sub-periods are distinguished in the main regression. Remarkably, the growth of labour productivity is related to the 1960 level of income per capita as a ratio to the US level, instead of to the initial level of labour productivity. When expanding the regression analysis, a distinction is made between conditioning variables, policy indicators and other potential explanatory variables.

Table 7.1   Explanatory variables

Conditioning variables	Policy indicators	Other variables
Income per capita	Change in inflation	Financial development
Life expectancy	Budget balance	Real exchange rate
Log of population	Sachs-Warner measure	Alternative measures for
Trade instrument	for openness[1]	openness
Geography		Educational indicators
Institutional quality		Investment share

Note: [1] This trade policy measure, computed in Jeffrey Sachs and Andrew Warner (1995), is widely used in empirical research.

Table 7.1 presents the most important variables, grouped according to the type of variable, as distinguished in Bosworth and Collins (2003). The conditioning variables express the position of the economy in the initial situation. Life expectancy is a measure for the health of the population. Population is included in the conditioning procedure as a dimension for country size. The trade instrument is a constructed variable that can be viewed as a measure of a country's predisposition for trade. The geography variable is based on a weighting of the number of frost days, on the one hand, and the percentage of tropical land area, on the other hand. Institutional quality is an important variable based on information in the International Country Risk Guide, in which corruption, law and order, risk of expropriation, government repudiation of contracts, and bureaucratic quality are measured and carefully weighted.

All conditioning variables are highly significant from a statistical viewpoint. This significance result does not hold for the policy indicators in the second column of Table 7.1, although this conclusion should be qualified somewhat for the budget-balance variable. Next, Bosworth and Collins (2003) investigate whether other variables play a significant role. Obvious variables, such as the investment ratio, the level of education and financial development hardly exert any influence. Alternative measures for the openness of the economy do not perform very well from a statistical point of view. However, a large number of studies argue that integration into the world markets is of crucial importance for economic growth. All in all, these results do not take one very far, as Bosworth and Collins (2003, p. 32) have to conclude: 'A striking aspect of these regressions is the relatively minor evidence of a direct role for conventional government policies. Instead, the most important determinants of growth appear to be factors that cannot be changed substantially in the short-run'.

One may ask what the relation is between the cross-country analysis of economic growth on the one hand and neoclassical growth theory, discussed in Chapter 3, on the other hand. As mentioned in earlier chapters, according to the neoclassical theory the growth rate of output depends on the growth rate of the number of workers, which corresponds with the increase in population, the growth rate of the capital stock and technological progress. This relationship can easily be transformed in a relation explaining the growth of output per worker by the growth of capital per worker and technological change. The latter variable can be defined as the change in total factor productivity (TFP). Applying the simple technique of growth accounting it is possible to establish both the contribution of change in capital per worker and of TFP change to the growth rate of output per worker. The contribution of the growth of capital per worker is obtained by multiplying this figure with the share of capital income in total output.[1] Next, the contribution of TFP change is found by subtracting the contribution of the growth rate of capital per worker from the growth rate of output per worker. Therefore, technological change is calculated as a residual. As a result of this procedure, the residual is not only a measure of technological change in a strict sense, but includes efficiency improvements and mutations in capital utilization as well. It should be noted in this connection that it is not necessary to make any assumption with respect to the bias of technological change (labour or capital saving).[2]

Bosworth and Collins (2003) combine both empirical methods in an original manner. The authors regress the contribution of the accumulation of capital per worker and of technological change, obtained through growth accounting, on the same set of explanatory variables as they did in the regression on output growth. This reveals 'the channels through which the variables influence growth' (Bosworth and Collins, 2003, p. 159). In Table 7.2 we present the results with respect to the regression coefficients of the independent variables. As such the numerical values of the regression coefficient are not that interesting, because they also depend on the dimensions of measurement of the variables concerned. However, the combination of regression coefficients on each row of Table 7.2 shows through which channels conditioning factors and policy variables influence economic growth. It should be noted that by construction the sum of the coefficient in columns two and three is equal to the value of the coefficient in column one.

As is apparent from the coefficients on initial income, 'the convergences process is evident both through capital accumulation and through the efficiency of resource use' (Bosworth and Collins, 2003, p. 159). The same holds true for the impact of geography and population size. Life expectancy and especially institutional quality work through the channel of TFP improvements. The policy variable budget balance has its primary

Table 7.2   Regression coefficients explaining growth, 1960–2000

Independent variable	Dependent variable		
	Growth output per worker	Contribution of capital per worker	Contribution of TFP
Constant	−1.64	−0.52	−1.12
	(−1.6)	(−0.6)	(−1.3)
Conditioning variables			
Initial income per capita	−6.24	−2.89	−3.35
	(−10.7)	(−6.2)	(−6.7)
Life expectancy	0.06	0.02	0.04
	(5.0)	(2.4)	(3.6)
Log of population	0.28	0.16	0.12
	(4.7)	(3.4)	(2.4)
Trade instrument	3.55	2.24	1.31
	(3.0)	(2.4)	(1.3)
Geography	0.48	0.22	0.26
	(3.9)	(2.2)	(2.5)
Institutional quality	2.34	0.34	2.00
	(3.6)	(0.7)	(3.6)
Policy indicators			
Inflation	−0.01	0.00	0.00
	(−1.1)	(−0.7)	(−0.6)
Budget balance	0.06	0.06	0.00
	(2.3)	(2.6)	(0.3)
Sachs-Warner openness	0.48	0.44	0.04
	(1.7)	(1.9)	(0.2)

Source: Retrieved from Bosworth and Collins (2003), Table 8; numbers in parenthesis are *t* statistics.

impact through capital accumulation, as may be expected in the case where savings are concerned. Not everything is as expected: 'One surprise is that the correlation of both the trade instrument and trade openness with growth appears to operate through capital accumulation rather than through TFP. Much of the theoretical literature has emphasized the efficiency gains from trade' (Bosworth and Collins, 2003, p. 159). However, it should be recalled that the policy variable openness is not statistically significant.

The outcome of the update in Bosworth and Collins (2003) implies that convergence ultimately depends on where the individual countries concerned stand initially. However, conditioning variables only offer a limited insight; these variables are not even necessary to reach this

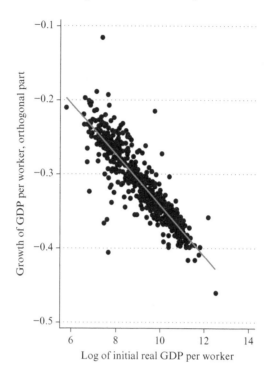

Source: Rodrik (2011b).

Figure 7.2   *Conditional growth regression (decadal regression for
            1970–2008)*

conclusion. Rodrik (2011b) shows that, in his sample, conditional convergence can be proved by the introduction of so-called fixed country-
effects. In this case, a dummy variable is introduced for every separate
country, which marks the specific position of that country. One should
note that this method is only possible if sub-periods are distinguished
in the sample period. This type of analysis is characterized as a *pooled*
cross-section time series analysis. A country-specific result can then be
obtained, as illustrated in Figure 7.2. The difference with the picture
sketched in Figure 7.1 is remarkable. It should be noted that in a cross-
section analysis of countries, as in Bosworth and Collins (2003), the
introduction of fixed country-effects does not make sense. However,
fixed country effects are a kind of black box. It could be maintained that
the Bosworth/Collins approach opens this box to some extent, but the
right thing to do is to combine cross-section and time series data. It then

remains to be seen whether the coefficients on country dummies remain statistically significant.

In anticipation of further statistical evidence, it may be concluded that convergence depends on national factors that are not easy to change in the short run. Therefore, it looks as if to make any progress, a historical narrative seems to be the only constructive option. Interestingly, this is not the only way out. Rodrik (2011b) shows that unconditional convergence does hold for labour productivity at the four-digit level of disaggregation for manufacturing over the period 1990–2007. Besides, this era is also the period in which the developing countries in Asia, but also in Latin America and in Africa, grow faster than the developed countries in terms of per capita GDP, for the first time since 1950. We will discuss the consequences of the findings of Rodrik in the next section.

7.2. STRUCTURALISM

The remarkable growth of developing countries in the period 1990–2007 is associated with more intensive globalization. In this context, Margaret McMillan and Dani Rodrik (2011, p. 2) notice: 'Developing countries, almost without exception, have become more integrated with the world economy since the early 1990s. Industrial tariffs are lower than they ever have been and foreign direct investment flows have reached new heights'. As a consequence, convergence becomes clearly visible in the manufacturing sector, as Rodrik (2011b) elaborates upon. This result becomes even more succinct, if one takes account of fixed country-effects. Besides, one should notice that the occurrence of unconditional convergence in the aggregate economy has not been investigated for the period 1990–2007. However, one can imagine that manufacturing, more than any other sector, is exposed to international competition.

Developing countries are featured by what may be called a *dual economy* – sharp differences with respect to labour productivity exist among the different sectors in the economy. These discrepancies are much bigger than in more advanced economies, as shown in Chapter 4 (Figure 4.10). Therefore, the economy-wide productivity would be much higher, if the developing countries were able to realize the sector pattern of the rich countries.[3] Of course, this would also mean lower employment in agriculture and also in the sheltered sector. McMillan and Rodrik (2011) calculate that, in this hypothetical case, average productivity would double in India, while productivity in China would almost triple. The effects are even much bigger for a number of African countries. However, such a theoretical construction is somewhat misleading. As far as advancing the efficient allocation of production factors is concerned, marginal productivities instead of average productivities ought to be compared. Moreover, such a reallocation affects the marginal productivities in the sectors concerned. Nevertheless, in developing countries, production factors are probably not allocated in line with the neoclassical paradigm. This phenomenon is attributable to a number of institutional factors, which differ across countries. As observed in section 4.3, Weil (2005) mentions a number of possible causes for the lack of factor mobility in backward countries.

The ongoing globalization puts pressure on the sector structure in developing economies. Catching-up leads to substantial growth of labour productivity in various manufacturing sectors. The other side of the coin is that employment in these sectors falls owing to savings on labour, while the question is justified as to whether all laid-off workers can be employed again in manufacturing. In this context, one may notice that part of the labour-saving is realized by the elimination of inefficient firms. The theory of the partial oligopoly shows that a profit-maximizing cartel benefits from setting the price so high that inefficient firms (the fringe) are enabled to operate in the market.[4] If the cartel is exposed to competition in the world market, then this is no longer possible. Besides, the question arises whether even the most efficient firms in developing countries are able to face global competition. On the one hand, the wages in these countries are comparatively low, but, on the other hand, productivity is also significantly lower than in advanced economies. The rise of labour productivity may yield the cost-savings that are necessary to survive in the world market. However, this mechanism does not necessarily mean that the firm concerned is able to expand in the world market.

According to McMillan and Rodrik (2011), the rise of labour productivity in the aggregate economy can be unravelled into two components. The first component consists of the weighted sum of the rise of labour productivity in the separate sectors. The weights are the shares of the employment in the sectors concerned in total employment. In the terminology of the authors, this first component is the *within* component of productivity growth. The second component is equal to the sum of the changes in the shares in the total employment, multiplied by the labour productivity in the sector concerned in the initial situation. This second component is coined the *structural change* term. One may assume the first component to be positive. The second component, however, might be negative. This is especially the case if employment falls in those sectors which are featured by a high level of labour productivity (production per worker): 'If the displaced labour ends up in activities with lower productivity, economy-wide growth will suffer and may even turn negative' (McMillan and Rodrik,

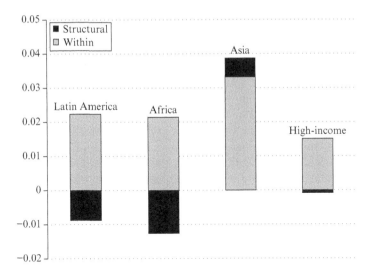

Source: Rodrik (2011b).

Figure 7.3 Decomposition of growth between 'within' and 'structural change' components, 1990–2005

2011, p. 13). Of course this holds even more so if the labour disposed of becomes unemployed.

The decomposition sketched above is applied to a sample of 38 countries and nine sectors in the period 1990–2005. The results of the analysis are summarized in Figure 7.3. A remarkable difference exists between Asia, on the one hand, and Latin America and Africa, on the other hand. In the latter continents, growth-reducing structural change occurs, while in Asia structural change contributes to the increase of economy-wide productivity growth. Growth-reducing structural change implies that labour is redirected from high-productive activities such as manufacturing and tradable services to low-productive services, informality and sometimes even to agriculture. The importance of the structural change term becomes manifest, if one realizes that a large part of the growth difference across continents is explained by the structural change term. Rodrik (2011, p. 29) provides further details: 'Asia's labour productivity growth in 1990–2005 exceeded Africa's by 3 percentage points (per annum) and Latin America's by 2.5 percentage points. Of this difference the structural change term accounts for 1.8 points (61%) in Africa and 1.5 points (58%) in Latin America'. In this connection, one should note that the number of countries in the sample is rather limited. For example, the nine

African countries together represent half of the population of the Sub-Saharan region. Additionally, the sample contains nine Latin American countries and ten developing Asian countries, including China and India. This comment does not take away that the authors have discovered an important phenomenon, which requires further investigation.

At first glance, one may think that the convergence of productivity in manufacturing is caused by the fact that, as McMillan and Rodrik (2011, p. 22) observe: 'All developing countries in our sample have become more globalized during the time period under consideration'. However, this observation is not in accordance with the structural development across the continents. The more intensive globalization is, of course, a world-wide phenomenon. This fact means that the way in which globalization is realized strongly differs across continents, depending on both the local circumstances and local politics. Import competition exposes local manufacturing to intensive rivalry. If domestic firms set prices above the price level in the world market, despite the lower wages, then the opening-up of domestic markets creates a major problem. In order to become competitive, domestic firms need to rationalize and cut costs. They may survive, owing to the increase in productivity. If so, they hold a defensive position and an expansion in the world market is not a priority.

According to McMillan and Rodrik (2011), it may be sensible to manage such downsides, in a world characterized by turbulent competition, as is accomplished in Asian countries. The major example is China that protects its state enterprises and, in the past, organized the emergence of its export-oriented industries in 'special economic zones'. This example is just one of many with respect to the two-track reform system that fostered the rapid growth of the Chinese economy. After China had joined the WTO, such opportunistic practices were no longer allowed. In order to remain competitive, Chinese authorities resorted to an undervaluation of the real exchange rate. In Latin America and in Africa, policymakers opted for a more integral globalization, with all the consequences attached to this approach for the local manufacturing sector. Moreover, these countries liberalized in a situation characterized by overvalued currencies, partly due to a policy aimed at disinflation. In this context, McMillan and Rodrik (2011, p. 23) note: 'Overvaluation squeezes tradable industries further, damaging especially the more modern ones in manufacturing that operate at tight profit margins'.

Another aspect that explains the differences with respect to development across the continents, according to McMillan and Rodrik (2011), is the pattern of specialization. Countries in Latin America and in Africa are well-endowed with natural resources and primary products. Although the sectors concerned are characterized by a high level of productivity, their contribution to the aggregate economy is rather limited. Alternatively formulated, these sectors contribute to growth-reducing structural change. In this context, Rodrik (2011b, p. 32) notices: 'This is yet another version of the natural resource curse'. However, without any further clarification, this explanation remains rather unsatisfactory. Specialization of countries in raw materials or minerals may lead to a high real exchange rate and, thus, harm the other manufacturing sectors, as implied by the notion of the 'Dutch disease'. But it remains to be seen whether a reliance on natural resources always has adverse consequences for economic growth.

Gavin Wright and Jesse Czelusta (2004) subject the idea of a resource curse to critical scrutiny by examining cases of mineral-based economic development in the past as well as in the more recent history. It appears from their investigation that resource abundance does not necessarily imply that countries rely on the realization of windfall profits and therefore realize poor macroeconomic growth. Sometimes this may happen on impact of a resource price escalation, as for instance in the 1970s. However, this period was rather special as Wright and Czelusta (2004, p. 36) point out: 'the experience of the 1970s stands in marked contrast to the 1990s when mineral production steadily expanded through purposeful exploration and ongoing advances in the technologies of search, extraction, refining, and utilization; in other words, by a process of learning'.

Michiko Iizuka and Luc Soete (2011) discuss the possibility that resource-abundant countries can realize high growth from a broader perspective. In their analysis of the catching-up process activities based on natural resources function as an engine of growth, especially in a number of Latin American countries. The authors state that many assumptions made earlier in the literature are no longer valid because economic activities connected with the exploitation of natural resources have changed more recently. More specifically they make the following points:

1) Natural resource production is no longer an 'enclave', but is related to other activities through forward and backward linkages.
2) Making use of new knowledge connected with biotechnology, nanotechnology and environmental sciences increases the potential for knowledge-intensive production activities.
3) New knowledge based on natural resource production opens the possibility to apply such knowledge in other sectors, leading to what is called 'lateral migration'.
4) Because of the particular nature of natural resource production one is required to deal with environmental conditions, which may induce local knowledge generation on climate, geography, soil, etc.
5) Because of the segmentation of the global market what matters is the nature of the product (quality, uniqueness, specialized) rather than

the type of product (manufacturing, agriculture). This implies that natural resource based products can be made attractive with adequate strategic marketing.

The theoretical discussion in Iizuka and Soete (2011) is supported by empirical research showing that Latin American countries with a higher proportion of natural based exports performed better in the period 2000–09 compared to countries with a higher proportion of manufacturing based exports. The natural resource boom in the world economy opens a window of opportunity for catching-up. To take advantage of this opportunity countries have to invest in knowledge-creating components such as human capital, institutions and R&D. Despite some promising results a warning seems in place: 'whether such policy initiatives can shift Latin American economies towards knowledge creation is a subject for further research, as these attempts are still at the incipient phase' (Iizuka and Soete, 2011, p. 14). In contrast, Wright and Czelusta (2004, p. 35) come to a more optimistic view on the same issue: 'in virtually all the countries we have examined, the public-good aspects of the infrastructure of geologic knowledge have justified state-sponsored or subsidized exploration activities, often with significant payoffs to provincial or national economies'.

Returning to the analysis of McMillan and Rodrik (2011) it can be concluded that their explanation for the differences with respect to structural development comes down in essence to elaborating on the infant industry theme. Attaining convergence in developing countries requires a form of industrial policy. This statement holds true, at least temporarily, since, in the course of time, the protected industry must be able to face competition in the world market. That such a change in policy is necessary in order to converge towards the technological frontier is made clear in Acemoglu et al. (2006). As discussed in section 4.2 developing countries have to switch in time from an investment-based strategy to an innovation-based strategy.

The infant industry theme is recurring regularly in the work of Rodrik. In this context, the author likes to point at the success-stories of the rich countries in the past, and at the growth of the so-called Asian Tigers (Hong Kong, Singapore, Taiwan). The core of the argument is that market imperfections ought to be overcome in order to create an industrial bridgehead. Rodrik (2011b, p. 37) once more lists these imperfections:

- learning externalities: spill-overs to other firms or industries;
- coordination externalities: lumpy and coordinated investments required;

- credit market imperfections: problems with financing projects;
- wage-premiums: monitoring and other costs that raise wage levels.

According to Rodrik (2011b, p. 38) market failures are rather acute in modern industries. As a consequence, 'growth requires remedies targeted at these "special" sectors rather than general policies'.

Keeping the example of China in mind, it seems that Rodrik is right. Countries that rely on industrial policy do well in economic terms. However, the emergence of India and, to a lesser extent, also Brazil seems to be more based on general policies aimed at the liberalization of markets and privatization of state enterprises. With respect to these developments, Rodrik (2011, p. 18) takes on a critical stance: 'As for India, its half-hearted, messy liberalization is hardly the example that multilateral agencies ask other developing countries to emulate'. However, it is not clear what is meant by 'messy liberalization' and it is even less clear in which way such a policy may lead to a growth-enhancing structural change, as found for India in McMillan and Rodrik (2011). Deeper insight at the microeconomic level seems necessary. Case studies about competition and innovation in developing countries may offer a deeper understanding.

7.3. GROWTH SLOWDOWNS

Catching-up is self-limiting and goes along with a decrease of the growth rate. The more imitation has been accomplished, the less there is to be learnt from the technological leader. Based on the theory that we have discussed in section 4.1, this is a gradual process. In the empirical literature the gradual decline in the growth rate of backward economies is not always taken into account. This applies also to the analysis of Bosworth and Collins (2003), discussed in section 7.1. The authors relate the growth rate of output per worker to per capita income in the base year in their update. Other variables are added to condition this relationship. The starting point of Bosworth and Collins (2003) is a cross-section of countries. Therefore, only one growth rate per country is taken into account – the growth rate in the period 1960–2000. In contrast, Rodrik (2011) makes a distinction between sub-periods. In this analysis, the growth rate falls in later periods, since the process of catching-up has already proceeded further. Besides, the growth rate may also increase, as conditions in a specific country improve. This has been the case in emerging countries since the 1990s, owing to an increasing degree of globalization.

In a recent study, which has even got attention in the columns of *The Economist* (see John O'Sullivan, 2011), Barry Eichengreen, Donghyun

Park and Kwanho Shin (2012) emphasize the growth slowdown that occurs when countries approach the technological frontier. The authors describe the resistance that countries then experience as follows: 'Periods of high growth in late-developing economies do not last forever. Eventually the pool of underemployment rural labour is drained. The share of employment in manufacturing peaks, and growth comes to depend more heavily on the more difficult process of raising productivity in the service sector' (Eichengreen, Park and Shin, 2012, p.43).

The authors define a 'growth slowdown' in period *t*, if the following conditions are satisfied:

1) the growth rate of real GDP is, on average, higher than 3.5 per cent over the preceding seven years;
2) the average growth rate of real GDP falls by more than two percentage-points in the seven years that follow;
3) per capita GDP in constant prices of 2005 exceeds $10,000 in period *t*.

The latter condition excludes those countries that are not yet successful in catching-up as identified statistically in Chatterji (1992) and Van Schaik and De Groot (1996), discussed in section 4.1. Eichengreen et al. (2012) estimate the probability of growth slowdowns based on a sample containing a large number of countries and data with respect to the period 1957–2007. The method applied is a so-called probit regression, in which the dependent variable is a binary one, in this case referring to either a growth slowdown or not. The chance that a growth slowdown occurs is, in particular, dependent upon per capita GDP. This chance appears to be highest at a per capita GDP of $15,389 in prices of 2005. Apart from per capita GDP itself, the square of this variable is also included in the regression analysis. Therefore, the probability distribution can be depicted as an inverted parabola, as one can see in Figure 7.4 below. Along the horizontal axis, the per capita income of those countries that realize a growth slowdown is measured. The peak of this inverted parabola is situated at a per capita GDP equal to $15,389, as already indicated. The average of the observations (the bars in Figure 7.4) is $16,740 in 2005 prices.

A specific value of per capita GDP is not very useful as an explanatory variable, but from another estimation, based on the ratio between a country's per capita GDP and per capita GDP of the technological leader, it appears 'that a growth slowdown typically occurs when per capita income reaches 58 per cent of that in the lead country' (Eichengreen et al., 2012, p.66). This outcome seems to suggest that a complete catching-up with the leader is difficult, if not impossible. Nevertheless, in Chapter 6 we have seen that most Western European countries did succeed in doing

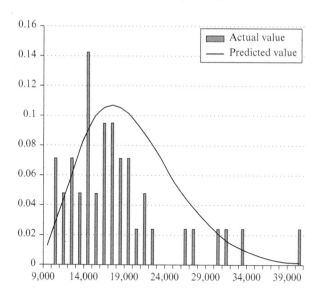

Source: Eichengreen et al. (2012).

Figure 7.4 Frequency distribution of growth slowdowns (oil exporters excluded)

so, if one assesses the situation using labour productivity (output per hour worked) as the relevant criterion. The criterion of Eichengreen et al. (2012) is production per capita, as a measure of technological knowledge, which is not the right indicator. The growth of the European economies indeed slowed down in the first half of the 1970s, as the authors conclude. However, a substantial part of this growth slowdown of GDP per capita was attributable to a decrease in the labour force participation rate. Due to lack of data, it remains an open question to what extent changes in the participation rate are important for other countries as well.

The authors investigate the effect of a number of other variables on the probability distribution of growth slowdowns. For a limited number of countries, data are available with regard to the share of manufacturing employment in aggregate employment. The peak probability appears to be reached at a share of employment in the manufacturing sector in total employment equal to 23 per cent. Furthermore, this research shows that countries which are more open in the domain of goods trade are less likely to experience slowdowns. Policy variables turn out not to be significant, except for a constructed measure of the undervaluation of the real exchange rate. Although this relation leaves much to be wished for from a statistical point of view, the authors conclude, nevertheless, that countries with more dramatically undervalued currencies are more vulnerable with respect to growth slowdowns. Some potential explanations are put forward, but these explanations remain speculative, due to the absence of a theoretical framework.

The analysis of Eichengreen et al. (2012) is partly inspired by the spectacular growth spurt of countries such as India, Brazil and, most of all, China. The title of the article does not include the expression 'Implications for China' accidentally. The geopolitical consequences of the growth of the emerging economies are of vital importance. We will return to this issue in Chapter 8. Against this background, the emphasis that Eichengreen and his co-authors put on a possible growth slowdown in China is understandable. This may have been an important consideration for the editorial board of *The Economist* to discuss the contribution of Eichengreen et al. (2012) in-depth. The question arises whether an abrupt growth slowdown in China is likely, keeping the results obtained by the authors in mind.

Closer examination of the data at first raises the suggestion that an abrupt growth slowdown is improbable. In 2007, per capita GDP in China was equal to 19.8 per cent of US per capita GDP, while the slowdown probability is at its maximum when this percentage equals 58. Suppose that China would continue to grow at an annual pace of 9.3 per cent, as has been the case in the not-too-distant past, while US per capita GDP grows annually by 1.9 per cent. Then, per capita GDP of China would still only amount to 35 per cent of the US level in 2015. Only in 2023, the ratio between Chinese and US per capita GDP would amount to 58. Based on these outcomes, one may conclude that the growth slowdown in China is something for the distant future. Data for the share of industrial employment in aggregate employment are not available for the years after 2002. The authors assume that this ratio rises by one percentage-point per year. 'If this is right', they conclude, 'it suggests that the share of employment in manufacturing is now within hailing distance of the 23 per cent where historical comparisons suggest that growth slows down' (Eichengreen et al., 2012, p. 80). Based on a regression equation in which a number of independent variables are statistically significant (per capita income, pre-slowdown rate of growth, trade openness and the composition of spending), the authors estimate the chance that China will have to face a growth slowdown to be 73 per cent.

The findings of Holz (2008) are the complete opposite. The author compares the structure of the Chinese economy with the economic structures of Japan, South-Korea and Taiwan. These countries are ahead of China in the process of catching-up by far. China appears to be in a stage of development in which these countries were three decades ago. In the period

Table 7.3   GDP growth 2000–2020 (annual percentage)

Country/Region	2000–10	2010–20	
	Historical	Base	Pessimistic
US	1.7	2.3	1.3
EU-15	1.2	1.5	0.6
China	11.4	8.5	5.0
India	7.6	8.7	5.0
Latin America	3.2	3.9	2.8

Source: Conference Board (2011).

1978–2005 in China the share of agricultural employment in aggregate employment has declined from more than 70 per cent down to 45 per cent. This comes down to an annual reduction by one percentage-point. At this pace, 'China has another 35 years to go before its agricultural labour share reaches the 10 per cent level at which the agricultural labour shares of Japan, Korea and Taiwan stabilize' (Holz, 2008, p. 1669). Other indicators point in the same direction and the author ultimately reaches the conclusion that 'China faces another 30 years of continued growth' (Holz, 2008, p. 1683).[5]

The difference in tone between Eichengreen et al. (2012) and Holz (2008), is characteristic for the great uncertainty with respect to the future of the Chinese economy. This discrepancy also resounds in the observations on the specific risks that threaten China, such as financial instability or social instability, due to the unequal income distribution. Given all these uncertainties, presenting various scenarios seems obvious. This approach has been followed, amongst others, by The Conference Board (2011). Table 7.3 contains scenarios for some countries/regions.

First, the left column presents the actual growth rates for the period 2000–10. Next, the middle column provides the estimates of The Conference Board according to the Base Scenario. Notably, these projections exhibit an acceleration of economic growth compared to the past, except for the Chinese economy. Despite this relative growth slowdown, the share of Chinese output in global output increases from 16 per cent in 2010 to 24 per cent in 2020. The impact of India on the world economy (eight per cent in 2020) clearly lags behind. Apart from this, the growth of the world economy is supported by the emerging economies and, more in particular, China and India. In elucidating these figures, The Conference Board (2011) states that 'a more pessimistic scenario for these countries, which could result from uncontrolled inflation, asset bubbles, or a failure to absorb large fluctuations in capital flows, could reduce global growth for 2010–20 by almost 2 percentage points'. The right column of Table 7.3 sketches what this means for the selected regions.

Frequently, the popular press attaches importance to the fact that the GDP of China will surpass US GDP at a certain stage. The exact year in which this will happen depends on the way in which the GDP of China is measured, using a yardstick for the purchasing power parity (PPP). Cross-country comparisons of GDP based on the actual exchange rate provide a distorted picture, since not all goods are tradable. In China, labour-intensive services are much cheaper than in the US. A conversion that makes use of PPP indices takes account of such factors. In the literature, various calculation methods are applied to determine the PPP-ratio. The Conference Board follows a method that yields 2012 as the year in which the GDP of China will exceed the GDP of the US. According to these calculations, the ratio of Chinese per capita GDP to US per capita GDP increases from 21 per cent in 2010 to 40 per cent in 2020 in the base scenario. These figures deviate from the ones presented in Eichengreen et al. (2012), which are based on the Penn World Tables 6.2. In these tables, alternative PPP indices are applied. Nevertheless, the general picture in the long run is clear. If China succeeds in maintaining its current high rate of economic progress, the country will equal the welfare level in the US sometime around the middle of the twenty-first century.

7.4.   EVALUATION

Globalization implies that an increasing number of countries operate in the world markets. One may expect the welfare level in poor countries to converge to the welfare level in rich countries. This hypothesis has not been confirmed by the facts in the twentieth century. On the contrary, divergence seems to have prevailed. The search for the explanation of this contrarian development leaves economic scientists puzzled. In this context, the following statement by DeLong (2001, p. 1) is characteristic: 'I confess that I do not know the answers, which has made this hard to think about'.

In order to obtain knowledge with respect to this complicated issue different methods can be chosen. Dowrick and DeLong (2003) opt for a descriptive method, at the core of which the notion of a 'convergence club' stands. Information concerning per capita GDP, as a ratio to per capita GDP of the world leader, on the one hand, and a measure for industrial development, on the other hand, is used to establish the membership of convergence clubs in the sub-periods distinguished. Globalization leads to a gradually expanding convergence club, but many countries dropped out during the 1950–2000 period for political reasons. In the view of Dowrick and DeLong entry into the convergence club stems from the ability to supersede major obstacles. Countries lag behind the developments in the industrialized world, because they are caught in a poverty trap: 'Poor countries remain poor, and so the purchase of investment goods from overseas that embody technology and assist in technology transfer remains expensive, and finding the resources to support mass education remains difficult' (Dowrick and DeLong, 2003, p. 218).

The statistical analysis of these issues aims at unravelling the above-mentioned obstacles that have to be overcome in order to realize convergence. The central idea is that convergence is conditional. The economic growth of countries is not solely determined by the relative position in terms of per capita GDP in the initial situation (unconditional convergence), but also by a number of variables that determine the conditions for convergence. Much statistical research has been done to trace these conditions. Bosworth and Collins (2003) assess the results by using an empirical framework that can be applied to a large group of countries over a relatively long period. Their sample contains 84 countries and the dependent variable is the average growth rate of output per worker during the period 1960–2000. The authors make a distinction between conditioning variables in a narrow sense and policy indicators, which should be considered as endogenous variables. The conditioning variables refer to the initial situation. These variables concern issues such as health, the size of the population, the geographical situation and the quality of the institutions. Together with per capita income in the initial situation, these variables constitute the correlation with output growth from a statistical perspective. Policy indicators such as the change in inflation, the openness of the economy and budget balance, are hardly significant or even insignificant. This finding means that economic growth is determined ultimately by items that cannot be affected substantially in the short run. As a consequence, convergence strongly depends on the specific conditions in which the countries find themselves. This conclusion is confirmed by Rodrik (2011b). The author works with a pooled cross-section time-series sample over the period 1970–2008. This approach offers the possibility to introduce fixed country-effects. Unconditional convergence in terms of GDP per worker is absent, but the introduction of country dummies suffices to invoke conditional convergence.

Ultimately, the descriptive and the statistical method lead to identical results. The possibilities to converge to a Western level of welfare are to a large extent dependent on country-specific circumstances. However, casuistry does not lead to general knowledge. In a pioneering study, McMillan and Rodrick (2011) offer a way out of this deadlock. The authors analyze the convergence of countries at a disaggregate level, in which nine sectors are distinguished in 38 countries. The analysis concerns economic growth in the period 1990–2005. In this era, the developing countries, with only a few exceptions, have integrated more deeply into the world economy. This is reflected in the spectacular growth rates of a number of countries, with China and India leading the pack.

The decomposition of the increase of productivity in a country into a *within* component and a *structural change term* is characteristic for the structuralist approach of McMillan and Rodrik (2011). First, the *within* component is equal to the weighted sum of the productivity increase in the individual sectors. The weights are the shares of the distinguished sectors' employment in aggregate employment. Second, the *structural change* component is defined as the inner product of productivity levels (at the end of the time period) and the change in employment shares across sectors. This term expresses the effect of the reallocation of labour between sectors. If labour moves from sectors with low productivity to sectors with high productivity, then aggregate labour productivity rises. In the reverse case, the aggregate labour productivity falls. In the latter case, one can speak of a growth-reducing structural change.

Owing to the ongoing globalization, productivity increases substantially in the exposed sectors of emerging countries. If these convergence sectors succeed in growing at such a rapid pace that their share in aggregate employment increases, then the aggregate labour productivity rises substantially. In contrast, if the labour-saving in the dynamic sectors is coupled with the dismissal of labour, then developing countries cannot avoid a growth-reducing structural change which leads to a lower overall rate of productivity growth. The latter has to do with the fact that, in these countries, productivity in the sheltered sectors falls considerably short of productivity in the exposed sectors. As a consequence, there is no efficient allocation of factors of production, but a situation that is usually characterized as a dual economy.

Empirical research makes clear that, in this respect, a major difference exists between Asia, on the one hand, and Africa and Latin America, on the other hand. In Asia, the structural change component is positive, whereas Africa and Latin America are confronted with 'growth-reducing structural change'. For the explanation of this discrepancy, three potential causes can be mentioned. First, Africa and Latin America have substantial natural resources at their disposal. The exploitation of these natural resources is very profitable, but these dynamic sectors yield little in terms of employment. However, this argument is disputed in Wright and Czelusta (2004) as well as in Iizuka and Soete (2011), because the exploitation of resources is often based on investment in knowledge and R&D with significant spillovers to the rest of the economy. Resource-abundant countries may thus realize high rates of growth. The notion of a resource curse may be a myth after all. Second, one may observe that the manufacturing sectors in Africa and Latin America are forced to operate efficiently and to dismiss workers, due to competition in international markets. In contrast, Asian-style globalization is based on a two-track reform: various import-competing activities are supported by the government, while new export-oriented activities are stimulated. China is the champion of such an opportunistic policy, in which the rationalization of firms that perform poorly is executed in stages. Finally, one may point at the importance of the real exchange rate. Countries in Latin America and in Africa are confronted with overvalued currencies, while the Asian countries favour their own industry via targeted competitive real exchange rates: China is a leader also in this respect.

The recent convergence of countries such as China, India and Brazil has caused disconcert in the Western world. In this context, it is often mentioned that the Chinese economy will soon surpass the US economy, in terms of the absolute size of GDP. Accurate research, which takes purchasing power parities into account, shows that China may outstrip the US in 2012. However, this development does not mean that China will match the US in terms of per capita GDP. In the meantime, many things may change. The latter observation takes a central place in the research of Eichengreen, Park and Shin (2012). The authors estimate, using a large sample of countries, at which per capita income the chance of a growth slowdown is at the highest level. Besides, other factors are considered that influence this probability. The pre-slowdown rate of growth, trade openness and the composition of spending appear to be of significant importance. Based on the obtained results, the authors estimate the probability that China will experience a growth slowdown at 73 per cent. In this respect, other scholars are less pessimistic. For example, Holz (2008) shows that China still has a long way to go before the relationship between key variables corresponds with these relations in Japan, South-Korea and Taiwan, countries that are ahead of China in economic development. The forecasts of The Conference Board for the period 2010–20 also point at continued strong growth of the Chinese economy. China is on its way. As stated above, the geopolitical consequences will be dealt with in Chapter 8.

NOTES

1. In the case of perfect competition the share of capital income equals the production elasticity of capital, which can be derived from the neoclassical production function.

2.   There is a difference in this respect with standard neoclassical growth theory, whereby
     one has to assume that technological change is labour-saving in order to establish bal-
     anced growth in the long run. See section 3.1 for the details.
3.   Chang-Tai Hsieh and Peter Klenow (2009) estimate the impact of the misallocation of
     inputs across firms in manufacturing on TFP in China (1998–2003) and India (1987–94).
     They find that moving to 'US efficiency' would increase TFP by 30–50 per cent in China
     and by 40–60 per cent in India.
4.   See, for example, Theo van de Klundert (1961).
5.   The interpretation of the presented data leaves something to be desired. In two diagrams,
     the annual growth rate of China, Japan, Korea and Taiwan is related to 'GDP per
     laborer per US GDP per laborer', whereby highly improbable values for the latter vari-
     able are presented along the horizontal axis.

8. Democracy at bay

8.1. A POLITICAL TRILEMMA

In Joseph Schumpeter (1942, p. 61), a fundamental question is asked: 'Can capitalism survive?' His answer was: 'No, I do not think it can'. As we know now, this answer did not prove to be true. Yet, maybe the question should have been formulated differently: can democracy survive? This formulation shifts the problem to a different playing field. The relationship between globalization and democracy is at stake, and no longer only the internal dynamics of the capitalist system, as in the works of Schumpeter. Globalization of markets implies that national governments have less say concerning the organization of their own economies. This development does not necessarily mean that the democratic control of market processes is moved to the background, but the danger is not unreal. For, exercising control at a global scale requires tailor-made political institutions. However the chance that such institutions will emerge and satisfy the requirements as well, does not seem great momentarily.

These observations correspond with the view of Dani Rodrik (2011a), in his recent evaluation of the process of globalization. Besides, an important difference exists between Schumpeter and Rodrik, as far as methodology is concerned. In his view, Schumpeter emphasizes that his 'No' actually does not matter at all. What really matters is the analysis of historical developments. The main issues concern 'tendencies present in an observable pattern' which show 'what would happen if they continued to act as they have been acting in the time interval covered by our observation and if no other factors intruded' (Schumpeter, 1942, p. 61). Rodrik's intentions are quite different as he starts searching for the most attractive variant of international capitalism. His approach is normative, and as such not altogether unusual in the science of economics. However, in contrast with many of his colleagues, Rodrik takes the trouble to make the value judgements, on which his deliberations rest, explicit. Prior to that, he reflects on international economic relations in the past and in the present.

Major room is reserved for the Bretton Woods regime that determined international monetary relations during more than two decades after World War II.[1] Thereby an agreement was negotiated with regard to a system of fixed exchange rates and the International Monetary Fund (IMF) was established to temporarily support countries financially. In case of a fundamental disequilibrium in a specific country, it was possible to adjust the exchange rate. An important part of the arrangement was that countries were allowed to put restrictions on international financial transactions. These capital controls were important, in order to create sufficient 'policy space' for a national monetary and fiscal policy.

International goods trade was regulated by the General Agreement on Tariffs and Trade (GATT). In contrast with the IMF and the World Bank, the GATT was not a formal organization, but a multilateral forum with a secretariat in Geneva. The countries that had signed this treaty agreed to reduce import tariffs substantially and to introduce the most-favoured nation principle, according to which all countries involved would benefit from the lowering of import tariffs by one of the participants ('the principal supplier'). Despite the great success of this trade liberalization, notable exceptions existed. Agriculture and services were kept out of harm's way, at least to a large extent. Moreover, regulation, in the form of anti-dumping rights, was introduced to protect countries from dumping. These arrangements were used often and eagerly. According to Rodrik (2011a, p. 74), this does not provide a reason to show the GATT in a bad light: 'to find fault with the GATT regime because it fell considerably short of free trade would be to judge GATT from an inappropriate perspective'. The regime offered countries the opportunity to avoid the disadvantageous sides of international trade, in the form of either negative external effects (for example, in the area of national health) or undesired implications for the income distribution.

According to Rodrik (2011a, p. 98), the Bretton Woods system with respect to financial transactions may be characterized as follows: 'As in the case of the trade system, the international financial regime was built around the belief that domestic economic needs would (and should) trump the requirements of the global economy'. If this would result in higher international transaction costs, this had to be taken for granted. Alternatively formulated, the main message of the Bretton Woods system is that national interests are not always secondary to the 'great' goal of efficient allocation of scarce resources worldwide. In order to appreciate what it is all about, it is useful to mention some characterizations ventured in the economic literature. For example, John Ruggie (1982, p. 393) characterizes the Bretton Woods system as: 'the compromise of embedded liberalism' in which 'its multilateralism would be predicated upon domestic interventionism'. According to Robert Skidelsky (2009, p. 171) Bretton Woods was 'the international expression of liberal/social-democratic political economy'.

The Bretton Woods system, with fixed exchange rates and the dollar as the world's reserve currency (dollar exchange standard) did not fit well with the inflationary financing of the Vietnam War by the US. In 1971, an overhang of dollars arose, which put pressure on the convertibility of the US dollar into gold. A devaluation of the US dollar became necessary. In 1973, the system of fixed but adjustable exchange rates was abandoned and it was replaced by a system of flexible exchange rates. Liberalization and capital mobility got a place at the top of the agenda. This was partly invoked by the stagflation of the 1970s. The combination of inflation and unemployment: 'pushed attention away from Keynes's focus on demand management to the supply side of the economy' (Rodrik, 2011a, p. 101). Confidence in market forces increased and, influenced by the wave of liberalization that had taken off in the 1980s, free goods trade and free labour mobility were stimulated. The world economy went into the direction of what Rodrik indicates as 'deep integration'. Skidelsky (2009) puts this development somewhat more in a historical perspective. Making reference to the political-economy cycle of Arthur Schlesinger Junior (1986), discussed in Chapter 2 of this book, Skidelsky considers the transition from a regulated towards a liberal market economy as a reaction to what one could indicate as the arrogance of power, the thought that everything can be arranged top-down. Remarkably, both authors do not relate these developments, either to the cycles caused by technological revolutions or to the shifts in the balance of power resulting from such technological revolutions.

The 'deep integration or hyperglobalization', which was achieved with the foundation of the World Trade Organization (WTO) in 1995 and the liberalization of international capital movements, puts democracy to the test. Within the framework of the WTO, the participating countries are subject to rather stringent rules: 'Under WTO, trade disputes began to reach into domestic areas that were previously immune from external pressures. Tax systems, food safety rules, environmental regulations, and industrial promotion policies were open to challenge from trade partners' (Rodrik, 2011a, p. 79). The decisions to be made in disputes in the area of international trade are reserved for the Court of Appeal in Geneva. In most cases, this Court decides that the agreements within the WTO-framework are binding. This implies that 'deep integration' prevails, resulting in a removal of the existing tension between trade policy and domestic regulation. Then free trade comes first and global rules replace domestic regulation.

Since the late 1980s, the IMF has strongly supported the freeing up of capital markets. The US and the UK, with their strong financial centres, benefited from the liberalization of capital movements and the deregulation

of the banking sector. Many economists argued that free capital movements were to be preferred above capital controls, because perfect capital
mobility fosters economic efficiency, despite the unavoidably greater financial instability. This view with respect to free movements of capital became
common knowledge and it was incorporated into the statutes of international organizations, such as the IMF and the Organisation for Economic
Co-operation and Development (OECD), a club of the richest countries in
the world with *de facto* political power on the international scene.

Power plays an important role in dealing with the institutional design
of economies, as we have argued repeatedly. Rodrik (2011a) partly agrees
with this line of reasoning. In this context, the author refers to Simon
Johnson, a former chief economist of the IMF, who draws a revealing conclusion when reflecting critically on past developments. Rodrik (2011a,
p. 130) summarizes his outpouring as follows: 'Banks may not have guns
and armies at their disposal, Johnson argued, but they had other means
that were equally effective: campaign contributions, the revolving door
between Wall Street and Washington, and an ability to foster a belief
system supportive of their interests'. Yes, as Rodrik argues, this may all
be true, but the opinions prevailing at the IMF were supported by the economics profession's best minds. Thus, economists exerted a great influence
on the liberalization strategy. If ideas rule the world, then Rodrik surely
has a point, but, in our view, money and wealth are just more important.
Economists frequently exhibit an inclination to overestimate the influence
of their discipline. If capital leaves its mark on the belief system, then it
becomes rather difficult for science to take an independent stance. The
voices of independent minds, such as Rodrik himself, then go unheeded in
the maelstrom of deregulation policy.

The historical developments induce Rodrik (2011a) to investigate which
options are available to manage the tensions between national democracies and global markets. To bring a clear focus to the choices that have
to be made, the author introduces the political trilemma of the world
economy. Figure 8.1 sketches these options in a schematic way. 'Pick two,
any two', as the maxim reads.

Hyperglobalization is not compatible with a well-functioning democracy at the national level. This means that hyperglobalization either comes
at the expense of democracy or that a new form of worldwide democracy
is designed. In the first case, the Golden Straitjacket applies, as Thomas
Friedman (2000) has coined it. Under this regime, countries have to satisfy
the following conditions: free trade, free capital markets, free enterprise,
and small government. The rules of the game are determined by the
requirements of the global economy. The result is that 'you can have your
globalization and your nation state, too, but only if you keep democracy

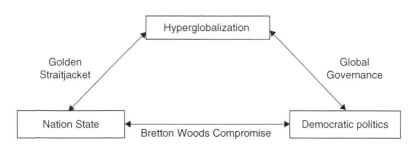

Source: Adapted from Rodrik (2011a).

Figure 8.1 *The political trilemma of the world economy*

at bay' (Rodrik, 2011a, p. 202). In the second case, one gives up the nation-state in order to make room for global governance. Of course, this formulation is somewhat exaggerated. The nation-state continues to exist, but it has to give up a significant part of its national sovereignty. The question arises, whether institutions can be created at the global level, featured by adequate accountability and legitimacy, so that democracy remains intact. This is not easy as the experience with the process of European unification makes clear. We will return to this issue in the next section.

The final conclusion is that one needs to reject hyperglobalization, provided that one wants to rescue democracy at the national level. The other side of the coin is that one has to search for new forms of international cooperation. If one would stick to the sovereignty of countries, then the cards have been shuffled: 'We have no choice but to settle for a "thin" version of globalization – to reinvent the Bretton Woods compromise for a different era' (Rodrik, 2011a, p. 205).

Finally, the 'thin' version of globalization is presented by Rodrik in the form of, what he calls, 'sane globalization'. As we have already stated, the author is so honest to account for value judgements, principles for a new globalization, underlying his normative approach. The chapter in which the principles are presented is titled 'Designing Capitalism 3.0'. Notably, the preceding versions of capitalism were, in his vision, based on minimal government influence (Capitalism 1.0) and the original Bretton Woods compromise (Capitalism 2.0). Capitalism 3.0 is based on the following seven principles:

1) Markets must be deeply embedded in systems of governance.
2) Democratic governance and political communities are organized largely within nation-states, and are likely to remain so for the immediate future.

3) There is no 'one way' to prosperity.
4) Countries have the right to protect their own social arrangements, regulations and institutions.
5) Countries do not have the right to impose their institutions on others.
6) The purpose of international economic arrangements must be to lay down the traffic rules for managing the interface among national institutions.
7) Non-democratic countries cannot count on the same rights and privileges in the international economic order as democracies.

On the basis of these principles, Rodrik expresses his views with respect to international trade, global finance, labour migration and the problem: how to accommodate China in the global economy. The latter problem will be dealt with in section 8.3. The topic of migration requires a specific approach. In the reflections on globalization made by Rodrik, it appears as a kind of *Fremdkörper*.

In the area of international trade, Rodrik pleads for a thorough revision of the WTO's Agreement on Safeguards. In the initial set-up, these safeguards were meant to offer protection against unfair competition. As we have remarked earlier, an independent panel judges whether claims, in this respect, are justified. According to Rodrik (2011a, p. 253) the number of reasons on which protection can be based ought to be extended substantially: 'Distributional concerns, conflicts with domestic norms and social arrangements, prevention of the erosion of domestic regulations, or development priorities would be among such legitimate grounds'. The WTO panels that assess such requests should then only deal with procedural issues. Thus, they ought to abstain from any judgement with regard to the contents of a case, but only audit the fulfilment of the conditions for democratic decision-making. Were all relevant parties taken into account? Was all available scientific knowledge in the field used? Was domestic political support sufficient to make an appeal to safeguard clauses? In addition, the author would prefer to abandon the existing regulation concerning the most-favoured nation treatment (in which tariffs need to apply to all participating countries) as well as the existing condition with respect to compensation by the country applying the safeguard.

The extension of the concept of 'safeguard' offers developing countries the opportunity to protect their industries temporarily in order to benefit from the learning curve (the infant industry argument). For rich countries with low import tariffs, the gains from trade resulting from a further reduction of tariffs are already limited. These gains do not balance against the possible disadvantages in the area of the environmental protection, social norms or the distribution of income. Domestic democratic considerations have to determine whether this is indeed the case.

Rodrik also pleads for a further regulation of global finance. The menu of options is broad: 'The measures under discussion include tighter capital-adequacy standards, restrictions on leverage, caps on executive pay, rules that facilitate bank closures, broader disclosure requirements, greater regulatory oversight, and limits on bank size' (Rodrik, 2011a, p. 260). If countries make different choices from this list, then the danger of regulatory arbitrage arises – a race to the bottom in the financial world. In order to prevent this, measures need to be taken to limit the jurisdiction of the so-called financial safe havens. Moreover, Rodrik advocates a small global tax on financial transactions. The aim of this tax is not to reduce the financial instability, but to generate resources to prevent climate change and health pandemics.

All in all, the proposals based on Capitalism 3.0 are idealistic and rather unrealistic. The proposals demonstrate what should happen to bend the ongoing process of globalization. However, this comes down to something of an uphill struggle. National democracies are subject to political power struggles, in which the resources invested are not restricted to national boundaries. Rodrik (2011a) wants to turn back time, but the world keeps on turning. As a result, democracy gets more and more under global pressure, whether one likes it, or not. An important example of the growing significance of international economic cooperation is the unification of Europe, which is discussed in the next section.

8.2. EUROPEAN UNIFICATION

To have influence on the global economy in the twenty-first century Europe needs to act as an entity. The foundation of the European Union (EU) was a first step in the direction of European unification. The free movement of goods, capital and labour requires new forms of regulation. This does not mean that a Golden Straitjacket has to be imposed as Friedman (2000) suggests with respect to directives of globalization. European integration is much more a matter of what Charles Sabel and Jonathan Zeitlin (2007) indicate as the invention of a 'new architecture of experimentalist governance'. In this view, goals such as full employment, social inclusion and a unified energy grid are determined in a collective action of the member countries and the EU institutions.

In such a setting there is an important role for the principle of subsidiarity, implying that lower-level decision-making units get a fair share of autonomy when applying the existing regulation. In return, these units must report to higher levels in the hierarchy and must also participate in peer reviews to compare their results with those of other units on the same level. Finally, within this framework, goals, metrics and procedures are frequently given a thorough going over and, if necessary, a revision. Deliberation and multi-level decision-making are features that define this framework of the EU more precisely. In this manner, the welfare state in a unified Europe could be maintained. Nevertheless, the question is whether democracy will not be put aside in this way to make room for a kind of technocratic governance system. In order to prevent this, decision-making ought to be based on sufficient forms of transparency and accountability, but according to Sabel and Zeitlin (2007, p. 10): 'the new architecture does not automatically produce democratic outcomes. It means rather that the new forms of decision making promote forms of accountability that are consistent with some aspects of democracy, though not necessarily furthering representative democracy in any traditional way'.

Such a fine-tuning of decision-making among European countries seems to be overshadowed by the problems the European Monetary Union (EMU) has got into since the euro-area peripheral countries were confronted with a sovereign debt crisis in 2010. The debt crisis is at the same time a 'balance-of-payments imbalance of a nature similar to the one that destroyed the Bretton Woods System' (Hans-Werner Sinn and Timo Wollmershaeuser, 2011, Abstract). The acute problem anno 2012 is how to save the EMU and its currency, the euro. The first question to be asked is: how was it possible that things got wrong to such an extent? The answer is that the EMU brought together two groups of countries with a quite different attitude of their inhabitants. The Northern countries, with Germany as the leading economy, followed a macroeconomic policy of restricting labour costs and government budget discipline. Contrary to these more or less Calvinistic guidelines, the Southern countries were in for a laissez-faire policy trusting with Catholic cheerfulness that the unavoidable adaptions enforced by markets would keep the economy on track. It should be recalled that Southern countries like Italy, Portugal and Spain were characterized in Chapter 6 as mixed market economies (MMEs) because strategic coordination in the labour market is less important in these countries than in coordinated market economics (CMEs), like for instance Germany, the Netherlands, Finland and Denmark. The group of countries causing problems in the context of the EMU is usually indicated as the GIIPS-countries (Greece, Ireland, Italy, Portugal and Spain). Putting together these countries therefore makes sense not only because of their economic position in the EMU but also because of their cultural inheritance.

Economic experts warned that the EMU should be restricted to core Europe (Germany, France, Benelux and Denmark), but politicians

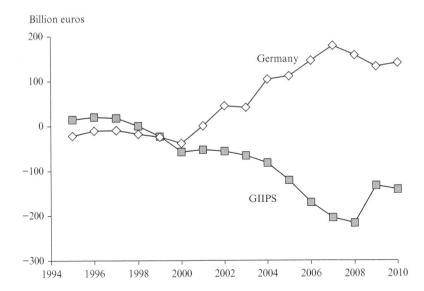

Source: Sinn and Wollmershaeuser (2011).

Figure 8.2 Annual current account balances

allowed the peripheral GIIPs-countries to enter. Moreover, Italy and later on Greece succeeded in satisfying the admission criteria with respect to government debt and the public budget deficit, owing to creative accounting. Apart from this, countries that should be refused to enter the union could block decision-making, because decisions in the EU at that time had to be taken unanimously.

Since the introduction of the euro the GIIPS-countries show increasing deficits on the current account of the balance of payments, as shown in Figure 8.2. In contrast, core countries like Germany realized surpluses on the current account. Before the GIPPS-countries entered the EMU the problems of overspending and of uncompetitive wage and price levels could be solved by depreciation of their own currencies. The consequences of depreciation take the form of high interest rates and a high level of inflation. But it also implied a silent and continuous restructuring of debt. After joining the EMU the valve of currency depreciation was no longer available and the inflationary growth process resulted in deficits on the current account. Until the financial crisis of 2008 these deficits could be financed by a net inflow of private capital, which is the normal market solution. But as the flow of capital ran dry, deficits had to be financed by printing money in the GIIPS-countries. This implies that deficits were to a large extent financed by Target credits through the Eurosystem. The term TARGET stands for Trans-European Automated Real-Time Gross Settlement Express Transfer. In Sinn (2011, p. 3) a Target credit is defined as 'a reallocation of ECB refinancing credit from the core, basically Germany, to the periphery, beyond the credit necessary to endow these countries with a monetary base for internal circulation'. The details of the mechanism are explained in Sinn and Wollmershaeuser (2011). As the ECB was running out of ammunition, the hidden rescue mechanism had to be supplemented by an open rescue mechanism in the form of credit granted by the European Financial Stability Facility (EFSF) and the International Monetary Fund (IMF). In addition, the European Central Bank (ECB) has purchased government bonds to extend the scope of the rescue operations.

The ECB determines the monetary policy of the EMU, but the macroeconomic equilibrium is also dependent upon saving and investment decisions. In this connection, government budget deficits are important as they fuel economic spending. To keep national governments under control the EMU was dressed up by a Stability and Growth Pact (SGP), which determines an upper limit for the budget deficit of three per cent of GDP. The question is whether under normal circumstances such a deficit is sufficiently large to trigger a recovery of the economy in times of a recession. Anyway, the SGP was put under severe pressure in 2003, when the core countries France and Germany broke the rule and were able to block sanctions on the basis of their political influence. The failure of the SGP is seen by many observers as the main cause of the Euro-crisis. Barry Eichengreen (2011, p. 17) summarizes this view in the following way: 'That the euro-area periphery ultimately descended into a full-blown sovereign debt crisis is seen, in the consensus view, as prima facie evidence of the inadequacy of the EU's Stability and Growth Pact'.

It may be tempting to blame the SGP for the sovereign debt crisis in the periphery-countries, but such a view passes over what really happened. First, there are important differences across these countries. The Greek and Portuguese debts resulted mainly from lax behaviour of the government. The Irish and Spanish debts originated to a large extent from the private sector. In the latter countries additional spending especially on residential and commercial real estate was financed by domestic banks that had to borrow from banks in the euro-area core. 'But that difference is irrelevant', Sinn (2011, p. 3) argues, because 'in the end it does not matter whether the inflationary growth process originated with the government or the private sector'. Second, the inflationary process referred to by Sinn resulted in a loss of international competitiveness of the periphery-countries as the spending boom drove up wages and prices above the levels prevailing in the core countries. Ultimately, the problems in the EMU

Table 8.1   Changes in wage costs and budget balance in deviation from Germany

	Greece	Spain	Italy	France	Belgium	Netherlands
Wage cost per unit of output	73	21	31	7	8	3
Government budget balance	−6.2	−5.0	−0.4	−2.9	−2.1	−2.7

Source: Adapted from Peter de Ridder (2011).

were manifested in the guise of a balance-of-payments crisis. Although Italy also exhibited current account deficits in 2008, 2009 and 2010 the country was able to finance these deficits by private capital imports until 2011. To illustrate the diverging developments in the core and the periphery in Table 8.1 the percentage increases in wage costs per unit of output and the changes in the government budget balance (in percentage points of GDP compared to 2000) over the period 2000–10 are presented for a selection of countries. Both changes are measured in deviation from the developments in Germany.

Rescue plans for EMU-countries in trouble are inevitable. The problem is that in case the rescue operations are too generous the stability of the Euro-area is at stake. Financing all deficits by printing money on a large scale under the auspices of the ECB may endanger the credit worthiness of the Eurozone as a whole, because the current-account imbalances are perpetuated. What may go wrong is indicated by Sinn (2011, p. 5) in a penetrating manner: 'So-called rescue programmes may, in fact, turn out to be incendiary channels through which the fire can expand and smother all public budgets in the Eurozone'. Whereas politicians opt for imposing a political debt constraint and common EU control, Sinn argues for measure to discipline debtor countries, so that markets can again perform their allocative function. To attain this goal assistance on a limited scale may still be necessary. Sinn (2011, p. 7) presents 'ten commandments for a renewed Eurozone' with the intention that 'the crisis countries will themselves then be able to decide whether they see a possibility of managing the real depreciation process, or whether they find the burden too large and prefer to exit the Eurozone'. To give an impression of what the author has in mind we present a list with ten 'commandments':

1)   No further government bond purchases by EFSF and ECB.
2)   Paying back the Target credit on the basis of transition rules.

3) New voting rights in the ECB weighted by ECB capital shares.
4) Unanimity for credit policies of the ECB.
5) Liquidity help for two years through the EFSF.
6) Slicing the problem in case of impending insolvency by an automatic haircut applied to maturing bonds.
7) Exit of Eurozone in case of full insolvency.
8) Basel IV: higher risk weights for government bonds.
9) Higher equity ratios for banks.
10) Bank recapitalization and partly nationalization for banks unable to fulfil the requirements.

It is remarkable that these rules contain no restrictions on government budget deficits. Market forces are supposed to discipline exuberant spending by government agencies. If high interest rates are not able to prevent insolvency the way out is to leave the EMU. However, such an exit option has important consequences for the other EMU member states. It therefore seems desirable to require that countries give up national sovereignty in the field of budget discipline. As is well-known in the economics literature international cooperation is problematic if there are no binding commitments to turn a non-cooperative game into a cooperative game. Matthew Canzoneri and Dale Henderson (1991, p. 4) analyzing the implications of monetary policy in interdependent economies, state what should be done in such cases: 'Sovereign policymakers may not be able to make such commitments, since the commitment requires the policymaker to submit to a higher authority. Generally, we identify a switch from non-cooperative to cooperative game structures with a loss of sovereignty'. What makes a non-cooperative game inferior in this connection are the cross-jurisdiction externalities. In case of a monetary union without a political union such externalities are extensive. The commandments of Sinn may internalize the externalities emanating from national central banks, but there is no guarantee that the actions of governments are aimed at the common good of a unified Europe. Loss of some parts of sovereignty seems therefore unavoidable if unification is on the agenda. However, this need not imply that democracy is jeopardized. Innovative governance architecture along the lines set out in Sabel and Zeitlin (2007) may lead to a form of deliberative democracy that makes Europe a forerunner on the global scale.

8.3.   CHINA AND THE WORLD ECONOMY

Sabel and Zeitlin (2007) point to the architectural similarities between the EU and the WTO. The main issue, in both cases, is to unite national legislation and the transfer of national sovereignty in a balanced way. In this context, countries are allowed to serve their own interests, provided that these interests are tested and accepted within the framework of international regulation. The membership of the EU and the WTO does not mean that national rules are replaced by supranational regimes. However, as Sabel and Zeitlin (2007, p. 58) formulate very precisely, these memberships do entail that: 'in joining these regimes, member states are agreeing to remake their rules, in domain after domain, in light of the efforts of all the others to reconcile their distinctive regulations with general standards in whose determination they participate and that are assumed to be attentive to the interests of others elsewhere'.

New developments in the world economy raise the need for international cooperation. Capitalism remains the driving force behind these developments, but the challenges in the domain of international governance are great. This attracts wider attention, for instance, as shown by the comments of Rogers Hollingsworth (2011) on a seminal article by Richard Nelson (2011) about the complex organization of capitalism. Hollingsworth concludes that Nelson, in his considerations about the organization of capitalism, restricts himself to coordination problems at the level of the firm and at the level of the state. According to Hollingsworth (2011, p. 5) this view is too narrow: 'As the institutions of capitalism are increasingly nested in multiple levels of the World, we are faced with the perplexing problem of how to govern a capitalist society which is embedded in a global system'. Therefore, one of the great challenges of our time is to create a new theory of how to design the institutions of capitalism which are nested in a world of unprecedented complexity, one in which individual agents, nation states, continental and global regions are all intricately connected. In contrast to Rodrik (2011a) the author does not elaborate upon this, but it is clear what is at stake. The main future challenges come from the economic development of China and other emerging countries in connection with issues, such as resource scarcity and climate change.

The most notable emerging countries are often referred to as BRIC-countries. The abbreviation BRIC stands for Brazil, Russia, India and China. Of course, China is the most important of these countries, in terms of the size of its area and its population, on the one hand, and its long and impressive history, on the other hand. As already noted in Chapter 7, China may surpass the US in terms of GDP in 2012. According to the forecast of The Conference Board (2011), the share of China in global output will be equal to 24 per cent in 2020. India will then clearly lag behind with a share that equals only eight per cent in 2020. Apart from that, it needs to be remarked, that per capita GDP in China will only be at 40 per cent of the US level in 2020, at least according to the Base Scenario of The Conference Board (2011). Nevertheless, China will be an important player on the world stage in the foreseeable future. Therefore, the question arises, whether conflicts can be avoided and to what extent the influence of China will lead to specific forms of a 'deliberative democracy'.

Before an answer to these questions may be considered, one needs to determine whether economic growth will foster democracy, not only in China, but also in the other emerging economies. According to the influential modernization theory, a causal relationship exists between per capita income and a representative democracy. Empirical research based on observations for countries over a number of periods (pooled regression) shows a significantly positive relation between a measure for democracy and per capita income. Various indices circulate as a measure for democracy. Daron Acemoglu, Simon Johnson, James Robinson and Pierre Yared (2008) show that this relationship vanishes if fixed country-effects are introduced. This conclusion implies that the original relationship is biased since country-specific historical circumstances influence both per capita income and the political route that a country has chosen.

The authors illustrate this result by comparing the developments in the US and in Colombia. In Colombia, the colonizers introduced a hacienda system, based on repression and inequality with respect to both income and political power. In such a system, there is little room for industrialization and growth. This lack of opportunity puts a stamp on subsequent developments. In the US, property ownership was wide spread and the distribution of power was rather equal, already from the beginning. This situation created a favourable climate for industrialization and growth. As stated above, the comparison between the US and Colombia is nothing more than an illustration, but the underlying vision, that countries follow diverging political-economic development paths starting from a certain critical juncture, is an appealing one. Then, in the absence of fixed country-effects, the established statistical relationship between democracy and per capita income is not a simple causal relationship, but the reflection of historical processes. This conclusion provides an explanation for the fact that rich countries are democratic today. However, it seems unlikely that history exhibits all possible paths. Is a development, characterized by high economic growth and restrictions on the representative democracy, ultimately not feasible? Or is our knowledge of history coloured by Western-based views and corresponding arrangements? In brief, does a viable variety of capitalism exist, based on the developments in China?

In the 'Varieties of Capitalism' literature, discussed in Chapter 6, there is no place for such a variant. Wrongly, according to Christopher McNally (2011), for Chinese capitalism is a very special type of capitalism. It is based on the age-old Confucian idea of *Guanxi* relations. *Guanxi* points at the existence of long-lasting reciprocal personal relations, which result in mutual trust. This implies that, in a system with few formal rules and an underdeveloped legal system, private entrepreneurs function well. Such a system does not only concern networks in the private sphere. In today's China, *Guanxi* has a special place with regard to the interactions between the private sphere and the public sphere. Entrepreneurs are part of the political elite, via party membership or the membership of other governmental organizations. Thus, they influence regulation and other institutions. Leaders of the communist party have a share in the welfare of the private sector. After the reforms of 1978, communism with its command economy has made way for a capitalist variety, in which Confucianism plays a mediating role. McNally (2011, p. 10) characterizes this situation as follows: 'Indeed, *guanxi* have facilitated the transition from a monolithic Leninist system to a more open and plural polity in which up-and-coming capitalists can exchange wealth for power'.

However, this polity does not mean that the top-down control disappears. The control by the state is upheld by creating an intentional vagueness with respect to regulation and institutions. This contrast between 'Leninist control and relentless accumulation' (McNally, 2011, p. 23) is contained by a 'deliberate ambiguity'. Thus, the political elite and the economic elite are ultimately indispensable partners. 'Deliberate ambiguity' is deeply rooted in the Chinese culture, according to McNally. Although the future of Chinese capitalism is uncertain, the author states that *Guanxi* capitalism is there to stay in China. The considerations of McNally are valuable. However, a rigorous analysis of the political elite along the lines presented in Chapter 2 is lacking. Apart from the political and economic elites, room needs to be reserved for the working-class in such an analysis. Regulation depends on the power of the various parties. 'Deliberate ambiguity' and *Guanxi* are also subject to change.

In Adrian Wooldridge (2012) the economic developments in China are placed in a broader perspective, i.e. that of state capitalism, which tries to meld the powers of the state with the powers of capitalists. State capitalism is a kind of mix between government influencing the operation of markets and the play of free markets. The way in which the government exercises control is mainly through their ownership of shares. There are of course different varieties of state capitalism as the political regimes across states are different. In China the communist party has its agency that holds shares in the biggest companies. Moreover, there is a new generation of managers that alternate between the corporate domain and the public sector. The authors of the survey on state capitalism mention the culture of *Guanxi* and corruption in one breath. This is typical for the critical attitude towards state capitalism as such. It is argued that the rise of state capitalism may encourage trade wars as liberal markets economies may contest subsidizing state enterprises. 'But turning companies into organs of the government, state capitalism simultaneously concentrates power and corrupts it' (Wooldridge, 2012, p. 18). Such a conclusion needs qualification as the implicit argument seems to be that under traditional capitalism democracy functions independently of the economic realm. This is not correct as the history of American capitalism, discussed in Chapters 2, 5 and 6, reveals. Moreover, the conclusion detracts attention from the main issue, whether state capitalism can remain sufficiently innovative when the possibilities for catching-up evaporate. To put it differently, is state capitalism as it functions nowadays in the BRIC-countries an example of an investment-based strategy, and have its institutions to be adapted once an innovation-based strategy is called for to prevent a growth slowdown or stagnation? But even so, there still may be a Chinese variety of capitalism based on a cultural influence which deviates from the Western world. The innovative potential of such a variety is difficult to assess.

The idea that China fundamentally differs from the Western world is also defended by Martin Jacques (2009). According to the author, China ought to be considered as a civilization-state and not purely as a nation-state. This conclusion means that the view on the world of the Chinese people is different in two ways; that is to say both inward-looking as well as outward-looking. As far as the first aspect is concerned, one may not expect that China is on its way to a Western form of democracy. Jacques (2009, p. 395) bases this conclusion on the characteristics of the Chinese society:

> An overriding preoccupation with unity as the dominant imperative of Chinese politics; the huge diversity of the country; a continental size which means that the normal feedback loops of a conventional nation-state do not generally apply; a political sphere that has never shared power with other institutions like the church or business; the state as the apogee of society, above and beyond all other institutions; the absence of any tradition of popular sovereignty; and the centrality of moral suasion and ethical example.

Based on these considerations, Jacques (2009, p. 237) expects 'an authoritarian Confucian rather than democratic polity'.

According to Jacques (2009), the attitude of China towards the rest of the world is determined by a new form of the tributary system, at least to a large extent. In the traditional 'tributary system', mighty China dominated its neighbour-countries. Acceptance of the Chinese superiority was accompanied by a policy of protection and non-intervention by China. The new form of the tributary system implies, among other things, that China makes use of its enormous potential to assure its needs with respect

Table 8.2 Resource scarcity

	Food	Oil	Water
Demand	Rise by 50 per cent (2030). Meat rises by 85 per cent.	Rise one per cent per year until 2030.	Rise by 32 per cent (2000–2025).
Supply	Productivity growth 1.1 per cent per year, and declining.	Debate on year of peak production: 2020?	Two-thirds world population in water-stressed conditions (2025).

to raw materials and food. The lease of territory and the construction of infrastructural projects with this aim, for instance in Africa, are exemplary for a 'relationship in neo-tributary terms' (Jacques, 2009, p. 376). In this context, the author notes that the emergence of countries like India and Brazil can contain the aspirations of China.

Activities, such as land lease in exchange for infrastructural construction, are not special in a world in which, according to Alex Evans (2010, p. 14): 'scarcity of land, food, water and oil is likely to be an increasing driver of change between now and 2030, and beyond'. To give an impression of what we are talking about, Table 8.2 briefly summarizes the drivers on the demand and the supply side with respect to resource use, as discussed in Evans (2010). The author draws from various sources. The projections with respect to demand for food stem from the World Bank. The estimate of the increase in the demand for oil is based on calculations of the International Energy Agency, while for the projections with respect to the demand for water a publication of the United Nations Educational, Scientific and Cultural Organization (UNESCO) is made use of. With respect to the supply side, the diversity of sources is just as large. The estimate of the productivity growth of food comes from a study of the US Department of Agriculture. Moreover, the food outlook is complicated by constraints on the availability of land as a result of intensifying competition between uses of land for different purposes. The discussion about the peak production of oil takes place in different bodies. The figures with respect to water-stressed conditions are derived from a publication of the International Water Management Institute. With such a diversity of sources, an exact confrontation of demand- and supply-figures is precluded. Nevertheless, Evans (2010) concludes that it is doubtful whether the projected increases in demand in various domains can be met. In this context, one may observe that the scarcity with respect to food and water is even reinforced by the climate change, the future size of which cannot yet be determined.

One should notice that many problems stemming from scarcity are strictly local, but this does not mean that the rest of the world will only watch passively. This will certainly not be the case, if these problems trigger armed conflicts at the regional level. Anyway, the challenges resulting from climate change and resource scarcity are immense, as Evans (2010, p. 17) concludes after a thorough inventory of the problems: 'At all levels from local to global, climate change and scarcity issues will force decision-makers to make choices between intensifying zero-sum competition and increasing co-operation in rules-based orders'.

Against this background, the question may be asked whether China may enjoy certain advantages in the future in the global competition, since decision-making at the national level may be more resolute than in the US or in Europe. This question is especially important, since China will take an independent position as a future superpower. The significance of this position for the international cooperation in the economic and financial area and for the solution of unavoidable conflicts remains to be seen. According to Jacques (2009, pp. 398–9) the emergence of China leads to a different approach to these problems:

> The profound differences in the values of China (and other Confucian-based societies like Japan and Korea) in contrast to those of Western societies – including a community based collectivism rather than individualism, a far more family-orientated and family-rooted culture, and much less attachment to the rule of law and the use of law to resolve conflict – will remain pervasive and, with China's growing influence, acquire global significance.

It is clear that cooperation by cultures that are as different from each other as the Chinese and the Western cultures may lead to tensions. To keep these tensions under control as much as possible, a form of 'sane globalization' with sufficient room for national interests seems desirable. Thus, we are back at the view of Rodrik, who, similar to Jacques, points out the great humiliation that China had to endure in the nineteenth century by the machinations of imperialist superpowers. The result of this past humiliation is that it 'made the Chinese leaders great believers in national sovereignty and non-interference in domestic affairs', which can be met by 'a light global touch' (Rodrik, 2011a, p. 279).

8.4.   EVALUATION

International economic relations become increasingly important, because transaction costs decrease, while the number of players in the world market increases. This development implies that much has to be arranged between countries mutually. Arrangements are made and the implementation is often left to international organizations and institutions, such as the WTO, the IMF, the World Bank and also the EU. Thereby, the question arises whether these supranational institutions can be controlled in a satisfactorily democratic way. Alternatively formulated: do nation-states give up part of their sovereignty without any compensation from a democratic point of view? If the answer is affirmative, then it implies that the increasing globalization is eroding democracy, i.e. democracy at bay. In order to prevent this, democracy itself ought to be globalized, but only a few commentators really believe in a government at the world level accompanied by a parliamentary system with adequate checks and balances. In practice, such a solution does not seem feasible. This observation corresponds with the view of Rodrik (2011a), which we discussed in section 8.1.

According to Rodrik, only two alternatives remain. Either national states submit to non-democratic rules, the Golden Straitjacket, or the national governments put the interests of their citizens first and make the necessary sacrifices in the economic domain, which are caused by restricting global market forces. Rodrik prefers the latter possibility and he even indicates this choice out of a collection of three variants (the political trilemma) as 'sane globalization'. Thus, the author opts for a normative viewpoint and deserves praise for making his set of value judgements explicit, because this is not always done properly in economics.

The aftermath of the financial crisis of 2008 has led to financial imbalances across countries. The US and the People's Republic of China are in a difficult position. The US wages wars and amasses debts. China has an undervalued currency and generates export surpluses. On balance, China finances the excessive spending of the US, but this situation does not seem to be sustainable. In the EU and especially in the EMU, large budget deficits characterize countries with a lack of budget discipline and countries with overinvestment in the real estate sector that has got out of hand. Going together in the Eurozone forces the participating countries in the monetary union (EMU) to search for a solution. The difficulty of this process is revealed in discussing the activities to overcome the debt crisis in section 8.2. According to Sinn (2012) the core of the problem is that the Southern periphery countries have too high price levels, and are therefore uncompetitive in the world market. As a consequence, the sovereign debt crisis is *de facto* a balance-of-payments crisis. Sinn proposes measures ('commandments') to restore market discipline, combined with temporary measures to restore liquidity and solvency in the periphery.

However, it seems doubtful that the EMU can be rescued without the participating countries giving up a part of their sovereignty. This should be in line with the idea that Europe has to function as an entity to have influence in the global economy of the future. At the same time this may induce countries to think about new forms of democracy. In the European Union (EU) there are already many supranational rules which the countries have agreed upon. In this context, Sabel and Zeitlin (2007) explore the characteristics of a 'deliberative democracy', in which national governments and European institutions reach decisions in mutual consultation and with a hierarchy of competences. The authors illustrate the shape that such a 'new architecture of experimentalist governance' may take using a number of examples from various policy domains, such as telecommunications, food safety, health care and competition policy.

According to Sabel and Zeitlin (2007), the EU might be exemplary for the international cooperation in other domains and under other circumstances, as we have discussed in section 8.3. It is important to be able to fall back on a model-to-follow when issues such as climate control and resource scarcity become more important. Moreover, climate change aggravates problems such as food scarcity and water shortages, which is made clear in an informative study of Evans (2010). The fact that the circumstances at the global level change rapidly also has to do with the expansion of emerging countries, the so-called BRIC-countries (Brazil, Russia, India and China). China will be an important player in the future, owing to the size of both its area and its population. In Chapter 7, we have seen that China will equal the US in 2012, as far as the size of GDP is concerned. Besides, it turned out that the Chinese economy may be expected to exhibit fast growth in the years to come. The political influence of the People's Republic of China will increase proportionally.

The question arises whether the rising welfare in China will lead to a more democratic regime. According to some economists, a causal relationship exists between per capita income and a measure for the degree of democracy in countries. However, Acemoglu, Johnson, Robinson and Yared (2008) show that this causality does not materialize. The authors argue that the relationship between per capita income and democracy is historically determined. Countries choose a specific development path, in which the political system and the economy, in mutual relationship, determine progress. Rich countries enjoy prosperity as they have opted for democracy and freedom from the beginning. Poor countries remain stuck with a non-democratic regime.

China grows rapidly, but it does not seem on its way to a representative democracy. Is this an indication for a development path that has not been explored yet in history? McNally (2011) thinks that this is indeed the case. With the *Guanxi* capitalism, China opts for its own political-economic system, a specific 'variety of capitalism'. An important characteristic of this variety of state capitalism, as Wooldridge (2012) typifies the situation in China, is indicated by McNally as 'deliberate ambiguity', which relieves the tension between relentless accumulation and Leninist control.

According to Jacques (2009), the attitude of China towards the rest of the world is determined by a culture, based on millennia-old Confucian values. China will assure its need for raw materials and food by expanding its sphere of influence. In this respect, the lease of land and the associated infrastructural projects in Africa are an example. Jacques (2009) considers this as a new form of the tributary system, which dominated the relationship between China and the neighbouring countries in the imperial era. Besides, the author stresses, taking the humiliations of the country in the nineteenth century into account, that China attaches a high value to its own sovereignty. The latter implies that the more powerful China becomes, the less the drive will be for an 'architecture of experimentalist governance' in international affairs, as analyzed in Sabel and Zeitlin (2007). At the same time, this means that binding agreements within the framework of international cooperation are difficult to attain. According to Rodrik (2011a) this is not a big problem as 'sane globalization' is the most favoured solution in the global economy. With this solution of the political trilemma countries can each realize their own preferred variety of capitalism.

NOTE

1. The name 'Bretton Woods' refers to a place in New Hampshire, US, where, in 1944, the international conference about the organization of the world economy was organized.

Conclusions

In the book the history of capitalism is examined from two different perspectives. First, emphasis is put on technological progress as the main engine of economic growth. It is shown that technological change occurs in an irregular fashion, which has important consequences for the design of the economy and for democracy. Second, attention is paid to the diffusion of capitalism across countries. The main question thereby is whether such a diffusion gives rise to varieties of capitalism, because countries have their own history determined by specific cultures.

Capitalism in its present form dates back from the Industrial Revolution in England, which took place after 1750. Technological change as such is not the main factor behind the fundamental revolution. After all, technological knowledge increased step-wise during the long history of mankind as, for instance, documented in Lipsey et al. (2005) by identifying major technological breakthroughs (general purpose technologies) since 9000 BC. What is decisive for the emergence of the capitalist system, is that markets are no longer embedded in social relations. Polanyi (1944) refers to this remarkable feature as 'The Great Transformation'. North et al. (2009) discuss such a fundamental change in terms of the transformation of 'natural states' into 'open access orders'. The characteristic for this revolutionizing change is that economic and political choices are no longer the prerogative of an absolute ruler with military power, but are based on free competition between organizations and groups of people. An essential condition for such a freedom of choice is that the property rights of economic agents are secured. In England these rights were established as a result of political reforms connected with the Glorious Revolution of 1688, when the parliament dominated by economic elites gained substantial power.

Under a system governed by relentless accumulation of capital the provision of an increasing amount of goods is based on the profit motive. This is often accompanied by undesirable side effects as well as by the crowding out of valuable social activities. Such negative externalities may relate to matters as endangering food and traffic safety, pollution of the earth and the atmosphere, and destruction of natural habitat. Other aspects of economic change that may arouse resistance are social exclusion, poverty and an unequal distribution of income and wealth. The consequence of the tension between freedom and conflict is that, according to Polanyi, capitalism is characterized by a 'double movement'. On the one hand, there is a laissez-faire movement necessary to extend the scope of the market system and to stimulate innovation. On the other hand, there is a countermovement that resists disembedding markets. The economic elite will push in the direction of laissez faire to secure their property rights. Underprivileged groups and the victims of competition-driven creative destruction will strive for political power to eliminate the harmful effects of capitalist accumulation by imposing regulation.

There is some irony in historical development, because as democracy evolves more fully it changes from a friend into an enemy of the economic elite. A parliamentary democracy is all right for them as long as the political power of capitalists is undisputed and, what Greif (2008) calls, coercion constraining institutions can be enforced. However, under a representative democracy with a majority of voters earning an income below the average the contract enforcing institutions, the expression comes again from Greif, may be under pressure. The majority may opt for redistribution and regulation, thus jeopardizing property rights from a different angle. As a consequence, a combination of capitalism and democracy appears to be a fragile alliance. Although at least in the US 'this remains a tension rather than a mortal antagonism' as Schlesinger (1986, p. 26) observes.

One could assume that both sides engaged in the double movement have an interest to find a compromise which results in a kind of a balanced growth path. The problem with this view is that technological change, the engine of capitalist expansion, is not a smooth process as assumed in neoclassical growth theory. Technological development goes along with the introduction of fundamental and far-reaching modernizations, identified among others by Lipsey et al. (2005) as general purpose technologies (GPTs). The introduction of GPTs can be described applying the metaphor of the logistic curve. The birth of a GPT can be characterized as a kind of 'big bang', after which the dispersion of new production processes, new products and new organizational devices elapses gradually. After some time the development gets momentum and may even lead to overinvestment in the dynamic sectors of the economy. If things are straightened out, economic growth may be balanced until the existing GPT reaches the point of maturity and the situation is ripe for the introduction of a new GPT.

There is another source of instability in the capitalist system. As emphasized by Minsky (1964) the system is prone to financial instability. The financial sector itself generates profitable innovations, which may seduce participants to take irresponsible risks. This may result in bubbles on asset markets or on the markets for real estate, which will burst in due time. Financial instability contributes to dynamics of regulation and deregulation that is typical for the capitalist system.

The different ideas on the functioning of capitalism are integrated in Perez (2002) by putting them in the context of the long wave theory. The existence of long waves, or Kondratieff cycles, is disputed from a statistical point of view, which is understandable as the number of observations for cycles of about 50-years duration is limited. Nevertheless, the concept of long waves may be useful in explaining history, provided that it is done with the required flexibility and carefulness.

Technological revolutions are a key concept in the theory of Perez (2002). The concept is related to the introduction of GPTs but is broader as technological revolutions are accompanied by a number of imbalances that cause tension in the real economy, as the author puts it. In the installation phase of a technological revolution these tensions have to be resolved and institutions have to be adapted to make room for new developments. As a rule this comes down to liberalization and deregulation of the economy. A recent example which may be remembered by many, is the promotion of market forces by President Reagan in the US and by Prime Minister Thatcher in the UK during the 1980s. In this case political power shifted from the old economic elite towards challengers who sought to restore the dynamics of the capitalist system. In the terminology of Polanyi (1944) this is a clear case of the first part of the double movement.

In the theory of Perez (2002) the Installation phase of about twenty-five years is followed by a Deployment phase of roughly similar length before the technological revolution comes to an end. The Deployment phase is more or less a period of balanced economic expansion. The real firework takes place during the transition from the Installation towards the Development Phase, which in the classification of Perez holds a special position and is called the Turning Point. The final part of the Installation Phase is characterized by different forms of excess and disequilibrium, which are caused by overoptimistic expectations. As the technological revolution comes into full swing people believe that a whole new era has arrived. There is no fear of things going wrong. The *adagium* 'this time is different', with which Reinhart and Rogoff (2008) mark this mentality, rules the world. Against this background firms overinvest and financial speculation takes a high flight. A crisis becomes inevitable, shaking the economy, and urging politicians to redress institutions. The second part of the double movement now appears on the agenda.

The expression 'turning point' in the theory of Perez (2002) is not well chosen as, for instance, appears from the developments during the Great Depression of the 1930s. The whole period from 1929 until 1942 is classified under the heading 'turning point'. Subsequently, Perez wonders why the Great Depression in the US economy lasted so long. The answer is that the New Deal of President Franklin Roosevelt was being systematically opposed in the political arena, because of capitalists supposed fear of socialism. The real reason was, of course, that the economic elite did not want to give up its profitable positions. The political struggle continued until the world changed dramatically because the Second World War forced the US to reconsider its position. Perez (2002, p. 126) makes clear what was at stake: 'It took the experience of collaboration in the military-industrial complex, during the Second World War, to understand that capitalists could coexist in a mutually beneficial relationship with a strong state that assumed an active and balancing role in the economy'. The events in the US contrast sharply with what happened in Germany, where huge investments in infrastructure and weapons led to a quick recovery after 1933. But in this case democracy was put completely aside.

The present crisis, which started in 2008, resembles in a number of ways the contingencies during the Great Depression. Now again recovery is not just around the corner as the government deficit problem in the US and the sovereign debt problems in Europe make clear. The reasons for recovery not to materialize are similar to those of the 1930s. Political disagreement stands in the way of the required reforms in the real economy as well as in the financial sector. However, the idea that preparation for war may be a way out does not give any comfort. Something has to be done and perhaps John Maynard Keynes (1936, p. 378), writing in the midst of a severe depression, may have a point when he concludes: 'I conceive, therefore, that a somewhat comprehensive socialization of investment will prove the only means of securing an approximation to full employment, though this need not exclude all manner of compromises and of devices by which public authority will co-operate with private initiative'. Even if Keynes is right, it remains to be seen in what way a political majority can be found to socialize investment in one way or the other. This illustrates again that capitalism and democracy in its traditional representative form of a one-person-one-vote system constitute a fragile alliance.

There is another way of recording the history of capitalism. It relates to the spread of the system over the globe, a process that is still under way. The main question hereby is whether the introduction of capitalism across countries gives rise to different varieties of capitalism, because countries have their own culture and history. Furthermore, if varieties exist will there be a tendency for these differences to fade away as temporary backward countries attain the welfare level of the rich economies?

As observed earlier, the Industrial Revolution occurred in England, and it took continental Europe and the US many years to follow the example for a number of, mainly political, reasons. Remarkably, England was leapfrogged by America around 1900. The European countries on the continent performed rather well during the second half of the nineteenth century. However, both world wars set Europe at a great distance from the American economy in terms of labour productivity. As a consequence, after the Second World War the European countries exhibited a large potential for catching-up. This potential could effectively be realized, because the existing institutions were geared towards cooperation in an environment characterized by mutual trust. Labour unions, employers' organizations and the government acted in concert to realize full employment and high rates of growth.

According to Hall and Soskice (2001) in continental Europe a special variety of capitalism took hold, which they typify as a coordinated market economy (CME). This variety can be compared to a liberal market economy (LME), prevailing in the Anglo-Saxon countries. Other scholars refer to the CME variety as the Rhineland model as opposed to the Anglo-Saxon model. A special feature of the Rhineland model is the importance attached to the redistribution of income and wealth. Alesina and Glaeser (2004) explain the difference in redistribution between Europe and the US from a political point of view. The political turmoil in Europe following the First World War gave socialist parties and labour unions the opportunity to gain political power and through this to put their mark on the design of the welfare state.

Catching-up is self-limiting and Europe has almost bridged the economic gap that separated it from the US. Many economists argue that at this point institutions need to be adapted to avoid economic sclerosis. In the terminology of Acemoglu et al. (2006), Europe has to transform its institutions which relate to an investment-based strategy towards a setting characterized as an innovation-based strategy. However, in a representative democracy it is not simple to get a majority supporting such a radical change. Moreover, it is not clear whether the argument implies that a CME should be rigorously transformed into a LME, or that adapting institutions to foster innovation is a matter of partial adjustment. This doubt is inspired by looking at the developments between 1870 and 1940. Both leading economies, the US and Germany, industrialized fast during this period, but along different patterns, as Chandler (1990, p. 12) makes clear: 'The basic difference between the two countries was, that industrial leaders in the United States continued to compete functionally and strategically for market share, while in Germany they often preferred to negotiate with one another to maintain market share at home and in some cases abroad. In the United States managerial capitalism was more competitive; in Germany it became more cooperative'.

Catching-up throughout the rest of the world is a mixed bag. In the twentieth century the initial picture is one of divergence with exception of the so-called Asian tigers (Japan, Taiwan, South-Korea and Singapore). These countries realized high rates of economic growth due to government support in several ways, for instance in the form of subsidized loans or tax incentives for investments. Since the early 1990s developing countries have been more fully integrated into the global economy as McMillan and Rodrik (2011) argue. As a result, many countries join the convergence club, to use the terminology of Baumol and Wolff (1988), with the so-called BRIC-countries (Brazil, Russia, India and China) in the lead. According to Wooldridge (2012) the BRIC-countries are characterized by a powerful new form of state capitalism, which constitutes in his opinion: 'One of the biggest changes in the world economy in recent years' (Wooldridge, 2012, p. 17). Under this variety of capitalism the government has a big say in economic development and the state owns some or many firms. Consequently, politicians have far more power than they hold under traditional varieties of capitalism. They can restructure entire industries and appoint captains of industry.

The most outspoken form of state capitalism is found in China, where democratic institutions in a Western sense are absent. The Chinese variety of state capitalism is sometimes referred to as *Quanxi* capitalism. It is a state of affairs whereby government officials and business leaders form an integrated elite. Some political leaders hold positions in firms and many business leaders serve in the party's Central Committee.

The BRIC-countries still operate at a great distance from the technological frontier, but as in the case of Europe the main question for many observers is: how can state capitalism in the course of time remain sufficiently dynamic when innovation in the neighbourhood of the technological frontier requires the freedom to experiment? In this connection, state-sponsored innovation is sometimes ridiculed as a 'boulevard of broken dreams', because such attempts have to fail.

Of course, there is empirical evidence to support the idea that innovation requires markets to operate freely. Technological revolutions take place when institutions favour challengers, which are able to eliminate incumbents in existing markets. Even if this is true, one could imagine that the authorities are aware of the problem when they want to direct capitalism. In the case of *directed capitalism* the state determines the strategy of economic development, leaving firms sufficient room to experiment and to innovate. Perhaps Keynes (1936) had something like this in mind in the quotation presented above. Moreover, under directed capitalism democratic decision-making may proceed along different lines than in a purely representative democracy. To elaborate on this suggestion the ideas discussed in Sabel and Zeitlin (2007) may be useful. Referring to the experience in the European Union the authors introduce the concept of a 'deliberative democracy', whereby decision-making is based on formal and informal deliberation among technical elites (civil servants, scientific experts, representatives of interest groups). This looks suspicious from a point of view whereby proportional representation is considered to be essential for democratic decision-making. However in the experimental design of Sabel and Zeitlin (2007) transparency, dynamic accountability and peer review should guarantee consensus through a process of socialization. The authors admit that 'a comprehensive democratic justification of this new governance architecture would be an independent project in political theory' but for the time being 'it destabilizes entrenched forms of authority in ways that may clear the way for an eventual reconstruction of democracy' (Sabel and Zeitlin, 2007, p. 46). The ideas on the 'socialization of investment' and a 'deliberative democracy' open avenues for reforming capitalism in the direction of a dynamically stable and at the same time innovative system.

State capitalism in China also will change, but it is unlikely that the country will adopt Western values and will embrace the liberal market economy. Jacques (2009) makes clear that the Chinese culture is deeply rooted in the Confucian value system. Moreover, China has its own millennia-old history of dealing with socio-economic development. Therefore, China may opt for a specific variety of capitalism, even in the long run. This is not to say that the country will not learn from experiences elsewhere, but it would be appropriate to think about learning in terms of a two-way traffic system as Jacques (2009, p. 220) emphasizes with respect to innovation in governance: 'Just as China can learn from the American federal system and the European Union (in which it is presently showing growing interest) in governing such a vast country, so China, accounting for one-fifth of the world's population, can offer the rest of the world a model for large-scale governance, which is likely to become increasingly important in a globalized world'.

With the BRIC-countries converging in economic terms the distribution of political and military power in the world will change. At the same time a number of important problems must be solved on a global scale. International trade between countries with different varieties of capitalism may cause problems with respect to what countries experience as unfair competition. The international mobility of capital must be regulated. An increasing demand for natural resources may induce conflicts on a local level, and the problem of climate change has to be addressed internationally. Given the large differences among participating countries, it may be wise to opt for some form of 'sane globalization', proposed by Rodrik

(2011a). Sane globalization consists of a thin layer of simple, transparent and common-sense rules to coordinate the economic activities of diverse nations. In such an environment there is sufficient room to pursue national goals and to protect one's own national institutions. It also set the stage for a peaceful cooperation between nations in the world economy.

Sane globalization does not exclude regional economic integration. For instance, if Europe wants to be a global player in the future, integration seems to be a necessary precondition. At present the difficulties of achieving a political union to support economic integration are almost insurmountable. Therefore, Rodrik (2011a, p. 220) who is sceptical about the possibility of global governance, summarizes the situation with respect to Europe as follows: 'At best, it is the exception that tests the rule'.

References

Abramovitz, Moses (1986), 'Catching up, forging ahead, and falling behind', *Journal of Economic History*, **46**, 285–406.

Acemoglu, Daron (2009), *Introduction to Modern Economic Growth*, Princeton and Oxford: Princeton University Press.

Acemoglu, Daron, Philippe Aghion and Fabrizio Zilibotti (2006), 'Distance to frontier, selection and economic growth', *Journal of the European Economic Association*, **4** (1), 37–74.

Acemoglu, Daron, Simon Johnson and James Robinson (2005), 'Institutions as a fundamental cause of long-run growth', in Phillipe Aghion and Steven Durlauf (eds), *Handbook of Economic Growth*, Volume IA, Amsterdam: Elsevier, pp. 385–554.

Acemoglu, Daron, Simon Johnson, James Robinson and Pierre Yared (2008), 'Income and democracy', *American Economic Review*, **98** (3), 808–42.

Acemoglu, Daron and James Robinson (2008), 'Persistence of power, elites, and institutions', *American Economic Review*, **98** (1), 267–93.

Akkermans, Dirk, Carolina Castaldi and Bart Los (2009), 'Do "liberal market economies" really innovate more radically than "coordinated market economics"? Hall & Soskice reconsidered', *Research Policy*, **38** (1), 181–91.

Albert, Michel (1991), *Capitalism contre capitalism*, Paris: Seuil.

Allen, Robert (2011), 'Why the industrial revolution was British: commerce induced invention, and the scientific revolution', *Economic History Review*, **64** (2), 357–84.

Alesina, Alberto and Edward Glaeser (2004), *Fighting Poverty in the US and Europe. A World of Difference*, Oxford: Oxford University Press.

Alesina, Alberto, Edward Glaeser and Bruce Sacerdote (2001), 'Why doesn't the US have a European-style welfare state?', *Brookings Papers on Economic Activity*, **32** (2), 187–278.

Baumol, William and Edward Wolff (1988), 'Productivity growth, convergence and welfare: Reply', *American Economic Review*, **78**, 1155–9.

Bénabou, Roland and Jean Tirole (2006), 'Belief in a just world and redistributive politics', *Quarterly Journal of Economics*, **121**, 699–746.

Blaug, Mark (1962), *Economic Theory in Retrospect*, Homewood, Illinois: Richard Irwin.

Block, Fred (2001), 'Introduction', in Karl Polanyi, *Great Transformation*, 2001 edition, Boston: Beacon Press, pp. XVIII–XXXVIII.

Block, Fred (2003), 'Karl Polanyi and the writing of *The Great Transformation*', *Theory and Society*, **32**, 275–306.

Bosworth, Barry and Susan Collins (2003), 'The empirics of growth: an update', *Brookings Papers on Economic Activity*, **34**, 113–206.

Bourguignon, François and Thierry Verdier (2010), 'The simple analytics of elite behaviour under limited state capacity', UNU-WIDER, Working Paper No. 2010/104.

Broadberry, Stephen, Giovanni Federico and Alexander Klein (2010), 'Sectoral developments, 1870–1914', in Stephen Broadberry and Kevin O'Rourke (eds), *The Cambridge Economic History of Modern Europe, Volume 2: 1870 to the Present*, Cambridge: Cambridge University Press, pp. 59–83.

Canova, Fabio (2004), 'Testing for convergence clubs in income per capita: a predictive density approach', *International Economic Review*, **45**, 49–77.

Canzoneri, Matthew and Dale Henderson (1991), *Monetary Policy in Interdependent Economies. A Game-Theoretic Approach*, Cambridge, Massachusetts: The MIT Press.

Chandler, Alfred O. Jr. (1990), *Scale and Scope, The Dynamics of Industrial Capitalism*, Cambridge, Massachusetts: Belknap Press.

Chatterji, Monojit (1992), 'Convergence clubs and endogenous growth', *Oxford Review of Economic Policy*, **8**, 57–69.

Chenery, Hollis, Sherman Robinson and Moshe Syrquin (eds) (1986), *Industrialization and Growth: A Comparative Study*, New York: Oxford University Press, for the World Bank.

Chenery, Hollis and Moshe Syrquin (1975), *Patterns of Development, 1950–1970*, London: Oxford University Press.

Clark, Gregory (2005), 'The condition of the working class in England, 1209–2004', *Journal of Political Economy*, **113**, 1307–40.

Conference Board (2011), *Global Economic Outlook 2011*, http://www.conference-board.org/data/globaloutlook.cfm (accessed 4 October 2011).

David, Paul and Theo van de Klundert (1965), 'Biased efficiency growth and capital-labor substitution in the US, 1899–1960', *American Economic Review*, **55**, 357–94.

Dawley, Alan (2005), 'The arbortive rule of big money', in Steve Fraser and Gary Gerstle (eds), *Ruling America: A History of Wealth and Power in a Democracy*, Cambridge, Massachusetts: Harvard University Press, pp. 149–180.

DeLong, J. Bradford (2001), 'The convergence club', http://www.j-bradford-delong.net/ (accessed 26 September 2011).

Djankov, Simeon, Edward Glaeser, Rafael La Porla, Florencio Lopez-de-Silanes and Andrei Shleifer (2003), 'The new comparative economics', *Journal of Comparative Economics*, **31**, 595–619.

Dowrick, Steve and J. Bradford DeLong (2003), 'Globalization and convergence', in Michael Bordo, Alan Taylor and Jeffrey Williamson (eds), *Globalization in Historical Perspective*, Chicago: University of Chicago Press, pp. 191–226.

Eichengreen, Barry (2007), *The European Economy since 1945. Coordinated Capitalism and Beyond*, Princeton: Princeton University Press.

Eichengreen, Barry (2011), 'European monetary integration with benefit of hindsight', *CPB Lecture* 2011, The Hague: Centraal Planbureau.

Eichengreen, Barry, Donghyun Park and Kwanho Shin (2012), 'When fast growing economies slow down. International evidence and implications for China', *Asian Economic Papers*, **11** (1), 42–87.

Emmott, Bill (2003), 'Pro-market, not pro-business', Special report: Capitalism and democracy, *The Economist*, 26 June, 1–8.

Evans, Alex (2010), 'Resources scarcity, climate change and the risk of violent conflict', *World Development Report 2011*, Background Paper.

Field, Alexander (2003), 'The most technologically progressive decade of the century', *American Economic Review*, **93**, 1399–1413.

Fourastié, Jean (1949), *Le grand espoir de XXe siècle: progrès tecnhnique, progrès économique, progrès social*, Paris: Presses Universitaire de France.

Fraser, Steve (2009), *Steve Fraser on the Crisis of Capitalism*, http://www.truthdig.com/arts_culture/item/20091105_steve_fraser_on_the_crisis_of_capitalism/ (accessed 8 February 2010).

Fraser, Steve and Gary Gerstle (2005), 'Introduction', in Steve Fraser and Gary Gerstle (eds), *Ruling America: A History of Wealth and Power in a Democracy*, Cambridge, Massachusetts: Harvard University Press, pp. 1–26.

Freeman, Chris and Francisco Louçã (2001), *As Time Goes By. From the Industrial Revolutions to the Information Revolution*, Oxford: Oxford University Press.

Friedman, Daniel (2008), *Morals and Markets. An Evolutionary Account of the Modern World*, New York: Palgrave McMillan.

Friedman, Thomas (2000), *The Lexus and the Olive Tree*, New York: Anchor Books.

Galbraith, John Kenneth (2004), *The Economics of Innocent Fraud*, Boston and New York: Houghton Mifflin Books.

Gelderen, Jacob van (1913), 'Springvloed: Beschouwingen over industrieele ontwikkeling en prijsbeweging' (Spring tides of industrial development and price movements), *De nieuwe tijd*, **18**, 253–77, 369–84, 445–64.

Gemert, Henk van (1987), 'Structural change in OECD countries', *De Economist*, **135**, 29–51.

Gerschenkron, Alexander (1962), 'The approach to European industrialization: a postscript', in Alexander Gerschenkron, *Economic Backwardness in Historical Perspective*, Cambridge, Massachusetts: Belknap Press, pp. 353–64.

Glaeser, Edward (2005), 'Inequality', *NBER* Working Paper 11511.

Glyn, Andrew (2006), *Capitalism Unleashed. Finance, Globalization and Welfare*, Oxford: Oxford University Press.

Goodwin, Robert (1967), 'A growth cycle', in Charles Feinstein (ed.), *Socialism, Capitalism and Economic Growth, Essays Presented to Maurice Dobb*, Cambridge: Cambridge University Press, pp. 54–8.

Greif, Avner (1989), 'Reputation and coalitions in medieval trade: evidence on the Maghribi traders', *Journal of Economic History*, **XLIX**, 857–82.

Greif, Avner (1993), 'Contract enforceability and economic institutions in early trade: the Maghribi traders coalition', *American Economic Review*, **83**, 525–42.

Greif, Avner (2005), 'Commitment, coercion, and markets: the nature and dynamics of institutions supporting exchange', in Claude Ménard and Mary Shirley (eds), *Handbook of New Institutional Economics*, Dordrecht: Springer, pp. 727–86.

Greif, Avner (2008), 'Coercion and exchange: how did markets evolve?', Stanford University. Paper prepared for a *Research Symposium on Property Rights Economics and Innovation*, organized by the Searle Center on Law, Regulation, and Economic Growth, Northwestern University.

Grossman, Gene and Elhanan Helpman (1991), *Innovation and Growth in the Global Economy*, Cambridge, Massachusetts: MIT Press.

Grossman, Herschel (2002), '"Make us a king": anarchy, predation, and the state', *European Journal of Political Economy*, **18** (1), 31–46.

Hall, Peter and Daniel Gingerich (2004), 'Varieties of capitalism and institutional complementaries in the macroeconomy. An empirical analysis', *Max-Planck-Institut für Gesellschaftsforschung*, Discussion Paper 04/5.

Hall, Peter and David Soskice (2001), 'An introduction to varieties of capitalism', in Peter Hall and David Soskice (eds), *Varieties of Capitalism: The Institutional Foundations of Comparative Advantage*, Oxford: Oxford University Press, pp. 1–70.

Helpman, Elhanan and Manuel Trajtenberg (1998), 'A time to sow and a time to reap: growth based on general purpose technologies', in Elhanan Helpman (ed.), *General Purpose Technologies and Economic Growth*, Cambridge, Massachusetts: MIT Press, pp. 55–83.

Hobbes, Thomas (1651), *Leviathan, or the Matter, Forme & Power of a Commonwealth Ecclesiastical and Civill.* Republication: Thomas Hobbes (1985), *Leviathan*, London: Penguin Classics.

Hollingsworth, Rogers (2011), 'Comment on "the complex economic organization of capitalist economies" by Richard Nelson', *Capitalism and Society*, **6**, Article 5.

Holz, Carsten (2008), 'China's economic growth 1978–2025: what we know today about China's economic growth tomorrow', *World Development*, **36**, 1665–91.

Hsieh, Chang-Tai and Peter Klenow (2009), 'Misallocation and manufacturing TFP in China and India', *Quarterly Journal of Economics*, **124**, 1403–48.

Iizuka, Michiko and Luc Soete (2011), 'Catching up in the 21st century: globalization, knowledge and capabilities in Latin America, a case for natural resource based activities', *UNU-MERIT*, Working Paper Series, 2011–071.

Iversen, Torben (2006), 'Capitalism and democracy', in B. Weingast and D. Wittman (eds), *The Oxford Handbook of Political Economy*, Oxford: Oxford University Press, pp. 601–23.

Jacques, Martin (2009), *When China Rules the World. The Rise of the Middle Kingdom and the End of the Western World*, London: Allen Lane.

Keen, Steve (1995), 'Finance and economic breakdown: modeling Minsky's "financial instability hypothesis"', *Journal of Post Keynesian Economics*, **17**, 607–35.

Keen, Steve (2009a), 'Household debt: the final stage in an artificially extended Ponzi bubble', *Australian Economic Review*, **42**, 347–57.

Keen, Steve (2009b), 'Bailing out the Titanic with a thimble', *Economic Analysis and Policy*, **39**, 3–24.

Keynes, John Maynard (1936), *The General Theory of Employment, Interest and Money*, London: MacMillan & Co.

Klundert, Theo van de (1961), 'Het tijdselement in de theorie van het partiële oligopolie' (The time dimension in the theory of partial oligopoly), *Maandschrift Economie*, **26**, 82–96.

Klundert, Theo van de (2010), 'On the determinants of institutional design', *European Journal of Political Economy*, **26**, 167–75.

Klundert, Theo van de and Ton van Schaik (1996), 'On the historical continuity of the process of economic growth', in Bart van

Ark and Nicolas Crafts (eds), *Quantitative Aspects of Post-War European Economic Growth*, Cambridge: Cambridge University Press, pp. 388–414.

Klundert, Theo van de and Sjak Smulders (1996), 'North-south knowledge spillovers and competition: convergence versus divergence', *Journal of Development Economics*, **50**, 213–32.

Kondratieff, Nikolai (1926), 'Die langen Wellen der Konjunktur', *Archiv für Sozial-wissenschaft und Sozialpolitik*, **56**, 573–609.

Korotayev, Andrey and Sergey Tsirel (2010), 'A spectral analysis of world GDP dynamics: Kondratieff waves, Kuznets swings, Juglar and Kitchin Cycles in global economic development, and the 2008–2009 economic crisis', *Structure and Dynamics: eJournal of Anthropological and Related Sciences UC Irvine*, **4** (1), 1–55.

Laffer, Arthur (2004), 'The Laffer curve, past, present and future', The Heritage Foundation, Background Report 1763.

Landes, David (1998), *The Wealth and Poverty of Nations. Why Some Are So Rich and Some So Poor*, London: Abacus.

Lind, Michael (2005), 'Conservative elites and the counterrevolution against the new deal', in Steve Fraser and Gary Gerstle (eds), *Ruling America: A History of Wealth and Power in a Democracy*, Cambridge, Massachusetts: Harvard University Press, pp. 250–85.

Lindert, Peter (2004), *Growing Public. Social Spending and Economic Growth since the Eighteenth Century: Volume I, The Story, Volume II, Further Evidence*, Cambridge: Cambridge University Press.

Lipsey, Richard, Kenneth Carlaw and Clifford Bekar (2005), *Economic Transformations, General Purpose Technologies and Long Term Economic Growth*, Oxford: Oxford University Press.

Maddison, Angus (1995), *Monitoring the World Economy 1820–1992*, Paris: OECD.

Marshall, Alfred (1890), *Principles of Economics. An introductory volume*, Basingstoke: MacMillan.

McMillan, Margaret and Dani Rodrik (2011), 'Globalization, structural change and productivity growth', *NBER* Working Paper 17143.

McNally, Christopher (2011), 'China's changing *Guanxi* capitalism: private entrepreneurs between Leninist control and relentless accumulation', *Business and Politics*, **13**, Article 5.

Milgrom, Paul, Douglass North and Barry Weingast (1990), 'The role of institutions in the revival of trade: the law merchant, private judges, and the champagne fairs', *Economics and Politics*, **2**, 1–23.

Minsky, Hyman (1964), 'Longer waves in financial relations: financial factors in the more severe depressions', *American Economic Review*, **54**, 324–35.

Minsky, Hyman (1982), *Inflation, Recession, and Economic Policy*, Brighton: Wheatsheaf Books.

Minsky, Hyman (1995), 'Longer waves in financial relations: financial factors in the more severe depressions II', *Journal of Economic Issues*, **XXIX**, 83–96.

Mokyr, Joel (1990), *The Lever of Riches. Technological Creativity and Economic Progress*, Oxford: Oxford University Press.

Nelson, Richard (2011), 'The complex economic organization of capitalist economies', *Capitalism and Society*, **6**, Article 2.

North, Douglass (1990), *Institutions, Institutional Change and Economic Performance*, Cambridge: Cambridge University Press.

North, Douglass and Robert Paul Thomas (1973), *The Rise of the Western World. A New Economic History*, Cambridge: Cambridge University Press.

North, Douglass, John Wallis and Barry Weingast (2006), 'A conceptual framework for interpreting recorded human history', *NBER*, Working Paper 12795.

North, Douglass, John Wallis and Barry Weingast (2009), *Violence and Social Orders. A Conceptual Framework for Interpreting Recorded Human History*, Cambridge: Cambridge University Press.

North, Douglass and Barry Weingast (1989), 'Constitutions and commitment: the evolution of institutions governing public choice in seventeenth-century England', *Journal of Economic History*, **XLIX**, 803–32.

Olson, Mancur (1982), *The Rise and Decline of Nations. Economic Growth, Stagflation, and Social Rigidities*, New Haven: Yale University Press.

O'Sullivan, John (2011), 'A game of catch-up', Special report: The World Economy, *The Economist*, 24 September 2011, 3–8.

Papenhausen, Chris (2007), 'Long waves of economic development and their causal mechanisms', Druid Summer Conference, Copenhagen.

Perez, Carlota (2002), *Technological Revolutions and Financial Capital. The Dynamics of Bubbles and Golden Ages*, Cheltenham, UK and Northampton, MA, USA: Edward Elgar Publishing.

Perez, Carlota (2009), 'The double bubble at the turn of the century: technological roots and structural implications', *Cambridge Journal of Economics*, **33**, 779–805.

Perez, Carlota (2010), 'The financial crisis and the future of innovation: a view of technical change with the aid of history', Working Papers in Technology Governance and Economic Dynamics, no. 28, *Tallinn University of Technology*, Tallinn.

Perlman, Michael (2011), 'Retrospective X-efficiency', *Journal of Economic Perspective*, **52**, 211–22.

Persson, Karl Gunnar (2010), *An Economic History of Europe. Knowledge, Institutions and Growth, 600 to the Present*, Cambridge: Cambridge University Press.

Phillips, Kevin (2002), *Wealth and Democracy. A Political History of the American Rich*, New York: Broadway Books.

Polanyi, Karl (1944), *The Great Transformation. The Political and Economic Origins of Our Time*, Boston: Beacon Press.

Prados de la Escosura, Leandro (2005), 'Gerschenkron revisited. European patterns of development in historical perspective', Universidad Carlos III De Madrid, Working Paper 05–79 (10).

Qian, Wen-yuan (1985), *The Great Inertia: Scientific Stagnation in Traditional China*, Beckenham, Kent: Croom Helm.

Reich, Robert (2007), *Supercapitalism, The Transformation of Business, Democracy and Everyday Life*, New York: Alfred A. Knopf.

Reinhart, Carmen and Kenneth Rogoff (2008), 'Banking crises: an equal opportunity menace', *NBER*, Working Paper 14587.

Reinhart, Carmen M. and Kenneth Rogoff (2011), 'From financial crash to debt crisis', *American Economic Review*, **101** (5), 1676–1706.

Ridder, Peter de (2011), 'De eurozone in crises', *Economisch Statistische Berichten* (ESB), **96**, 762–65.

Rodrik, Dani (2011a), *The Globalization Paradox: Why Global Markets, States, and Democracy Can't Coexist*, Oxford: Oxford University Press.

Rodrik, Dani (2011b), 'The future of convergence', Harvard University, Paper prepared for the *2011 Jackson Hole Symposium of the Federal Reserve Bank of Kansas City*, 25–27 August, 2011.

Romer, Paul (1986), 'Increasing returns and long-run growth', *Journal of Political Economy*, **94**, 1002–27.

Rosenberg, Nathan (1994), *Exploring the Black Box. Technology, Economics, and History*, Cambridge: Cambridge University Press.

Rowthorn, Robert and Ramana Ramaswamy (1999), 'Growth, trade and deindustrialization', *IMF Staff Papers*, **46** (1), 18–41.

Ruggie, John (1982), 'International regimes, transactions, and change: embedded liberalism in the postwar economic order', *International Organization*, **36**, 379–415.

Sabel, Charles and Jonathan Zeitlin (2007), 'Learning from difference: the new architecture of experimentalist governance in the European Union', *European Governance Papers (EUROGOV)*, No. C–07–02.

Sachs, Jeffrey and Andrew Warner (1995), 'Economic reform and the process of global integration', *Brookings Papers on Economic Activity I: 1995*, 1–96.

Sala-i-Martin, Xavier (2006), 'The world distribution of income: falling poverty and . . . convergence, period', *Quarterly Journal of Economics*, **121**, 351–97.

Schaik, Ton van and Henri de Groot (1996), 'Phases of economic growth and industrial structure', Tilburg University, Department of Economics, January 1996.

Schaik, Ton van and Theo van de Klundert (2013), 'Employment protection legislation and catching-up', *Applied Economics*, **45** (8), 973–81.

Schlesinger, Arthur. Jr. (1986), *The Cycles of American History*, Boston: Houghton Mifflin.

Schumpeter, Joseph (1912), *Theorie der wirtschaflichen Entwicklung*, Leipzig: Dunckner and Humblot.

Schumpeter, Joseph (1939), *Business Cycles*, Philadelphia: Porcupine Press.

Schumpeter, Joseph (1942), *Capitalism, Socialism and Democracy*, New York: Harper and Row.

Sinn, Hans-Werner (2011), 'How to rescue the euro: ten commandments', *VOX*, http://www.voxeu.org/article/how-rescue-euro-ten-commandments (accessed 27 January 2012).

Sinn, Hans-Werner and Timo Wollmershaeuser (2011), 'Target loans, current account balances and capital flows: the ECB's rescue facility', *NBER*, Working paper 17626.

Skidelsky, Robert (2009), *The Return of the Master. Why, sixty years after his death John Maynard Keynes is still the most important thinker in the World*, London: Allen Lane.

Smulders, Sjak and Theo van de Klundert (1995), 'Imperfect competition, concentration and growth', *European Economic Review*, **39**, 139–160.

Smulders, Sjak and Theo van de Klundert (2004), 'Monopolistic competition and economic growth', in Steven Brakman and Ben Heijdra (eds), *The Monopolistic Competition Revolution in Retrospect*, Cambridge: Cambridge University Press, pp. 307–31.

Solow, Robert (1956), 'A contribution to the theory of economic growth', *Quarterly Journal of Economics*, **70**, 65–94.

Spufford, Peter (2002), *Power and Profit. The Merchant in Medieval Europe*, New York: Thames & Hudson.

Swan, Trevor (1956), 'Economic growth and capital accumulation', *Economic Record*, **32**, 334–61.

Syrquin, Moshe (1988), 'Patterns of structural change', in Hollis Chenery and T.N. Srinivasan (eds), *Handbook of Development Economics*, Vol. I, Amsterdam: Elsevier, pp. 205–68.

Tabellini, Guido (2010), 'Culture and institutions: economic development in the regions of Europe', *Journal of the European Economic Association*, **8** (4), 677–716.

Temin, Peter (2010), 'The Great Recession and the Great Depression', *NBER*, Working Paper 15645.

Visser, Hans (2010), 'Minsky, Fisher and the credit crisis', *Kwartaalschrift Economie*, **7**, 555–66.

Weil, David (2005), *Economic Growth*, Boston: Addison Wesley.

Wersching, Klaus (2010), 'Schumpeterian competition, technological regimes and learning through knowledge spillover', *Journal of Economic Behavior and Organization*, **75**, 482–93.

Wolff, Salomon de (1924), 'Prosperitäts- und depressionsperioden', in O. Jenssen (ed.), *Den Lebendige Marxismus*, Jena: Thüringen Verlagsanstalt, pp. 13–43.

Wooldridge, Adrian (2012), 'The visible hand', Special report: State capitalism, *The Economist*, 21 January 2012, pp. 3–18.

World Value Survey (1995), World Value Surveys Association.

Wright, Gavin and Jesse Czelusta (2004), 'The myth of resource curse', *Challenge*, **47**, 6–38.

Index